WORTH DOING

Fallenness, Finitude, *and* Work
in the Real World

W. DAVID BUSCHART
and RYAN TAFILOWSKI

FOREWORD *by*
KELLY M. KAPIC

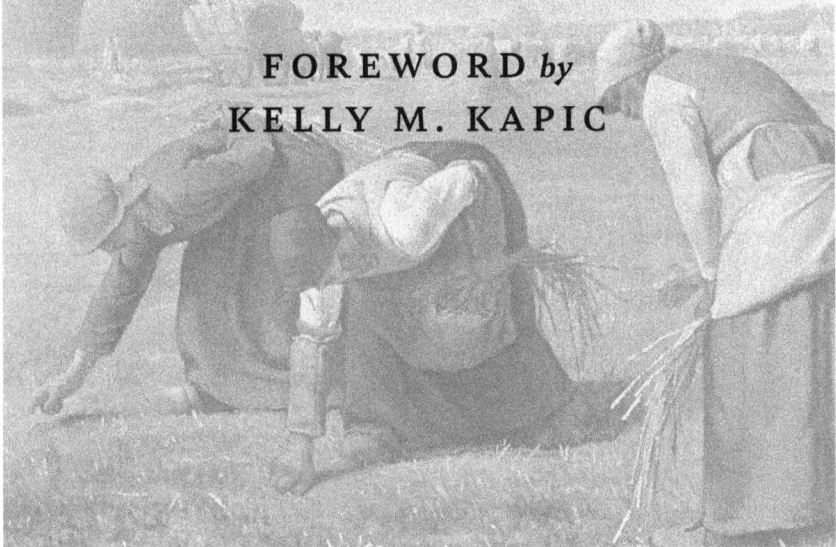

ivp
Academic
An imprint of InterVarsity Press
Downers Grove, Illinois

InterVarsity Press
P.O. Box 1400 | Downers Grove, IL 60515-1426
ivpress.com | email@ivpress.com

InterVarsity Press® is the publishing division of InterVarsity Christian Fellowship/USA®. For more information, visit intervarsity.org.

Scripture quotations, unless otherwise noted, are from the New Revised Standard Version Bible, copyright © 1989 National Council of the Churches of Christ in the United States of America. Used by permission. All rights reserved worldwide.

The publisher cannot verify the accuracy or functionality of website URLs used in this book beyond the date of publication.

Cover design: Faceout Studio, Spencer Fuller
Interior design: Jeanna Wiggins
Image: © duncan1890 / DigitalVision Vectors via Getty Images

ISBN 978-1-5140-0948-2 (print) | ISBN 978-1-5140-0949-9 (digital)

Printed in the United States of America ∞

Library of Congress Cataloging-in-Publication Data
A catalog record for this book is available from the Library of Congress.

31 30 29 28 27 26 25 | 12 11 10 9 8 7 6 5 4 3 2 1

Honoring my late parents,

William Arthur Buschart and Margaret Mae Buschart,

who, without the benefits of higher education,

worked long and hard to provide for our family,

in both body and spirit. And they provided so well.

DB

To Adrienne, the wife whom I love and

with whom I have shared all the days of this vain life

that God has given us under the sun, and

my constant companion in my toil at which I toil under the sun.

RT

CONTENTS

FOREWORD

Kelly M. Kapic

CONSIDER HOW YOU SPEND most of your average day. Most of us primarily spend it doing work, which may or may not involve paid employment. The authors here define *work* as "a definite and intentional field of activity," which covers stay-at-home parents, politicians, truck drivers, or community activists. But whether your labor is tedious or ever changing, whether it brings much or little financial gain, how should we think and feel about our relationship to work?

Many people in business have tried to provide answers by writing bestsellers that describe *The 48 Laws of Power*, *Think and Grow Rich*, or *The Magic of Thinking Big*: each volume in its own way promises strength, success, and an ever-growing movement into greatness. Christians can be tempted to laugh at books like this, but our own responses sometimes make similar mistakes. Both the world and the church have struggled to think well theologically about our work, primarily for two reasons.

First, some Christian people and traditions have approached work by separating it so far from our faith that their followers can't connect how they spent most of their waking hours (doing work) with what they consider the spiritual part of their lives (e.g., church attendance, quiet times). Work is often reduced to our ability to generate income, but few people in any significant way relate it to our faith, except for the rare chance we might get to evangelize a non-Christian colleague in the lunchroom. This approach to work suffers from an underdeveloped doctrine of creation. I will return to this shortly.

Second, other Christian people and traditions have approached this faith-work connection by exhibiting the beauty and goodness of our work as emerging from God's calling for our lives; unfortunately, in the process, they sometimes present a romanticized view of human labor and ignore the difficulties. Although this presentation begins as an inspiring vision, it can eventually lead to deeper disillusionment. Especially when sprinkled with inspiring biblical verses, the result often looks more like a baptized speech from Steve Jobs than a kingdom vision provided by Jesus. This approach to work suffers from an underdeveloped doctrine of the fall.

The first approach downplays the goodness of God's creation, while the second minimizes the complex and painful ways sin has affected every area of life, including our work. One view risks losing a sense of God's delight in our participatory role in his creation and the joy we can experience in our labor for God and for the good of his world, while the other view risks ignoring the painful reality that work is often dull or tedious, or all too often appears relatively insignificant.

We avoid these two pitfalls—neglecting either the goodness of creation or the pain of the fall—not just by mentioning that both are true but by carefully working out the implications of these two factors, and, beyond that, by taking into account the full narrative of the biblical story, which includes creation, fall, redemption, and consummation. And this brings me to the beauty of this volume you now hold in your hands.

David Buschart and Ryan Tafilowski have put together a wonderfully thoughtful book that both builds on what others have done and puts it together in a rich and fresh way. They take account of both the goodness of creation and the effects of the fall, working out the implications of the tension between them. This allows them to be both inspiring and realistic, both cautious and hopeful. Holding themes together without picking between them allows for a conversation about labor that will resonate with the landscaper and the bank president. Along the way, they highlight other themes that are too often neglected or downplayed.

For example, Buschart and Tafilowski rightly emphasize the Creator-creature distinction. Unlike so many business books by both secular and

Christian authors, they maintain that only God is *infinite* and that we humans are *finite* by the Creator's good design. Unlike God, we are limited by space, time, knowledge, and power. Our limits are not part of the fall but part of what God unambiguously calls "good." For various reasons, this aspect of our nature is now difficult for most of us to believe these days. Two recent popular books have the same title: *No Limits*, one by Olympic swimmer Michael Phelps and the other by popular Christian leadership author John C. Maxwell. While I am confident that neither would have believed they were prompting people to think they were gods, in practice telling people they should not have limits sets them up for failure and self-condemnation, since all of us by our nature have limits. Of course we can grow, whether we push our limits to increase our muscle mass or our intellectual powers, but that push for growth easily gets inflated into a kind of search for divine power. Many of us find it hard to be comfortable with enough, as the authors of this present book advise. But rightly framing our limits actually helps foster human flourishing, community life, and the power of meaning.

Offering those of us who are not superheroes something more grounded and relatable than other books, *Worth Doing* reminds us of how God intentionally made us to recognize our limits in a good and healthy way. Further, Buschart and Tafilowski also take into account sin's effects on the created order, helping us identify how the fall has affected every aspect of our lives, from our internal world to the disordered social structures that we daily have to navigate. We no longer live in Eden: as they remind us, all of us work east of Eden. Overpromising people that our work should *always* perfectly align the world's needs with our personal desires and gifts can—even if well-intentioned—breed impossible expectations and produce uninformed and even cruel outcomes.

Thankfully, Buschart and Tafilowski provoke a conversation we need to have about how we, as Christians, should think and feel about our work. They question the clichés that call us to "love" what we do (this, they believe, can be a subtle form of ideology—and maybe idolatry as well) because that demand can introduce unbiblical assumptions into our relationship with our work. Too often these unquestioned assumptions have led us to devalue the dignity of work that may not be particularly enjoyable but still provides shelter and food for ourselves and others. And too often we have assumed greater leverage and agency for the average worker than is often afforded to laborers around the globe in difficult situations. We need to know when our vision of work and life is more driven by TED talks than by Jesus' kingdom vision; if we don't double-check our assumptions, we risk leading people astray with false promises that undermine communion with God and others.

This book presents a healthy perspective: it encourages us to live in the middle. It reminds us that we experience neither the creation as it was before the fall nor the full harmony and freedom that will come in future glory, when reconciliation will be complete and God will make all things right. We live in this uncomfortable middle space, but our God is with us in this space and has good work for us to do. We do not live in a noncompromised creation or in an idealistic future. We live here and now, in a fallen and broken world as fallen and broken people. We can and should look forward (eschatology) and backward (creation/ protology), but the authors also remind us to look side to side in our here and now. God has placed us in a particular place, in a distinct culture and time, with its own weaknesses and strengths. This middle space is not only where we live; it also deserves our attention. Here is a vision for blue-collar workers and educated elites, for teenagers and seventy-five-year-olds. This is not merely a vision but a treatment that resonates with our real lives.

1

INTRODUCTION

Theologians must be reminded of the harsh, complicated, and tiring
circumstances and conditions under which work is often done—
along with the rest of our lives in the quotidian.
VELI-MATTI KÄRKKÄINEN, *CREATION AND HUMANITY*

Lord God, almighty and everlasting Father,
you have brought us in safety to this new day:

Preserve us with your mighty power,
that we may not fall into sin,

nor be overcome by adversity; and in all we do,

direct us to the fulfilling of your purpose;
through Jesus Christ our Lord. Amen.
A MORNING PRAYER, FROM THE BOOK OF COMMON PRAYER

IT'S ALL A MATTER OF PERSPECTIVE. OR IS IT?

The workers laying sewer pipe were sweaty, dirty, and weary. They had been digging, lifting, fitting, and securing pipe since seven o'clock that morning. And there was additional aggravation. During the previous night a portion of one of the walls of the trench that ran down the middle of the busy street had partially collapsed, so much of the morning had been spent digging that section again. It was now approaching noon, and they were looking forward to sitting down with their thermoses and lunch pails. Just as they emerged from their trench and climbed onto the sidewalk to have lunch, they happened to notice a group of three nicely dressed people emerge through the glass doors of the steel-and-glass office building and walk past them. One was talking on her cellphone and the other two were overheard comparing two possible restaurants for lunch. "Must be nice," said one of the trench workers. "Sit in a nice chair, at a desk, in an air-conditioned office. Get up when you want to get a cup of coffee or to talk with someone. 'Work' a few hours and then go to a nice restaurant for a three-drink lunch. And the company probably pays for it. People like that have no clue what it's like to work in the real world."

Later that day, at about four o'clock, the ad agency team was visited by a vice president. She informed them that their client had changed the timeline for the launch of their new product and that, as a result, the team's marketing presentation would need to be ready to deliver in just four days, rather than two weeks. As soon as she walked out of the room and people had blurted out their feelings about this, they huddled among themselves and grudgingly concluded they had to stay and continue to work well into the evening. Individual team members began to send texts and make phone calls, canceling dinner engagements, informing spouses that they would not be home until late, and reassuring children that they would be at the next game. One of the workers had wandered to the window and rather blankly stared out as he briefly spoke with his wife. Having finished his phone call, he began to turn back into the room and just happened to look down from the sixteenth-story window and see the trench workers. He watched as they loaded tools and equipment into a secure storage box. They then slowly made their way to their truck, laughing and slapping each other on the back along the way. They got into the truck and drove off. The ad agency worker glanced at his cellphone. The time was four-fifteen. "Must be nice," he thought. "Quit work at four o'clock, having had quite a few breaks throughout the day. Then, precisely at four o'clock, not a minute later, you hop into the company truck and take off. They'll probably stop at a bar for a few beers before they go home, and when they get home, they're home—no lingering worries about unfinished responsibilities or the office politics of the next day. 'Punch the clock' and you're done. People like that have no idea what it's like to work in the real world."

This kind of thinking, and feeling, is not limited to people who lay sewer pipe or craft advertising campaigns. It's not too difficult for anyone to look across the landscape of paid work and see people who don't appear, from the perspective of the viewer, to work in the real world. Some businesspeople look at academics and think their excessive job security (under the cover of tenure) and paid time off (during sabbaticals) are just a couple of the inefficient and costly excesses of higher education. Some academics look at many businesspeople with envy over their financial remuneration, benefits packages, and numerous perks. Some laypeople wish they could work just one day a week and have complete freedom to manage their schedules, the way they think pastors do. Some pastors long for the shorter hours with higher pay and less close-up scrutiny that so many people in their congregations enjoy. And almost everyone, except professional athletes, thinks that professional athletes are so grossly overpaid that they can easily retire in their early thirties and never have to work again.

The real world. It is a phrase we often use when comparing various people's situations in life, including our own, or when we want to impress on a young person what they can expect when they enter adulthood. (Because the adult world is the real world.) Furthermore, it is not uncommon that directly or indirectly, paid employment is often at the center of the notion of the real world. After all, for many people, work is where we spend most of our time.

However, the real world is not simply a notion. It is the real world. It is the world in which all of us and each of us lives. It is the world in which all of us and each of us works, both paid employment and mundane but necessary tasks, some of which are invigorating and interesting, others of which are stultifying and frustrating. It is the world—particularly as it bears on and shapes work—that we hope readers will understand and navigate a bit better as a result of this book. A genuinely Christian understanding and navigation of the real world will be distinctively theological, and we here pursue a contribution to the theological foundation and framework for approaching work in the real world. The chapters that follow will address rather specific and discrete theological issues. Specifically, this book will address itself to one key question: Is there a theology of work—a way of understanding the nature and purpose of human labor in light of the Christian faith—capable of speaking to work the way that we experience it: a mixture of pleasure and pain, fulfillment and futility, beauty and boredom, satisfaction and stress, finitude and fallenness? Is there a theology that might resonate both for workers with high degrees of autonomy and prestige *and* those who do not naturally find much meaning in their work or whose work is degrading? In short, is there a theology of work for the real world?

TOWARD A THEOLOGY OF WORK FOR THE REAL WORLD

Over the last two decades, evangelical accounts of the theology of work have proliferated. Indeed, the faith and work movement has become a cottage industry unto itself, complete with a vast literature, dozens of organizations, and a bustling conference and media scene.[1] However, as both its critics and proponents have observed in recent years, even though the faith and work movement has exploded among what Andrew Lynn has termed "creative class Evangelicals," it has struggled to gain traction among blue- and no-collar workers. "Many conversations about calling and work among professionals," explains Jeff Haanen,

---

[1]For a more comprehensive description of the faith and work movement in which we seek to situate our account, as well as its foundational literature, see the appendix.

entrepreneur and founding CEO of the Denver Institute for Faith and Work, "assume a certain amount of choice and agency that are foreign to most working-class men and women."[2] In short, the preponderance of faith and work resources has been devised by and for the creative class.[3] Indeed, from its inception, the faith and work movement has always focused on "the great professions": "law, education, medicine and the social sciences . . . commerce, industry and farming, accountancy and banking, local government or parliament, the mass media."[4]

But as it stands now, the movement has yet to produce a theology that might resonate with other kinds of workers, those who populate not "the great professions" but "the ordinary professions." Whether and to what extent this can be done remains an open question. However, in what follows we aim to address this lacuna in the faith and work literature through some constructive proposals rooted in two key methodological emphases: the recovery of finitude as a genuine good of creation (and therefore a genuine good in our working lives) and greater attention to and a more sober reckoning of how sin has distorted work. As we will argue at length, all human work east of Eden is undertaken *in medias res*—that is, in the middle of a story that is already unfolding. We labor, as it were, between two gardens, exiled from Eden and not yet residents of that future garden-city, the new Jerusalem. To put it another way, we come onto the scene in chapter two of a four-act drama, sometimes called the grand narrative: creation (chapter one) → fall (chapter two) → redemption (chapter three) → consummation (chapter four). Though we have been told about chapter one, none of us ever experienced it, and

---

[2]Jeff Haanen, "God of the Second Shift," *Christianity Today*, December 2018, 10.

[3]Andrew Lynn mounts this argument at length in *Saving the Protestant Ethic: Creative Class Evangelicalism and the Crisis of Work* (Oxford: Oxford University Press, 2023), especially chapters 1 and 5. However, even more sympathetic interpreters of the faith and work movement, such as David W. Miller, concede that its current iteration emerged in earnest only when evangelicals achieved social, political, and economic prominence starting in the 1980s. See Miller, *God at Work: The History and Promise of the Faith at Work Movement* (Oxford: Oxford University Press, 2007), 65-75.

[4]John Stott, *Christian Mission in the Modern World* (Downers Grove, IL: IVP Academic, 1975), 31-32. Quotation edited slightly.

though we've heard rumors of chapter four, none of us has ever seen it. Accordingly, any realistic theology of work will need, first, to attend to the sheer finitude of human creatures, our fundamental boundedness, while also reckoning with the phenomenology of sin, the ways in which sin twists and malforms the very fabric of reality. A realistic theology of work, then, will need to make the experience of finitude methodologically prime, since the experience of finitude is universal, and it will need to make fallenness methodologically prime, since the experience of the majority of workers reflects Genesis 3, not Genesis 1–2.

In light of these considerations, we propose here a revision to the ways in which the grand narrative described above is typically deployed in faith and work literature. As we shall discuss, most evangelical approaches ground the theology of work in protology (chapter one) while also drawing heavily on eschatology (chapter four), with sustained reflection also on redemption (chapter three). However, we suggest that at least part of the reason the faith and work movement has stalled out in its attempt to translate its message for blue- and no-collar workers is due to some key theological deficiencies to which we address ourselves in this book. In the first place, our revision will involve greater emphasis on an oft-overlooked aspect of chapter one of the grand narrative, since many of these theologies of work have not attended sufficiently to *creational finitude* and its impact on work, sometimes conflating finitude and fallenness. Yet, in the second place, existing accounts almost universally situate their theologies of work in the doctrine of creation, emphasizing human co-creation with God as the primary meaning of the *imago Dei*. Such a move, however, may inadvertently exclude workers who do not experience their work in these terms.

We aim to address these deficiencies in the form of two overarching emphases. In the first part of the book, we offer a more robust account of human finitude as a foundational element of the Bible's view of work. Accordingly, a realistic theology of work may and should appeal to protology, of course, but this must include an adequate and accurate reckoning of finitude, which is entirely proper to creaturely existence, as it does so. In the second half, we propose a methodology that more accurately reflects our present experience of work—which is beset by enmity, absurdity, and tragedy—by grounding it primarily in the doctrine of the fall (chapter two of the grand narrative) and only secondarily in the doctrine of creation. With this restructuring in place, we then gesture toward some ways in which the prevailing theology of work might be recalibrated to speak to the experience of a broader range of workers.

To anticipate the full breadth of the argument that follows in these pages, we propose a theology of work grounded primarily neither in protology nor eschatology, but rather a theology of work *from the middle, for the middle*—a theology rooted firmly in what David Kelsey calls "the quotidian."[5] That is to say, although the Bible offers multiple theologies of work, the faith and work movement, broadly speaking, is concerned mainly with two: the dignity-agency-power narrative rooted in Genesis 1–2 (protology), which relies on an interpretation of the *imago Dei* that (over)emphasizes human creativity and often ignores or understates human finitude, and the perfection-of-human-culture narrative glimpsed in Revelation 21 (eschatology). Our constructive proposals for a more realistic theology of work, expounded at length in chapter six, are from and for the middle, situated between protology and eschatology, and will revolve around three main theses. First, we consider creaturely work, finite though it is, in relationship to God's freedom and transcendence as sustained by God's presence. Second, we aim to affirm the instrumental value of work—not merely so-called intrinsic values—as biblically based, theologically viable, and pastorally helpful. Third, we situate human work within a broader anthropology that does not identify the *imago Dei* primarily with the capacity for creative co-labor with God but rather with a christological teleology in

---

[5]David H. Kelsey, *Eccentric Existence: A Theological Anthropology* (Louisville, KY: Westminster John Knox, 2009), 1:190.

which the saints are conformed fully to the image of Jesus Christ. This methodological shift will therefore also involve deconstructing two harmful work mythologies that are at risk of being unwittingly reinforced by the faith and work movement: "You Are What You Do" and "Do What You Love," both of which rest on dubious anthropological foundations and a questionable theology of vocation. Paradoxically, we argue that, ultimately, a realistic and healthy theology of work will be a theology in which work is *de-emphasized* and *de-centered*.

That is where our argument leads. Our analysis will begin, however, with a diagnosis of the various ways in which the grand narrative has been operationalized to build a theological understanding of work, since the vast majority of evangelical accounts of work use this framework. Although this paradigm is no doubt useful and illuminating, its application to work entails certain risks, namely the risk of distorting the Bible's full theology of work by focusing too narrowly on protology or eschatology. To put it starkly, of all the many recent theologies of work that deploy the grand narrative as an interpretive device, we know of not one, popular or scholarly, that does not situate its account of work in chapter one of the grand narrative.[6] Moreover, as we will show, these heavily protological accounts of work are almost always accompanied by an eschatology that envisions the perfection of human work and culture in the new heavens and the new earth. Before

---

[6]Of course, not all theologies of work employ the grand narrative as a framework, but most do. Faith and work literature has proliferated over the last two decades and is therefore voluminous, but here are some key works representative of the methodological decision to ground a theology of work in chapter one: Ross Chapman and Ryan Tafilowski, *Faithful Work: In the Daily Grind with God and for Others* (Downers Grove, IL: InterVarsity Press, 2024); John Mark Comer, *Garden City: Work, Rest, and the Art of Being Human* (Nashville: Thomas Nelson, 2017); Andy Crouch, *Culture Making: Recovering Our Creative Calling* (Downers Grove, IL: InterVarsity Press, 2008); James M. Hamilton Jr., *Work and Our Labor in the Lord* (Wheaton, IL: Crossway, 2017); David H. Jensen, *Responsive Labor: A Theology of Work* (Louisville, KY: Westminster John Knox, 2006); Timothy Keller with Katherine Leary Alsdorf, *Every Good Endeavor: Connecting Your Work to God's Work* (New York: Penguin, 2016); Tom Nelson, *Work Matters: Connecting Sunday Worship to Monday Work* (Wheaton, IL: Crossway, 2011); Amy Sherman, *Kingdom Calling: Vocational Stewardship for the Common Good* (Downers Grove, IL: InterVarsity Press, 2011); R. Paul Stevens, *Work Matters: Lessons from Scripture* (Grand Rapids, MI: Eerdmans, 2012); Ben Witherington III, *Work: A Kingdom Perspective on Labor* (Grand Rapids, MI: Eerdmans, 2011).

proceeding, we would note that our proposals are not intended to replace existing approaches to the theology of work entirely, but rather to revise them with a more accurate and adequate account of finitude and fallenness, which, in turn, will result in a more vital and pastorally viable theology of work for the real world.

THEOLOGY OF WORK: THE GRAND NARRATIVE

One cannot approach work (or any other matter) in a distinctively Christian way without that approach being theological. To think about and perform work in the light of God and his creation is to think and act theologically. To think about and perform work in the light of the Bible is to think and act theologically. To think about and perform work in the light of the gospel is to think and act theologically.

The challenge, then, is not whether Christians' views of and approaches to work will be theological, but whether they will be theologically true and wise. The challenge is to approach work in ways that are congruent with who God is, and with the way God has made human beings as well as the rest of creation. The challenge is to approach work in ways that comport with the teaching of the Bible. The challenge is to approach work in ways that testify to and advance the gospel of Jesus Christ. An authentically Christian response to these challenges will be by its very nature theological. It is with a view toward that theological address of work that we offer this book.

In addition to the explicitly theological challenges, there are also existential challenges to be addressed. The theology of work must be formulated in ways that acknowledge and address the wide range of human work experiences. We make no claim that this book addresses the entire range of human work experiences. We do, however, desire to make a constructive contribution to the theological address of work already under way. We seek to do this by thinking about and responding to work in the light of the realities of finitude and fallenness. Obviously, this is not the first book on the theology of work. Equally obvious, it will not be the last. What we say here falls within helpful trajectories already taken in the theology of work, while at the same time we offer some revisions and proposals that will help advance the further maturation of the theology of work. Furthermore, beyond the theology of work itself, it is our desire that this theology might help Christians think and act faithfully in relation to their work. We include ourselves among those Christians who feel the need to think deeply and act faithfully in and through our work.[7] For now, we will explore one of the most common ways, and potentially a very helpful way, of theologically framing human work. It is often referred to as "the story of the Bible" or "the grand narrative."

In recent years scholars in a variety of disciplines and with diverse subjects in view have formulated simple yet theologically comprehensive frameworks for their projects by tracing out the overall progression of the biblical canon. The number of chapters in the narrative may vary, as may the titles given to the chapters may vary, but the same fundamental storyline is clearly present. In *Visual Faith*, William Dyrness moves from creation to fall to redemption to eschatology in his discussion of beauty.[8] Responding theologically and ethically to the question "How should we think of the earth?" Steven Bouma-Prediger, in *For the Beauty of the Earth*, structures the core of his answer in accord with the narrative of creation, fall, redemption, and culmination.[9] The late pastor Timothy Keller frames his response to racial injustice and the concluding chapter of his book *Generous Justice* in terms of creation, fall, redemption, and

---

[7]For those who might be inclined to chuckle and say, "But you're professors, and professors don't know what real work is," we would humbly invite you to revisit the opening paragraphs of this chapter.

[8]William A. Dyrness, *Visual Faith: Art, Theology, and Worship in Dialogue* (Grand Rapids, MI: Baker Academic, 2001), 74-80.

[9]Steven Bouma-Prediger, *For the Beauty of the Earth: A Christian Vision for Creation Care*, 2nd ed. (Grand Rapids, MI: Baker Academic, 2010), 112-19. For other examples of discussions of creation care framed in terms of the grand narrative, see Daniel L. Brunner, Jennifer L. Butler, and A. J. Swoboda, *Introducing Evangelical Ecotheology: Foundations in Scripture, Theology, History, and Praxis* (Grand Rapids, MI: Baker Academic, 2014), 117-41, and Mark Liederbach and Seth Bible, *True North: Christ, the Gospel, and Creation Care* (Nashville: B&H Academic, 2012), 29-134.

culmination.[10] This rendering of the narrative or story of the Bible is not isolated to the arena of faith and work, nor is it the naive construction of people who are unsophisticated in biblical studies.

As the subtitle of his book indicates, Old Testament scholar Christopher J. H. Wright casts his landmark study of the mission of God as "the unlocking of the Bible's Grand Narrative."[11] He writes,

> The Bible presents itself to us fundamentally as a narrative, a historical narrative at one level, but a grand metanarrative at another. It begins with the God of purpose in creation, moves on to the conflict and problem generated by human rebellion against that purpose, spends most of its narrative journey in the story of God's redemptive purposes being worked out on the stage of human history, finishes beyond the horizon of its own history with the eschatological hope of a new creation. This has often been presented as a four-point narrative: *creation, fall, redemption,* and *future hope.*[12]

Similarly, Craig Bartholomew and Michael Goheen believe that "the true story of the whole world" is told in "the drama of Scripture."[13] They present this drama in six "acts": act 1, God establishes his kingdom: creation; act 2, rebellion in the kingdom: fall; act 3, the King chooses Israel: redemption initiated; interlude, a kingdom story waiting for an ending: the intertestamental period; act 4, the coming of the King: redemption accomplished; act 5, spreading the news of the King: the mission of the church; and act 6, the return of the King: redemption completed.

So, when authors writing on the theology of work discern in the Bible a version of this grand narrative and regard this narrative as providing a theological resource for a large and complex arena of Christian thought

---

[10]Timothy Keller, *Generous Justice: How God's Grace Makes Us Just* (New York: Riverhead Books, 2010), 120-23 and 170-89.

[11]Christopher J. H. Wright, *The Mission of God: Unlocking the Bible's Grand Narrative* (Downers Grove, IL: IVP Academic, 2006).

[12]Wright, *Mission of God*, 63-64, emphasis original. Note that the phrase "the God of purpose" in this quotation, rather than "the purpose of God," is not a typographical error. It is an expression of Wright's belief that "this whole worldview is predicated on teleological monotheism."

[13]Craig B. Bartholomew and Michael W. Goheen, *The Drama of Scripture: Finding Our Place in the Biblical Story*, 3rd ed. (Grand Rapids, MI: Baker Academic, 2024).

and action, they are not alone. As we shall see below, the majority of faith and work authors have, each in their own way, drawn on the grand narrative to frame the theology of work.[14] In *The Other Six Days*, Paul Stevens writes, "Taken as a whole the covenant mandate gives us a comprehensive vision for the human vocation." He delineates this mandate in Scripture in the following fourfold manner: creation one consists in design (Gen 1–2) and fall (Gen 3), and creation two consists in substantial salvation (Eph 1–3) and final salvation (Rev 21–22).[15] One of the more influential voices in recent conversations about Christian faith and work is that of Amy Sherman. In *Kingdom Calling*, she sets forth "The Basics of a Biblical Theology of Work" and implicitly but clearly traces the overall arc of the grand narrative. Sherman begins with creation, stating, "*Work is something we were built for, something our loving Creator intends for our good.*"[16] Moreover, God the Creator, God himself, is "a worker." God is good, and his giving of work to do is itself a good gift. These creational affirmations are set alongside—or more to the point, *before*—a reality that impacts but does not negate the creational truths. This juxtaposed reality is the fall. Sherman correctly observes that "the curse of Genesis 3 brought toil and futility into work. Ever since, our experience of work involves pain as well as pleasure." Thankfully, this is not the end of the story. The "intrinsic value" of work perseveres beyond the fall as human beings "participate in God's own work,"

---

[14]In his analysis of methodologies in the theology of work, Darrell Cosden does not observe the four chapter grand narrative. He does, however, see prominent roles for the first and fourth chapters—creation and consummation—in literature in the theology of work. He observes that "a common feature among Protestants generally and also among those particularly viewing work as vocation is a strong appeal to and dependence on the various doctrines surrounding the initial creation, or, protology." And for theologians such as Jürgen Moltmann and Miroslav Volf "their eschatological orientation means that from protology, work is perceived as teleologically directed and oriented toward the future new creation rather than backward toward the restoration of the initial creation." See Darrell Cosden, *A Theology of Work: Work and the New Creation*, foreword by Jürgen Moltmann (Milton Keynes: Paternoster, 2004), 41, 46. For a more extended representative account of theologies of work that deploy the grand narrative, see chap. 5.

[15]R. Paul Stevens, *The Other Six Days: Vocation, Work, and Ministry in Biblical Perspective* (Grand Rapids, MI: Eerdmans, 1999), 101.

[16]Sherman, *Kingdom Calling*, 102, emphasis original.

his redemptive work, providential work, justice work, and revelatory work. Indeed, "Christians need to have a big conception of God's redemptive work. . . . God's salvific work is not limited to individual salvation but concerns his mission of restoring the whole of the created order (Col 1:19-20; Eph 1:9)." And humans participate with God in his work. She concludes her brief biblical theology with eschatology. "Our work lasts," she observes and, citing Isaiah 60 and Revelation 21:24, posits that "work—pleasurable, fruitful, meaningful work—will be an eternal reality." Finally, in an appendix to the book, Sherman summarizes the Bible's answers to basic worldview questions in the following fourfold manner: "creation," "fall," "redemption," "restoration."[17]

Two other oft-cited books come from two pastors and the director of a church faith and work center who have been significant participants in a variety of Christian faith and work endeavors. The first four chapters of Tom Nelson's *Work Matters* explicitly follow the grand narrative: chapter one, "Created to Work" (creation); chapter two, "Is Work a Four-Letter Word?" (fall); chapter three, "The Good News of Work" (redemption); and chapter four, "Work Now and Later" (culmination). "Scripture presents the gospel to us," writes Nelson, "in the broader story line of redemptive history."[18] "The Bible places work within the literary framework of an unfolding progression in God's redemption of the physical world"—a progression from creation, through sin and death, through the redemption of both workers and their work, into "a great future in store for [God's] image-bearing workers."[19] Timothy Keller was the pastor of Redeemer Presbyterian Church in New York City, and he was instrumental in Redeemer's establishment of the Center for Faith and Work. Katherine Leary Alsdorf was the founding director of the center. Together they cowrote *Every Good Endeavor*, and the overall structure of the entire book is a progression from creation through fall to redemption. They wrote the book this way because they believe that

---

[17]Sherman, *Kingdom Calling*, 103, 235, 104, 244.
[18]Nelson, *Work Matters*, 53.
[19]Nelson, *Work Matters*, 66-67.

"People cannot make sense of anything without attaching it to a story line."[20] "If you get the story of the world wrong," they say, "you will get your life responses wrong, including the way you go about your work." And, "the Christian story line, or worldview, is: creation (plan), fall (problem), redemption and restoration (solution)."[21]

As a final example, James Hamilton has explicitly framed his book *Work and Our Labor in the Lord* in accord with "the salvation-historical storyline, i.e., the worldview story of creation-fall-redemption-restoration."[22] The first chapter, "Creation: Work in the Very Good Garden," includes the definition of "a righteous job" as "one that does not exist to commit or promote sin but to accomplish the tasks God gave to humanity at the beginning: fill, subdue, rule."[23] This is followed by a chapter devoted to fallenness and flourishing in "Work after the Fall," and a third chapter that describes God's redemptive response, "Redemption: Work Now That Christ Has Risen." In the fourth and final chapter Hamilton offers a vision of work "in the new heavens and the new earth." "God will make the world new," he writes, "and we will do new work" of "ruling and subduing, working and keeping, exercising dominion and rendering judgment, all as God's people in God's place in God's way." Thus, Hamilton sets forth a view of work "as it was meant to be, as it is, as it can be, and as it will be."[24]

THE SHAPE OF THIS BOOK

The theological vision we seek to cast is not entirely new. We believe that this book falls within helpful trajectories already taken with regard to faith and work, particularly the theology of work. Among these helpful trajectories is the desire to think about and act on work in the light of a biblically faithful and biblically comprehensive framework, such as the

[20]Keller and Alsdorf, *Every Good Endeavor*, 155.
[21]Keller and Alsdorf, *Every Good Endeavor*, 156, 162.
[22]Hamilton, *Work and Our Labor*, 12.
[23]Hamilton, *Work and Our Labor*, 22. See Genesis 1:26-28.
[24]Hamilton, *Work and Our Labor*, 91, 13.

grand narrative. At the same time, we believe that the potential for the grand narrative to provide wise real-world guidance for thought and action in relation to work has not been adequately realized, and in some respects the way that the grand narrative has been applied has been misleading and unhelpful. Some scenes in the Story have been misunderstood. Some have not been adequately portrayed or acted on. In some instances there has been a compounding of both. We believe that through closer attention to these sometimes misunderstood and overlooked scenes and chapters in the Story a more adequate—a more realistic—theology of work can be formulated and applied. Specifically, in what follows, we will aim to recover a robust understanding of creational finitude, an oft-overlooked aspect of chapter one of the grand narrative, while situating our account of work primarily within the doctrine of sin and the fall (chapter two) and not exclusively in the doctrine of creation (chapter one). Moreover, a more complete and accurate understanding of these scenes and narrative chapters will meaningfully address a wider range of work situations in which people find themselves in the real world.

So what are these misunderstood and undervalued scenes in the Story? Finitude and fallenness. The truth about finitude is anchored in chapter one of the grand narrative, creation. Finitude is one of the characteristics of God-made creation, both human beings and the rest of creation. Moreover, finitude *perdures through the fall*. While the realities of sin may exacerbate and compound our creaturely limitations, the fall into sin did not fundamentally alter the finite structure of human existence. So while we are skeptical of some protological claims—accounts of work, for instance, that simply point to Genesis 1–2 as a blueprint we can follow in our world—it is theologically legitimate to appeal to finitude as one enduring aspect of our good and proper creaturely existence, since it is neither a product of the fall nor does the fall radically transfigure creational finitude itself. The story of fallenness constitutes chapter two of the grand narrative. And just as finitude pertains to both human beings and nonhuman creation, so too does fallenness. In here singling out chapter one of the grand narrative, creation, and chapter two of the grand narrative, fall, we do not mean to say that we will look at these two chapters only. The grand narrative is *a* narrative. It is cumulative, with each chapter remaining significant for the unfolding of subsequent chapters, and each of the subsequent chapters presuming and often looking back to earlier chapters. Each chapter of the narrative matters. And all the chapters together matter. So while our attention will be focused on revised interpretations of chapter one (creation) and chapter two (fall), we want never to lose sight of each chapter's role in and significance for the entire Story. Reality demands it.

Reality also demands that, to a greater degree than is generally the case in the theology of work, we pay close attention to finitude and fallenness. Upon reading those two words someone could gain the mistaken impression that we are here pursuing a vision for work that encourages mediocrity or discouragement or, even worse, a hopelessness with regard to work or a stoic resignation to exploitative or dehumanizing work. Any of these conclusions would indeed be mistaken. We seek to advance the theology of work by bringing some critical realism to bear. Alister McGrath indicates that critical realism simply reflects "the way things really are."[25] Not the way we wish they were. Not worse than they are. Simply the way they are. And among the realities of our world—the world in which all work is done—are finitude and fallenness. These two by no means constitute the totality of the real world, nor the totality of work in the real world, but they are nevertheless ever-present conditioners of everyone's work that, in our estimation, are too often misunderstood or overlooked, or both. If one's view of finitude and fallenness is such that one despairs over the potential for good work in this world, then one has a view of finitude and fallenness very different from that which will be found in the chapters that follow. Simply put, work that is limited by finitude and plagued by fallenness

---

[25]Alister E. McGrath, *A Scientific Theology*, vol. 1, *Nature* (Grand Rapids, MI: Eerdmans, 2001), 73.

is still good enough to be *worth doing*—and worth doing "with all your might" (Eccles 9:10 NIV). Indeed, that is the title of this book. And we mean it.[26]

Toward these ends, the book proceeds as follows. The two chapters that immediately follow this introduction are devoted to finitude. Chapter two advances a Christian theology of finitude with a view of applying this doctrine to our understanding of work. Traditionally, finitude is not a major locus of theology. A brief sampling of both the tables of contents and the indices of comprehensive systematic theologies will illustrate this, as will a sampling of major theological dictionaries and encyclopedias.[27] This chapter sets forth a modest yet constructive Christian theology of creational finitude. Chapter three then brings this theology to bear on the realities of work. In so doing we seek to constructively modify the theology of work, not least the appeal to chapter one of the grand narrative, creation.

The next two chapters are devoted to the fall. Chapter four sets forth a theology of the fall that we will then deploy as a framework for our interpretation of work in the real world. Unlike the topic of finitude, the fall and its consequences have been a major topic of theological reflection throughout the history of Christianity and continue to be so into the present. Consequently, unlike the chapter on the theology of finitude, chapter four is of necessity more selective in its treatment, focusing on what we call a phenomenology, rather than a genealogy, of sin. In other words, this chapter seeks to describe the conditions sin creates (and in which all work is undertaken), namely enmity, absurdity, and tragedy. In this way, chapter four provides the constructive foundation

---

[26]Both of us enjoy and cherish the opportunity to work as seminary professors, which work includes, but is by no means limited to, research and writing . . . such as our work on this book. And, just like everyone else, we regularly experience the realities of finitude and fallenness in our work, including our work on this book. With the exception of a footnote or two, we have chosen not to feature our own experience here in the book, but simply want to assure readers that we share with you the experience of finitude and fallenness in our work.

[27]A recent exception to this generalization is Daniel J. Treier, "Finitude," in *Evangelical Dictionary of Theology*, 3rd ed., ed. Daniel J. Treier and Walter A. Elwell (Grand Rapids, MI: Baker Academic, 2017), 317-19.

for chapter five, in which a robust theology of fallenness is applied to the theology of work. We seek in this chapter to advance the theology of work in ways that correspond more closely to the real world in which most people work day-by-day.

In chapter six we step back, if you will, from focusing specifically on finitude and fall and revisit the grand narrative as a whole, exploring the ways in which the theologies of finitude and fall developed here can deepen and expand the application of the grand narrative to the theology of work. It is our hope that ultimately this deepened and expanded theology will provide encouragement and guidance for workers and their work. We offer here theological perspective that we hope will enable workers to see creational finitude clearly when they are constrained by the reality of it and to respond to it hopefully—recognizing it for what it is and not for what it is not. We present here theological reflection that, when workers are confronted with the reality of fallenness, we hope will equip them to think rightly about it and engage it redemptively. Along the way, we will gesture toward some constructive possibilities for work in the real world.

Finally, we conclude this introduction with a few words about words. People use a variety of terms to talk about their work: *job, career, position, employment, occupation, ministry, calling,* and *vocation,* to name some of the more common terms.[28] More often than not, when people talk about their work they are referring to that which they do for pay—gainful employment. How does one describe the work, though, of a stay-at-home parent, the effort of someone who is unemployed to obtain a paying job, or the activity one engages within retirement? In order to have clarity in our conversation about finitude and fallenness we need to define the terms related to work that we will use here and briefly explain why we chose these terms.

---

[28]For a helpful discussion regarding the importance of work-related terms and how they are defined, see Amy Wrzesniewski, Clark McCauley, Paul Rozin, and Barry Schwartz, "Jobs, Careers, and Callings: People's Relations to Their Work," *Journal of Research in Personality* 31 (1997): 21-33.

Work encompasses activity engaged in all the dimensions of a person's life. We here use the term *work* to refer to a definite and intentional field of activity.[29] This activity may or may not be done for financial remuneration. For example, when someone engages their place of employment on Monday morning, they are working. This is work. When that same person comes home that evening and mows their lawn, this too is work. Other examples of work include volunteering at church or a local school, coaching a youth sports team, or raising children. The word *job* refers to a gainfully employed field of activity. In this more specific work context, monetary compensation accompanies work. Specific jobs include being a teacher, firefighter, contractor, engineer, doctor, barista, or farmer. Those who work a full-time job, string together part-time jobs, or operate within the gig economy often spend a significant portion of their waking hours engaged in work that is gainful (or, too often, less-than-gainful) employment. These forms of work, financially remunerated employment, will most often be the focus of our attention in this book. While terms such as *vocation* and *calling* are often associated with work, we avoid their use because of the wide range of functional meaning associated with them.[30] We will address calling and vocation specifically at different points in our book, but we will not use these terms outside of these instances of focused attention.

---

[29]We adapt this phrase from Max Weber, *The Protestant Ethic and the Spirit of Capitalism* (New York: Routledge, 2000), 209. Dietrich Bonhoeffer also cites Weber and uses the same phrase to describe the scope of responsibility a person has to follow Christ in the whole of their life. See Dietrich Bonhoeffer, *Ethics*, trans. Reinhard Krauss, Charles C. West, and Douglass W. Stott, vol. 6 of *Dietrich Bonhoeffer Works* (Minneapolis: Fortress, 2009), 289 and 292.

[30]See also Scott Waalkes, "Rethinking Work as Vocation: From Protestant Advice to Gospel Corrective," *Christian Scholar's Review*, 44, no. 2 (Winter 2015): 135-53; Lori Brandt Hale, "Bonhoeffer's Christological Take on Vocation," in *Bonhoeffer, Christ and Culture*, ed. Keith L. Johnson and Timothy Larson (Downers Grove, IL: IVP Academic, 2013), 175-90; and William W. Klein and Daniel J. Steiner, *What Is My Calling? A Biblical and Theological Exploration of Christian Identity* (Grand Rapids, MI: Baker Academic, 2022).

2

GOOD

A Theology of Finitude

We disdain limits.

Tish Harrison Warren, *Liturgy of the Ordinary*

We must divest ourselves of the idea that limitation implies
something derogatory, or even a kind of curse or affliction.

Karl Barth, *Church Dogmatics*

God saw all that he made, and it was very good.

Genesis 1:31

TOWARD A THEOLOGY OF QUOTIDIAN WORK

This is the first of two chapters devoted to finitude. The second of these chapters will explore the relationship between finitude and work. In preparation for this, the present chapter explores the theology of finitude. Two primary motives animate this chapter. The first is, quite simply, to offer theological perspective on finitude. Finitude, human and other forms, is an inescapable characteristic of all of life for all people. Consequently, it is not surprising that from time to time it has captured the attention of theologians. Recently, it has received fresh attention in the context of theological explorations of human embodiment.[1] And rightly so. From telling children that they can be whatever they want to be to coaching people with the encouragement that there are no limits to keep them from "success" to tacitly thinking that finitude is evil, there are facts of embodied life worthy of considered, theological reflection.

The second motive that propels this chapter is the need not merely to think theologically but, as we do so, to think accurately and wisely about finitude. This will involve both setting forth what we understand to be the truth about finitude and correcting certain misunderstandings. Because finitude is part of "the air we breathe" it often is not consciously thought about.[2] In turn, it can tacitly come to be regarded as insignificant. Given that finitude is an ever-present condition of life, there may be times when the reader thinks that we are here simply stating the obvious. If so, that is because from time to time we will be simply stating the obvious, stating it so that it is not allowed to be tacitly overlooked, misunderstood, or denied.

The faith and work movement has done little to advance the theological account of finitude in relation to work. There is a recognition of finitude reflected, at least implicitly, in most discussions of sabbath, which are common in theology of work literature, and, perhaps more explicitly, in economic discussions of scarcity and competition, which are sometimes engaged within the theology of work.[3] However, a thicker understanding

---

[1]The theme of human embodiment has received renewed theological attention in recent years, often, though not always, prompted by scholars with particular interest in gender or race or social justice. For examples of recent treatments by evangelical scholars, see Jill Firth and Denise Cooper-Clark, ed., *Grounded in the Body, in Time and Place, in Scripture* (Eugene, OR: Wipf and Stock, 2021); Kelly M. Kapic, *You're Only Human: How Your Limits Reflect God's Design and Why That's Good News* (Grand Rapids, MI: Brazos Press, 2022); Gregg R. Allison, *Embodied: Living as Whole People in a Fractured World* (Grand Rapids, MI: Baker, 2021), 59-72; Sean McGever, *The Good News of Our Limits: Find Greater Peace, Joy, and Effectiveness Through God's Gift of Inadequacy* (Grand Rapids, MI: Zondervan Reflective, 2022); and W. David O. Taylor, *A Body of Praise: Understanding the Role of Our Physical Bodies in Worship* (Grand Rapids, MI: Baker Academic, 2023).

[2]This phenomenon is itself a manifestation of finitude. We cannot—and thankfully, do not need to—think about "everything" all the time or even some of the time. See, for example, Scott A. Small, *Forgetting: The Benefits of Not Remembering* (New York: Penguin Random House, 2021).

[3]For a helpful discussion of this see Brent Waters, *Just Capitalism: A Christian Ethic of Economic Globalization* (Louisville, KY: Westminster John Knox, 2016), especially 40-54, 184-86.

and more comprehensive appreciation of the significance of the theology of finitude for the theology of work is largely absent. It is hoped that this chapter will help to lay a foundation for such integration.

The chapter will unfold in four steps. First, we will briefly note our cultural context with respect to limits. Second, we will observe the sheer fact of finitude, including the dimensions of space, time, and human capacities. Third, with a view toward a proper assessment of and response to finitude, we will reflect theologically on the origin and destiny of finitude. Finally, we will consider both challenges and gifts of finitude.

A BENT AGAINST BOUNDARIES: DENYING LIMITS

Finitude consists in boundary or limit. It is associated with a beginning and/or an end, whether spatial, temporal, or ontological. The dominant zeitgeist of contemporary culture with respect to finitude or limitations is not difficult to discern. As Tish Harrison Warren succinctly observes, "We disdain limits."[4] Those people whose profession involves getting other people's attention and moving them to some kind of action—such as marketers, coaches, and motivational speakers—know what to say and what to offer in order to attract people to their enterprises. The world of sports revolves around winning and offering to people, both athletes and spectators, coaching in what it takes to win, both in and beyond the arena. One of the most accomplished athletes of our time is the Olympic swimmer Michael Phelps, and when it came time for him to cowrite a book presenting his story and keys to his success it was titled *No Limits*.[5] Competitors in the business arena pursue winning with similar types of mindset, typified in articles such as "Your Potential Success Is Limitless, Despite What You've Been Told," which guides readers to recognize that "there is no limit to how much success can be created! It is infinite. You can always have as much as, or as little as, you

---

[4]Tish Harrison Warren, *Liturgy of the Ordinary: Sacred Practices in Everyday Life* (Downers Grove, IL: InterVarsity Press, 2016), 145.
[5]Michael Phelps and Alan Abrahamson, *No Limits: The Will to Succeed* (Glencoe, IL: Free Press, 2008).

want. . . . Unfortunately, most people look at success with scarcity and limitations."[6] Perhaps reflecting the glass ceiling that for too long kept women from positions of senior leadership, the "no limits" mindset is sometimes curated specifically for women. "You know what's stopping you, how to use the tools to eliminate what's stopping you," writes Karen Luniw on her website "No Limits Business Woman."[7] None of these people are cited here as intellectual authorities in the philosophy or phenomenology of finitude, and it would be unfair to assume that the language recounted above was intended to be an expression of onto-logical literalism. They do, however, provide a glimpse into a common mindset in our culture, even if not always so explicitly expressed.[8]

With a broader field of vision than mere self-help or individual success, utopian visions of human existence—ways of being that break the bonds and the bounds of human life as it is usually understood—have been promulgated since well before the time of Christ. The twentieth century saw fresh interest in a new level of such thinking, often referred to as *transhumanism*. When one moves from motivational speakers and life coaches to people focusing on the intersection of humanity and technology, the claims become slightly more modest but far more serious and substantial. According to their website and under a banner reading "Transhumanism," Humanity+ is an "international nonprofit membership organization which advocates the ethical use of technology to expand human capacities." The tagline for the homepage is "Don't limit your challenges—challenge your limits." Humanity+ seeks to advance "the ethical use of technology . . . to expand human capacities." "In other words," Humanity+ says, "we want people to be

[6]Grant Cordone, "Your Potential Success Is Limitless, Despite What You've Been Told," *Entrepreneur*, November 18, 2015, www.entrepreneur.com/article/252830.

[7]"Karen Luniw—No Limits Business Consulting," www.attractmorenow.com, accessed March 6, 2025.

[8]Amid the predominant self-help voices constantly urging and promising more there are those who acknowledge reality and forthrightly name finitude and limits. See for example Oliver Burkeman, *Four Thousand Weeks: Time Management for Mortals* (New York: Farrar, Straus and Giroux, 2021).

better than well." The website states, "Technologies that support lon-
gevity and mitigate the disease of aging by curing disease and repairing
injury have accelerated to a point in which they also can increase human
performance *outside the realms of what is considered to be 'normal' for
humans*."[9] Similarly, the "immutable principles" of the United States
Transhumanist Party, a political party, include "support[ing] significant
life extension achieved through the progress of science and technology,"
and "support[ing] efforts to use science, technology, and rational discourse to reduce and eliminate various existential risks to the human
species."[10] They assert that "No coercive legal restrictions should exist
to bar access to life extension and life expansion for all sentient entities,"
and hope that "Involuntary aging shall be classified as a disease."[11]

These examples of perspectives on finitude provide a window into our
cultural context. They reflect a way of thinking that is widespread
enough that people can make a living and organizations can be formed
by encouraging this way of thinking. Even if one regards some of these
illustrations as extreme, they correspond to widely held aspirations, to
a bent or orientation with respect to human life and reality. Furthermore,
this bent or orientation is not, at its core, unique to our cultural context.
It is characteristic of the human condition. In general, not least in the

---

[9]"Elevating the Human Condition," www.humanityplus.org/, accessed May 15, 2020, emphasis
added. There is an acknowledgment that there are ethical issues that require adjudication:
"Because these technologies, and their respective sciences and strategic models, such as block-
chain, would take the human beyond the historical (normal) state of existence, society, including bioethicists and others who advocate the safe use of technology, have shown concern and
uncertainties about the downside of these technologies and possible problematic and dangerous outcomes for our species."
[10]"Transhumanist Bill of Rights—Version 3.0," https://transhumanist-party.org/tbr-3/, accessed
May 19, 2020. The party's proposed "Bill of Rights" is predicated on the view that "science and
technology are now radically changing human beings and may also create future forms of advanced sapient and sentient life." The rights enumerated in this document are set forth as the rights
of "sentient entities," which includes "human beings, including genetically modified humans;
Cyborgs; Digital intelligences; and Intellectually enhanced, previously non-sapient animals."
[11]"All nations and their governments will actively seek to dramatically extend the lives and im-
prove the health of their citizens by offering them scientific and medical technologies to overcome involuntary aging." Articles V and VI, *Transhumanist Bill of Rights*, https://
transhumanist-party.org/tbr-3/, accessed May 19, 2020.

modern West, we disdain limits.[12] From the story told in Genesis 3 onward, human beings hate, or at the very least resent, limits of every sort. Yet, the fact of limits, the fact of finitude, remains.

CREATION . . . OLD AND NEW:
THE REALITY OF FINITUDE

To adopt a posture that is fundamentally against all limits is to adopt a posture that is fundamentally against creation as God, the Creator, designed and made it. God made the world, and the human beings who inhabit it, finite. Dietrich Bonhoeffer suggests, "The creatureliness of human beings . . . can be defined in simply no other way than in terms of the existence of human beings over-against-one-another, with-one-another, and in-dependence-upon-one-another."[13] This finitude, and the corresponding dependence, is not merely a matter of quantity but also one of quality, of ontology. As David Kelsey notes, the creaturely realm as a whole and each and all the creatures within it are "limited in being." And the dependence or contingency of limited human beings is ultimately, most fundamentally, dependence and contingency in relation to God. This is, he stresses, "an ontological, not a numerical claim. . . . The ontological finitude of the creaturely realm, however infinite its number, is a function of its radical dependency for its existence on God's ongoing creativity." The creation's and creatures' relation to the Creator is "radical-dependence-for-being."[14] This is human existence in the real world, the world in which every human being lives and works. To see, to acknowledge, and to embrace this is to have what Kevin Vanhoozer refers to as "evangelical imagination." That is, "to live not in a

---

[12]One can understandably wonder whether cultural contexts that place an especially high value on and strongly emphasize freedom—particularly individual freedom for individual persons— provide rich soil for the flourishing of a bent against boundaries, against limits.

[13]Dietrich Bonhoeffer, *Creation and Fall: A Theological Exegesis of Genesis 1–3*, ed. John W. de Gruchy, trans. Douglas Stephen Bax, *Dietrich Bonhoeffer Works*, vol. 3 (Minneapolis: Fortress, 2004), 64.

[14]David H. Kelsey, *Eccentric Existence: A Theological Anthropology*, 2 vols. (Louisville, KY: Westminster John Knox, 2009), 1:201. Also Paul Tillich, *Systematic Theology* (Chicago: University of Chicago Press, 1951), 1:198.

fantasyland but in the only real world there is: the world created by God's word; the world into which God's word has entered and will return."[15] Contrary to excessively subjective epistemologies, merely thinking something does not "make it so." The finitude of this world created by God's word entails what are, for human beings, limitations both extrinsic and intrinsic.[16]

Extrinsic limits. There is a *givenness* to the world. It is created, but we did not create it. If we are to live, we have to live in and with it, in keeping with its creation design. Even more fundamentally, we must and can live in relationship to the Creator. This is, as described by David Kesley, our "ultimate context." "The ultimate context into which [human beings] are born is God's relating to them as their creator."[17] The distinctively Judeo-Christian claim in this regard is that the God of Abraham, Isaac, and Jacob created the world and created human beings to live in and with this world. This is a foundational component of the "stern realism" of Christianity.[18] The evangelical imagination commended by Vanhoozer as well as the *realist* cosmologies of Thomas Torrance and Alister McGrath call on us to face the world, to embrace our existence with and before God, *as it is*.[19] And this includes embracing the reality of limitations. The fact that human beings are *creatures* of the divine Creator and that the world in which we live is the *creation* of this same

---

[15]Kevin J. Vanhoozer, *Hearers and Doers: A Pastor's Guide to Making Disciples Through Scripture and Doctrine* (Bellingham, WA: Lexham Press, 2019), 110-11. For Vanhoozer, an evangelical imagination is a "biblically disciplined" imagination, "ruled by the story of the gospel—[which] frees us to see, judge, and act in faith, in accordance with the way things really are rather than the way secular science or Madison Avenue say they are" (113, 110).

[16]Veli-Matti Kärkkäinen, *Creation and Humanity*, A Constructive Theology for the Pluralistic World, vol. 3 (Grand Rapids, MI: Eerdmans, 2015), 426. David Kelsey conceives what we here refer to as *extrinsic* limitations as *proximate contexts*, with the *ultimate context* being "God's hospitable generosity, creatively relating, to us" (Kelsey, *Eccentric Existence*, 1:175, 190).

[17]Kelsey, *Eccentric Existence*, 1:160.

[18]This term is adopted from David Bebbington's description of a Christian view of history (David W. Bebbington, *Patterns in History: A Christian Perspective on Historical Thought*, 4th ed. [Waco, TX: Baylor University Press, 2018], 58).

[19]Thomas F. Torrance, "Incarnation and Space and Time," in *Space, Time and Incarnation* (Edinburgh: T&T Clark, 1997), 52-90; and Alister E. McGrath, *A Scientific Theology*, vol. 1, *Nature* (Grand Rapids, MI: Eerdmans, 2001), 71-77.

Creator is fundamental to existence and fundamental to everything that is said in what follows below.

Space + time = particularity. Space and time are widely present in and often at the forefront of discussions of finitude, including theological discussions. In *Theology of Culture*, Paul Tillich observes that "time and space are the main structures of existence to which all existing things, the whole finite realm, are subjected. Existing means being finite or being in time and space."[20] Similarly, Brent Waters affirms that there is "an inextricable relation between time and place." We are "in place within time, and time is marked by being in place."[21] This is an inextricable connection characterizing embodied life. Embodied life is always *particular* life. As Treier observes, "Our Creator has given us bodies with which to engage a world, so our finite lives must always be particularized."[22] This is the character of embodied existence—it is particularized existence within space and time. We have particular relationships with particular people and we engage in particular activities in particular places at particular times. This person is not some other person. This place is not a different place. Now is not another time.

Some people find the implications of this problematic, speaking of "the scandal of particularity."[23] It can be employed to critique, for example, the view that the Jews occupy a unique place in salvation history

---

[20]Paul Tillich, *Theology of Culture*, ed. Robert C. Kimball (New York: Oxford University Press, 1959), 30. In *Systematic Theology* Tillich discusses finitude in relation to four "categories": time, space, causality, and substance. He identifies time as "the main category of finitude." (*Systematic Theology*, vol. 1, *Reason and Revelation, Being and God* [Chicago: University of Chicago Press, 1951], 193; also 82.)

[21]Brent Waters, *Common Callings and Ordinary Virtues: Christian Ethics for Everyday Life* (Grand Rapids, MI: Baker Academic, 2022), 55 and 61.

[22]Daniel J. Treier, "Finitude," in *Evangelical Dictionary of Theology*, 3rd ed., ed. Daniel J. Treier and Walter A. Elwell (Grand Rapids, MI: Baker Academic, 2017), 318b. "Particularity" is a recurring theme in Barth's discussion of vocation in the *Church Dogmatics* (see, for example, *Church Dogmatics*, III.4, 597, 599, 620, 633, 639).

[23]As with any phrase, the intended meaning of "the scandal of particularity" needs to be understood in context. Some authors employ the phrase in the process of negatively critiquing or rejecting a proposition. In such instances "scandal" is intended rather literally—the view being critiqued is regarded as utterly unacceptable. Other authors may adopt and adapt the phrase in a rather tongue-in-cheek fashion for rhetorical effect, regarding the view in question not as unacceptable but as being of some, perhaps even much, merit.

(a uniquely privileged people), or the claim that the Son of God was incarnated as a first-century (a particular time) Jewish (a particular group of people) man (a particular gender), or the fact that Jesus Christ, and no other savior, is *the* way, *the* truth, and *the* life (Jn 14:6). These and other *theological* views or assertions are conditioned by the *historical* realities of which they speak—realities within the finitudes of space and time, realities associated with embodiment. Speaking of the "scandal" of particularity, Beth Felker Jones notes that particularity "offends our sense of fairness and propriety." But she goes on to observe that in the particularity of God incarnate in Christ, "God's love reaches into our specificity, our particularity."[24] Barth suggests that "the calling or vo-cation" of each person consists in the "particularity, limitation and re-striction in which the God who calls and rules always finds man, and by which man must orientate himself to be obedient."[25] The realm of space and time is the realm in which fallen, particular human beings exist, and it is into this realm of particularities that God redemptively intervenes. Every day, throughout the day, conscious of it or not, our lives are carried out within innumerable particularities. And none of them is beyond the reach of our heavenly Father. Our Father reaches down and out from his ultimate context into our finite, contingent, proximate context.[26]

In a study of the incarnation of God in Christ, Thomas Torrance writes, "space and time were produced along with the creaturely world as orderly functions of contingent events within it." "Whatever we do," he writes, "we cannot contract out of space and time."[27] In God's creation order, to be in place is to be in time and to be in time is to be in place. While there admittedly are a variety of ways in which the extrinsic limits

---

[24]Beth Felker Jones, *Practicing Christian Doctrine: An Introduction to Thinking and Living Theologi-cally* (Grand Rapids, MI: Baker Academic, 2014), 137. Jones goes on in this context to note that God's salvific work in Christ "encompasses bodies as well as souls."

[25]Barth, *Church Dogmatics*, III.4, §56, 597. On the scandal of particularity, also see Katherine Sonderegger, "Finitude and Death," in *T&T Clark Companion to the Doctrine of Sin*, ed. Keith L. Johnson and David Lauber (New York: Bloomsbury, 2016), 394-95.

[26]Kelsey, *Eccentric Existence*, 1:190, 201.

[27]Torrance, *Space, Time and Incarnation*, 60, 62; also see 67, 74.

of human finitude can be conceived, we will here consider these limits in relation to the created realities of space and time.[28]

Space. To be human is, as God intended, to be located. To be human is to be here. It is to be somewhere, always. There are times when we are precisely where we want to be and times when we wish we were somewhere else. But always and wherever, we are here. And the accompanying reality is that at any given moment we are not there. This is our finitude with regard to space, and it is universal, true for all people at all times and—somewhat ironically—in all places. Note that these observations about finitude with regard to space are inextricably related to the reality of finitude with regard to time, expressive of the particularity discussed above. In God's good design, no one can be both here and there at the same time, but this is not an evil. Life is the gift of *being somewhere.*

Reflecting the uniqueness of human beings, the interaction of human beings with space often has a unique generative outcome: the creation of *place.*[29] Place is a particular finite space within space, but it is more. It is space that is particularized by virtue of its use by particular human beings. And this particularization brings with it meaning and significance. As Brent Waters accurately observes, "Unlike temporary space, the significance or value of place is not derived from its utility. Rather, people bestow meaning and value on a place over time. Place becomes a landmark demarcating important events in the lives of individuals or associations." As a result, human beings not only transform space into place but place shapes us, informing our thoughts and feelings, our actions and even our identity.[30] Indeed, as Craig Bartholomew rightly

---

[28]For example, Karl Barth discusses finitude under the heading of "Freedom in Limitation" and in relation to time, vocation, and honor (see Barth, *Church Dogmatics*, III.4, section 56), while Daniel Treier describes finitude by identifying ten "relational spheres" ("Finitude," 318a-b).

[29]For two extended and thoughtful treatments of space and place, see Craig G. Bartholomew, *Where Mortals Dwell: A Christian View of Place for Today* (Grand Rapids, MI: Baker Academic, 2011), and Eric O. Jacobsen, *The Space Between: A Christian Engagement with the Built Environment* (Grand Rapids, MI: Baker Academic, 2012).

[30]Euntaek David Shin, *Rest: A Theological Account* (Waco, TX: Baylor University Press, 2024), 34.

states, "One of the glories of being human and creaturely is to be implaced."[31] Thus, Waters laments that "there is a growing preference for space over place" because mere space is "not an adequate substitute that can displace place entirely." As embodied beings with agency, human beings are emplaced beings. "Human flourishing requires physical places where embodied humans congregate to collectively undertake certain tasks and establish relationships over time."[32] This is just one example of the goodness of finitude. Rather than space being a problem, humans flourish in specific, *even-more-limited* spaces within space—namely, places.

Time. Then there is time.[33] Our embodied selves cannot be simultaneously present *both* now *and* then. Human life is carried out moment by moment, always in the present. Through the gift and power of memory we can recall, even if incompletely, the past, and through the gift and power of imagination we can contemplate potential futures. That which has happened in the past informs and helps shape the present, and the way in which one anticipates the future informs and contributes to the shape of what one thinks and does in the present. But our finitude with respect to time is such that in each moment, we live and move and have our embodied being in the present.[34]

This succession of present moments unfolds from birth, through the days of our lives, to death. There is legitimate debate and considerable diversity of opinion among theologians and biblical scholars regarding the precise relationship between God's original creation design, the impact(s) of the fall, and bodily death. However, whether one believes

---

[31]Bartholomew, *Where Mortals Dwell*, xi.

[32]Waters, *Common Callings*, 176.

[33]In the present discussion, time is regarded as substantival and tensed. It is beyond the scope of this study to explore scientific and philosophical theories of time. For an introductory survey of views of time with particular attention to matters of theology, see Gregory E. Ganssle, ed., *God and Time: Four Views* (Downers Grove, IL: IVP Academic, 2001). For a challenging and poignant theological exploration of human disability and time, see John Swinton, *Becoming Friends of Time: Disability, Timefullness, and Gentle Discipleship* (Waco, TX: Baylor University Press, 2016).

[34]This is an adaptation of the language and imagery of Acts 17:28. It is not intended to be either a quotation or direct application of the verse itself.

that human bodily death was part of God's creation design in Eden or that human bodily death was not part of God's original creation design but is rather a result of the fall, the now-universal reality of human bodily death is, in earthly terms, the final and most dramatic manifestation of human finitude. Ultimately, humans have been, are, and will remain "finite in their ongoing radical dependence on God's creativity."[35] Our lives on earth have a beginning and an end, and in between we remain mortal, "existing," notes Ephraim Radner, "in a way that we cannot maintain of our own."[36] As is the case with most other limits, we push back against the finitude of the span of our lives. For most of us throughout most of our lives, whatever the number of our days, we would like more. This is understandable and, with appropriate humility, right and good because God made us as *living* creatures.

The uniqueness of the finitude of embodied life on earth is that God has provided for it ultimately to be overcome. In Jesus Christ God has provided for eternal *embodied* life. As will be explored later in this chapter, redeemed and glorified human existence will be embodied finite existence—transformed and glorified but bodily and finite nonetheless.

Incarnation and the incarnation. One can refer to the denial or attempt to reject human embodied finitude as *de-incarnation* or *disincarnation*, a form of abstraction from concrete particularity.[37] To be human is to be incarnate, embodied. This is the specific form in which the Creator made human beings "very good." Genesis 2:7 says, "Then the LORD God formed man from the dust of the ground and breathed into his nostrils the breath of life, and the man became a living being." The Lord did not simply breathe—he breathed *into*. He breathed into a being fashioned from "the dust of the ground." He breathed into nostrils. In recounting the history of God with his covenant people, from slavery in Egypt to the reign of David, the psalmist says that the Lord "remembered

---

[35]Kelsey, *Eccentric Existence*, 1:508.
[36]Ephraim Radner, *A Time to Keep: Theology, Morality, and the Shape of a Human Life* (Waco, TX: Baylor University Press, 2016), 38.
[37]On abstraction, see Kelsey, *Eccentric Existence*, 1:413.

that they were but flesh, a wind that passes and does not come again"
(Ps 78:39). Knowing that human spirit and body are inextricably interrelated, Proverbs wisely observes and counsels, "A tranquil mind gives
life to the flesh, but passion makes the bones rot," and "A cheerful heart
is a good medicine, but a downcast spirit dries up the bones" (Prov 14:30;
17:22). This intimate interrelation of soul and body is well known by the
apostle Paul. He calls on the Christians of the church at Rome to "present
your bodies as a living sacrifice, holy and acceptable to God, which is
your spiritual worship" (Rom 12:1).

The unique and redemptively significant instance of human embodiment between creation and consummation is the incarnation of
God in Jesus Christ.[38] In the case of the incarnation of the Son of God,
"the time, space and life of Jesus *is* the time, space and life of God without
ceasing to be the time, space and life of creation."[39] The word *incarnation* succinctly affirms the reality and, on elaboration, the goodness
of human embodiment. God took on human embodiment and did so
without being corrupted by sin. The author of the book of Hebrews
proclaims that the incarnate Christ was "tempted in every way, just as
we are—yet he did not sin" (Heb 4:15 NIV) and the early church faithfully carried this tradition forward. The fathers of the Council of Chal-
cedon (AD 451) clearly testified that the incarnate Christ was "actually
God and actually man, with a rational soul and a body," indeed "like us
in all things apart from sin." Human embodiment does not itself morally
corrupt the nature related to it. In Christ, human embodiment and a
nature and life devoid of sin were conjoined.

Though Jesus was without sin, he was, as Hebrews says, "tempted in
every way, just as we are." It would be wrong to oversimplify and reduce
all of Jesus' temptations to a form of wrestling with finitude. However, it
also would be a form of de-incarnation not to recognize that Jesus

---

[38]For an extended study of the incarnation with specific focus on two facets of finitude that we
focus on here—i.e., space and time—see Torrance, *Space, Time and Incarnation*.

[39]Ron Highfield, *The Faithful Creator: Affirming Creation and Providence in an Age of Anxiety*
(Downers Grove, IL: IVP Academic, 2015), 183, emphasis original.

experienced some of his temptations due to the finitudes associated with embodied human existence. Finitude entails various forms of dependence or contingency, which sometimes constitute the occasion for temptation. Both Matthew and Luke report that having gone without food for forty days and forty nights, Jesus "was famished" (Mt 4:2; Lk 4:2). He wanted and needed food. Aware of this, "The tempter came and said to him, 'If you are the Son of God, command these stones to become loaves of bread'" (Mt 4:3; see also Lk 4:3). This constituted a genuine temptation precisely because it targeted a particular finitude, a particular dependence—the physical need for physical food.[40] Jesus did not succumb, rebuking the tempter by testifying that "One does not live by bread alone, but by every word that comes from the mouth of God" (Mt 4:4; see also Lk 4:4). The inclusion of the word *alone* (μόνῳ) is significant. Jesus' statement is neither a denial of the need for physical food nor a denial of the rightness of such a need, but rather an indication that there is also another kind of food on which humans are dependent for life as God intends it.

Persistent, the tempter called on the Son of God to provoke the law of gravity and then to seek supernatural aid to evade its God-created natural consequences. Responding again from Scripture, Jesus obediently refrained from putting the Father "to the test" (Mt 4:7; Lk 4:12). A third time the tempter sought to entice Jesus to break God-given boundaries—to gain for himself a form and degree of control and glory, "all the kingdoms of the world," which were beyond the ordained bounds of his incarnate life (Mt 4:8-9; Lk 4:5-7). The same word *alone* or *only* is once again important, this time in an affirmative sense. Echoing Deuteronomy 6, Jesus says, "Worship the Lord your God, and serve only him" (Mt 4:10; Lk 4:8). The tempter leaves him, angels come to him and, in the context of Jesus' mode of life being conditioned by finitude, they "provide for Jesus' needs."[41]

---

[40]Some expositors refer to the episodes in the wilderness as testing or trial. We think that those understate the nature and gravity of what took place, and so we refer to them as temptations.

[41]Craig S. Keener, *A Commentary on the Gospel of Matthew* (Grand Rapids, MI: Eerdmans, 1999), 144.

All of this unfolds in keeping with the context of God-designed creation, which is both shaped by finitude and fundamentally good. "Again and again," writes Barth, "we must point to the fact that in Christ God Himself has entered the limitation and singularity of man."[42] Consequently, Jesus was subject to temptation, in part due to various kinds of limitations expressive of embodied human finitude. The temptations were, in significant measure, temptations to exceed human limits—to have more—but Jesus incarnated sinless perseverance and submission to God the Father by not exceeding these limits. Goodness, holiness, obedience to God the Father were realized within, not beyond, the bounds of Jesus' embodied life.

Intrinsic limits. The finitude of embodied human life consists not only in relation to that which is external to the person but also to that which is intrinsic to the person herself or himself. This is expressive of the fact that, as noted above, human finitude is not merely quantitative but ontological. Its intrinsic limits might even be said to be *intimate* to the person. We will here explore intrinsic limits by considering human capacities—that is, *human resources for embodied agency* such as *physical* abilities and energy, *intellectual* capabilities and energy, *psychological and emotional* capacities and energy, and *social and relational* skills and energy.

Sometimes humans possess one or more of these capacities in breathtaking measure, as is evident when a soldier slogs through deep sand and into enemy fire in service of a wounded comrade or a musical composer is celebrated when the premiere of her orchestral composition begets tears and cheers in a concert hall. Whenever we encounter people and actions of exceptional measure they should be duly appreciated and celebrated. There is nothing wrong with "pushing the limits" when done for good reason and in healthy measure. This acknowledged, we should neither demand nor expect more of such people and actions than accords with the realities of finitude. These kinds of achievements, and the people who bring them about, have, as we all do, their limits. If, for

---

[42]Barth, *Church Dogmatics*, III.4, 577.

example, there are dozens of comrades in need of help, even the noblest and most able of soldiers may not be able to even attempt helping them all, and not every musical composition by even the most revered composer always leaves every hearer cheering and in appreciative tears. All soldiers and composers, all of us, have limits. To say this is simply an acknowledgment of who we are as creatures. And we say this remembering that "God saw everything that he had made," including man and woman as finite beings, "and indeed, it was very good" (Gen 1:31).

We above considered the extrinsic finitudes associated with space and time, and space and time will be ever-present in and inform, sometimes implicitly, our consideration of human capacities. Furthermore, we recognize that the various capacities of human beings are inextricably integrated and interactive—human beings live and work as whole persons. So when we briefly focus on one capacity for the purposes of discussion, the other capacities need to be kept, whether explicitly or implicitly, within our peripheral vision.

Our *physical capacities* are finite. This is part of the reason we are struck by and celebrate the accomplishments of world class athletes. They achieve feats of which the rest of us can only dream. It is amazing, particularly in our era of hyper-specialization, to watch one athlete compete in a decathlon—ten discrete track-and-field events—and to undertake all of these events within a period of just two days.[43] It is incredible to see a weightlifter snatch-lift 225 kilograms (= 496 pounds) and clean-and-jerk 267 kilograms (= 589 pounds)—a total of 492 kilograms (= 1,085 pounds) in just two lifts.[44] Though not usually thought of as athletes, the physical achievements of firefighters are both amazing and awe-inspiring—going up stairs, wearing seventy-five pounds of gear and carrying equipment, in over 1,000-degree temperature. They are rightly lauded for pushing limits and rightly celebrated for going beyond

---

[43] The Olympic decathlon includes 100-meter dash, running long jump, shot put, high jump, 400-meter run, 110-meter hurdles, discus throw, pole vault, javelin throw, and 1,500-meter run.

[44] "World Records," International Weightlifting Federation, www.iwf.sport/results/world-records/ (accessed March 6, 2025).

the limits of the rest of us. However, even the most highly trained, deeply committed athletes eventually come up against physical limits. There are no specialized one-sport athletes who can jump forty feet, no weight-lifters who can clean-and-jerk one thousand pounds, and part of the job of captains of firefighting teams is to assess risk and know when not to direct their fighters into a building. Recognizing limits such as these takes nothing away from these kinds of remarkable accomplishments, for everyone has limited physical capacities.

All of us do, of course, observe physical finitude in everyday life. "Our powerful need for sleep is a reminder that we are finite," observes Trish Harrison Warren. "Our need for sleep reveals that we have limits."[45] Many college students and tech entrepreneurs are well acquainted with all-nighters, but eventually college students skip a class in order to sleep and tech entrepreneurs take advantage of the couch in the open work-space. We need to sleep. And most people who have experienced even moderate sleep deprivation over an extended period of time recognize that this deprivation negatively impacts other capacities, such as intel-lectual acuity and psychological and emotional well-being.

We need food, water, and air. When someone either refuses or is re-fused food or water for an extended period, the quality of their physical existence and functioning of their faculties declines. They must even-tually either receive nourishment or die. Our limit regarding air is the most restrictive of all. Ordinarily, a human being cannot live if their brain is deprived of oxygen for more than fifteen minutes, and that is a mar-ginal extreme.[46] (As you are reading this, try holding your breath. How many seconds before you take a breath?) These are not the only manifes-tations of our embodied embedding within the creation, and their sig-nificance is often overlooked precisely because they are so common, so mundane. But they are indicative of a very important fact of life: we are, by God's design, finite creatures whose very bodily existence is

---

[45]Warren, *Liturgy of the Ordinary*, 144.
[46]"How long does it take to die from no oxygen?," UCSB Science Line, http://scienceline.ucsb. edu/getkey.php?key=3643 (accessed June 29, 2020).

contingent, dependent on creation. In light of this, Kelsey observes that "we are born into a vocation from God, mediated through the quotidian, to be wise in our practices for the well being of the quotidian."[47]

To acknowledge and attend to limits and dependencies is simply to live in the real world and in no way negates the affirmation that human beings are "fearfully and wonderfully made" (Ps 139:14). Creational finitude is a fact of embodied human existence as God created it. It does not constitute an evil or moral failure. The physical needs identified here constitute an inescapable form of dependence, of contingency, of vulnerability . . . against which we so often want to press. They are the most concrete, tangible indicators that we are neither utterly independent nor sovereign. For over forty years theologian Frances Young has cared for her seriously disabled son, through whom she experiences a kind of "privileged access to the deepest truths of the Christian religion." Among these truths is the fact that "human beings are vulnerable—indeed, there is a scale of disability on which we all find ourselves, and acknowledgment of dependence is the key to independence."[48] Because human beings are, as God intends, physically embodied beings, our physical limitations and the dependence that accompanies them are the most tangible forms of finitude.

Yet no one lives on bread alone (recall Mt 4:4). There is more to being human—though not less—than being embodied. This is why Jesus commands "You shall love the Lord your God with all your heart, and with all your soul, and with all your mind" (Mt 22:37; also see Deut 6:5; Lk 10:27). In the context of the present discussion we cannot overlook the fact that this call to "all" is itself grounded in the fact of human finitude. We do not have the capacity to genuinely worship two gods. If one gives all of oneself to God, one has nothing to give to another god.

Human finitude extends to the nonphysical dimensions of human being. Our *intellectual and cognitive capacities* are finite. We do not and

---

[47]Kelsey, *Eccentric Existence*, 1:213.

[48]Frances Young, *God's Presence: A Contemporary Recapitulation of Early Christianity* (Cambridge: Cambridge University Press, 2013), 3, 128.

cannot know everything, and this limitation is both quantitative and qualitative. What's more, we don't know what we don't know. Nonetheless, there are those who believe that given enough time and resources human beings can solve any problem. This outlook entails confidence in more than the intellect but clearly does not entail less than essentially unbounded confidence in the human capacity to "figure things out." On an individual level, an extreme level of confidence in one's capacity to know can find expression in arrogance (and ironically in ignorance) and, in pathological fashion, in narcissism. The other extreme is to have no substantial confidence in the human capacity to know, whether in all or just some domains. For example, someone may have a high degree of confidence in the ability of humans to attain "scientific" knowledge but little or no confidence in our ability to apprehend knowledge of God, if there is a God. Most people are skeptical in some measure in the sense that they believe that there are some realities about which we simply cannot know; but these domains of ignorance are of such number and nature that we still know enough to carry on life and work. Being a pure or absolute skeptic, believing that one cannot know anything about anything, is simply not a viable posture from which to carry on any semblance of a meaningful human life.

Philosophers Robert Roberts and Jay Wood commend intellectual life that is marked by love of knowledge, firmness, courage and caution, humility, autonomy, and generosity. While most of these virtues are relevant to the finitude of human intellect, we here briefly draw on their discussion of autonomy. Roberts and Wood describe intellectual autonomy as a combination of "a wise dependence, a willingness and ability to tap the intelligence and knowledge of others as needed" and "an intelligent ability to stand one's own ground against bullying, as well as gentler forms of pressure to conform."[49] Of particular interest

[49]Robert C. Roberts and W. Jay Wood, *Intellectual Virtues: An Essay in Regulative Epistemology* (Oxford: Oxford University Press, 2007), 258. Above we acknowledged that while we would focus on one capacity at a time, in fact the capacities are interrelated, and human beings act as whole persons. Roberts and Wood observe that "autonomy is not a property of the intellect as

to the present discussion is their inclusion of *dependence*—a manifestation of finitude—as an essential ingredient of intellectual *autonomy*. Rightly understood, "the intellectual life is a network of deep dependencies."[50] No individual person, large group of people, or institution can know everything about everything, so effective and meaningful intellectual pursuit inevitably includes dependence on other people and the resources they produce. Thus, intellectual autonomy should manifest itself in gratitude. Being aware of one's "debt," the intellectually autonomous person "sees [this] indebtedness as a good and fitting thing."[51]

Our *psyches and emotions* have limits. Consider the following list of suggestions from staff of Mayo Clinic for managing anger: "Think before you speak. . . . Once you're calm express your anger. . . . Get some exercise. . . . Take a timeout. . . . Identify possible solutions. . . . Stick with 'I' statements. . . . Don't hold a grudge. . . . Use humor to release tension. . . . Practice relaxation skills. . . . Know when to seek help."[52] That is a substantial ten-item list for addressing a single emotion, an emotion for which there is an entire multibillion-dollar industry, anger management. Whether or not one thinks that anger is just a symptom, not the cause, and whatever one thinks the root of anger is (or isn't), we all know that our capacity to absorb insult or injury or injustice is limited, and that if not managed wisely this emotion can boil over into hurtful or dangerous fits, even homicidal rage.

In the face of life's challenges most of us experience one or more of the following: feeling sad, losing interest in activities, loss of sleep or too much sleep due to being emotionally upset, feeling worthless,

---

a faculty or part of a person, but a property of the thinker, the epistemic agent," and that "the emotions and desires" are "an integrating factor in the intellectual life" (280).

[50]Roberts and Wood, *Intellectual Virtues*, 261. They rightly observe that "knowledge builds upon knowledge; information and deeper understanding raise more questions, the pursuit of which uncovers more information and deepens our understanding."

[51]Roberts and Wood, *Intellectual Virtues*, 285.

[52]Mayo Clinic, "Anger Management: 10 Tips to Tame Your Anger," www.mayoclinic.org/healthy -lifestyle/adult-health/in-depth/anger-management/art-20045434 (accessed July 1, 2020).

feeling guilty, entertaining thoughts of suicide.[53] Experiences such as these can interfere with, even bring an end to, cherished relationships, employment, or simply carrying out basic functions of everyday life. The degree to which someone experiences these kinds of emotions and the degree to which these experiences become debilitating varies from person to person, and not every experience of so-called bad emotions is in fact bad or necessarily unhealthy.[54] However, while emotional capacities and psychological dynamics vary from person to person, most people have what are sometimes colloquially referred to as their "limits." When this point is reached, people are often prompted, even driven, to take action of some kind. The action may be helpful and healthful or it may be harmful and damaging, but it is action taken because emotional and psychological pressures have crossed a personal threshold, a limit.

We all have and experience *social or relational* finitude, both quantitative and qualitative. Perhaps the most familiar variation in this regard is the difference between introversion and extroversion. Introverts need more time alone, away from other people, than extroverts to maintain their equilibrium. Yet human beings are social beings, and introverts need, as we all do, interaction with other people to maintain psychological and emotional health. Extroversion does not guarantee such health, but it more vividly illustrates that human beings are social creatures who need (a word indicative of finitude) relationship with other people. Whatever one's personality, there are limits—both too much and too little—with regard to social interaction. There are also qualitative limits. People have varying degrees of social intelligence, the

---

[53]These are some of the kinds of experiences associated with depression. See American Psychiatric Association, "What Is Depression?," www.psychiatry.org/patients-families/depression /what-is-depression (accessed July 1, 2020).

[54]For a sampling of Christian wisdom that supplements or challenges some popular understandings of emotional and psychological limits, see Dennis Okholm, *Dangerous Passions, Deadly Sins: Learning From the Psychology of Ancient Monks* (Grand Rapids, MI: Brazos Press, 2014); Douglas Groothuis, *Walking Through Twilight: A Wife's Illness—a Philosopher's Lament* (Downers Grove, IL: InterVarsity Press, 2017); David G. Benner, *Healing Emotional Wounds* (Grand Rapids, MI: Baker Books, 1990); and C. S. Lewis, *A Grief Observed* (New York: HarperCollins, 1961).

ability to understand and conduct interpersonal relationships. Yet once again there are limits, as no one has perfect and complete social intelligence such that both they and all their interlocutors are always pleased with and built up by virtue of their interaction. Each of us needs relationship with other people, and there are limits to both the number and quality of our relationships.

"As creation is utterly dependent on the sovereign God for its existence," observes Beth Felker Jones, "so is humanity." She continues, "Unlike God, we humans are characterized by finitude. In contrast to God, who is all in all, we are limited, bound, and dependent."[55] We are dependent on God for the breath of life itself. We are dependent on God's revelation, in all its manifold forms, for knowledge and understanding of God, the world, and ourselves. We are dependent on the Spirit of God to sustain our spirits.

CREATION . . . OLD AND NEW: THE ORIGIN AND FUTURE OF FINITUDE

At the outset of this chapter we observed the human tendency to reach beyond limits, intensified in the "no limits" zeitgeist of contemporary Western culture. Considering this it will be worthwhile to briefly note both the origin and future of finitude before identifying, in the final section of this chapter, challenges and gifts of creational finitude. The origin of finitude has been alluded to or referred to throughout this chapter and will be addressed here more briefly than the future of finitude.

As previously indicated, the finitudes that we are here considering are *creational* finitudes. These are not the result of human agency but rather are integral to God's creation design. These finitudes, such as the ones described in the preceding pages and including those directly related to human beings, have been characteristics of creation from the beginning. They are not the result of human sinfulness or the fall. This recognition of these finitudes as *creational* is essential to an accurate assessment of

---

[55]Jones, *Practicing Christian Doctrine*, 99.

and wise response to these finitudes—including, as will be explored in the next chapter, our response in the form of work.

From the earliest centuries it has been a fundamental affirmation in all streams of Christianity that the God of the Bible is "Maker of heaven and earth, and of all things visible and invisible" (Constantinopolitan Creed). And this has been accompanied by embrace of Scripture's statement that "God saw everything that he made, and indeed, it was very good" (Gen 1:31). Whatever our experience might incline us to think or human cosmologies might propose, all of creation as designed and made by God is fundamentally good. And this good creation as designed and made by God is finite. Thus, Kelly Kapic can conclude his book-length study of human limits, *You're Only Human*, by saying, "God made us to be limited creatures, able to freely participate in his work, confident in his presence, and grateful for his promises and provision. Let us appreciate *the goodness of our finitude* as we rest in the love and provision of our infinitely good God. May it be so."[56] By virtue of God's creational goodness, this is the nature of creational finitude. But what is the future of finitude? Does it have a future? Or will the consummating, eschatological work of God include releasing creation, particularly human beings, from the limitations of finitude? Is the nature and character of finitude such that salvation includes the elimination of all human finitude? Responses to these questions constitute a second foundation underlying the affirmation of the goodness of creational finitude.

All comparisons of the present age and the eschatological future entail a combination of continuity and change. This is true of both what might be called *micro* matters, such as the material dimensions of the resurrection of an individual person, and *macro* or cosmic matters, such as the realization of the new heavens and new earth. In this regard there is wide-ranging diversity among the many theological visions of the eschatological future, but virtually all, if not all, include both affirmation

[56]Kapic, *You're Only Human*, 222, emphasis added. Also see Shin, *Rest*, 28; and Daniel J. Treier, *Proverbs and Ecclesiastes* (Grand Rapids, MI: Brazos Press, 2011), 129 and 182.

that the eschatological future is in some fashion continuous with the present and affirmation that it is in some fashion discontinuous with the present.[57] As Stanley Grenz observes, "the biblical vision of the culmination of the cosmos entails an interplay of continuity and discontinuity with the present order."[58] Our purposes here can be served by considering two fundamental matters, one of which is cosmic in scope and the other of which is more narrowly focused: the future of the relationship between the Creator and creation, and, with reference to human beings in particular, the future of our bodies.

There is an ontological distinction between Creator and creation, and this distinction is both fundamental and eternal. As Jones rightly observes, "The divine-human difference is deeper than the fabric of creation itself."[59] This difference and distinction is not merely one of roles or relationships or capacities, as significant as those are. It is a distinction that has to do with the very nature of the beings involved. God is God. Creation is not God. Human beings are not God. Creatures, including human beings, are creatures. God is not a creature. As Barth says, there is "an infinite qualitative distinction."[60] And, to the immediate point here, this ontological distinction will continue into the eschatological future.

At the very center of the apostle John's vision of the new heavens and new earth is God, seated on a throne. All those present worship him (see Rev 19:1-10). John reports that "the home of God is among mortals. He will dwell with them; they will be his peoples, and God himself will be with them" (Rev 21:3). There is no dissolution, not even a blurring,

---

[57]For just two examples, amillennial views, relatively speaking, envision a high degree of continuity between the present and the future, while dispensational views envision a high degree of discontinuity. For an introduction to the heuristic of continuity and change, including its application in eschatology, see John S. Feinberg, ed., *Continuity and Discontinuity: Perspectives on the Relationship Between the Old and New Testaments: Essays in Honor of S. Lewis Johnson, Jr.* (Westchester, IL: Crossway, 1988).

[58]Stanley J. Grenz, *Theology for the Community of God* (Grand Rapids, MI: Eerdmans, 2000), 645.

[59]Jones, *Practicing Christian Doctrine*, 122.

[60]Karl Barth, "Preface to the 2nd Edition," in *The Epistle to the Romans*, 2nd ed., trans. Edwyn C. Hoskyns (London: Oxford University Press, 1933), 10. Barth here acknowledges indebtedness to Søren Kierkegaard.

of the ontological distinction between God and those who worship God. God remains God and creatures remain creatures. As Amos Yong says, the new heavens and new earth will be "the dwelling place of God *and God's creatures.*"[61] It is true that God will "wipe every tear from their eyes" and that "Death will be no more; mourning and crying and pain will be no more" (Rev 21:4). Hallelujah! But none of this constitutes a change in the basic fact of the finitude of creaturehood. Creatures are, and will be, in need of the sustenance, care, and healing that only God the Creator can provide. This is the Creator caring for and definitively healing his creatures, *as creatures.*

Redeemed and glorified human existence will be embodied existence—embodied life. As we contemplate this glorified bodily existence, we do so mindful that we see now partially and dimly (1 Cor 13:9, 12). We also remind ourselves that, as was and is the case with Christ's resurrected body, this glorified bodily existence will consist in both change and continuity, and it will be helpful to structure our thoughts here along these lines.[62] First, consider ways in which our glorified eschatological existence will be one of dramatic change, of transformation beyond our present comprehension. One indicator is the use of the term καινός ("new"). For example, both Peter (2 Pet 3:13) and John (Rev 21:1) use this term when writing of the new heavens and new earth, and John also employs this term when speaking of the "new Jerusalem" and a "new name" (Rev 3:12). This is strong language. When thinking of change and continuity, a term like "new" clearly speaks of change—indeed, in the case of Christian eschatology, profound change.

In 2 Corinthians 5:17, using the same term, καινός, twice, the apostle Paul proclaims that "if anyone is in Christ, there is a new creation: everything old has passed away; see, everything has become new!" Taken out of its larger context and in a superficially literal way, this verse could seem to suggest a state of pure discontinuity, a transition of absolute

---

[61] Amos Yong, with Jonathan A. Anderson, *Renewing Christian Theology: Systematics for a Global Christianity* (Waco, TX: Baylor University Press, 2014), 50, emphasis added.
[62] For another example of this structure see Grenz, *Theology for the Community*, 645-46.

change with no continuity. "Everything" has "become new!" Similarly, in Ephesians 4:22-24, Paul reminds his readers that they have been taught to "put away your former way of life" and "to be renewed [αναστροφήν] in the spirit of your minds, and to clothe yourselves with the new [καινόν] self, created according to the likeness of God in true righteousness and holiness." These passages refer to the present stage of salvation history, rather than the eschatological future as in the Petrine and Johannine passages identified above, and they reflect Paul's, not Peter's or John's, use of καινός. However, while we cannot allow Paul's use of καινός to be artificially read into its use by Peter and John, brief consideration of Paul's view of the *new* can complement our understanding of it in Peter and John's eschatological passages.

Paul's understanding of καινός is clearly not ontologically *comprehensive and absolute*, 100 percent change with no continuity; rather, he intends truly dramatic change *in particular respects* that are *accompanied by, grounded in*, a kind of continuity or sameness. The first ten verses of 2 Corinthians 5 describe the present reality for Paul, one in which God "has given us the Spirit as a deposit, guaranteeing *what is to come*" (2 Cor 5:5 NIV, emphasis added). At the time of writing 2 Corinthians, Paul was neither experiencing nor portraying his *present* existence and life as one that was absolutely and comprehensively *new*. Indeed, in the next verse he indicates that "as long as we are at home in the body we are away from the Lord." Paul's contrast between the present and the fulfilled eschatological future in 2 Corinthians 5 as well as Ephesians 4 is a description of the new *quality and character of life in relationship with Christ*; it is *not an ontological statement about transformation away from human creatureliness.*[63] This is congruent with what can be observed in the book of Revelation. As Richard Bauckham says in describing John's apocalyptic vision, "the eschatological new" is "the

---

[63]Similarly, in conjunction with Gal 5:6, Paul's reference to the *new creation* in Gal 6:15 (cf. Gal 3:28) is a reference to a change in dispositions or relationship, not a change in creational human ontology. See Craig S. Keener, *Galatians: A Commentary* (Grand Rapids, MI: Baker Academic, 2019), 458-60, 573-75.

qualitatively quite different life of the eternal age to come."[64] The
newness spoken of here is dramatic and profound, but it does not consist
in eradicating human creatureliness. Rather, Paul is pointing at and
toward redeemed existence for human beings as creatures.

This profoundly new life will be accompanied by equally significant
continuity. The Christian promise of salvation is one of resurrection and
glorification. It is *not* one of *substitution*. Christian hope is grounded in
the fact that the body of Jesus that went into the tomb was the same
body that exited the tomb. As the apostle Paul so forcefully proclaims
in 1 Corinthians 15, this is "of first importance": "Christ died for our sins
in accordance with the scriptures . . . he was buried . . . he was raised on
the third day in accordance with the Scriptures" and then appeared to
followers and the apostles (1 Cor 15:3-8, 12-13, 19). The Christian hope,
grounded in this reality of Jesus Christ's resurrection, is that the bodies
of those who have died on earth but are alive in Christ will be raised to
new, eternal life. This is neither the setting aside nor the annihilation of
the old body and putting another in its place. That would be substitution. This sure hope is resurrection.

As Edith Humphrey observes, "the character of the new creation offered to us in the NT [is] in some ways entirely new and in other ways
in continuity with the best that we know."[65] She writes, "all that we call
nature is no mere backdrop for our lives, but a reality of which we are,
and will remain, a part. We will not become disembodied spirits, but
will retain that link with the material world that God has declared to be
'good'—though there will be more substance and glory than we can
imagine."[66] The assured hope for those who are in Christ is that, as was
the case with Jesus, the same body that goes into the grave is the same
body that is raised to glorification. To be sure, these bodies will be

---

[64]Richard Bauckham, *The Theology of the Book of Revelation* (Cambridge: Cambridge University Press, 1998), 49.
[65]Edith M. Humphrey, "New Creation," in *Dictionary for Theological Interpretation of the Bible*, gen. ed. Kevin J. Vanhoozer (Grand Rapids, MI: Baker Academic, 2005), 537a.
[66]Humphrey, "New Creation," 537b.

transformed, glorified, significantly different from our present bodies (Phil 3:21). The biblical vision of the eschatological future is one in which "creation is not confined for ever to its own immanent possibilities," writes Bauckham. Rather, creation, including human bodies, "is open to the fresh creative possibilities of its Creator."[67] Yet as Michael Horton rightly observes, "Instead of making us something *more than* human, grace saves and liberates humans to become *more human*: finally to glorify and enjoy God forever."[68] Redemption into and including glorification does not leave the good of "the beginning" behind. Creational finitude was part of that good beginning. There is no need for it to be eradicated in order for human beings to be redeemed and glorified, to enjoy and participate in God's new heavens and earth. Those who are redeemed in Christ will worship God their Creator as finite creatures. As Treier observes, "those limits that remain . . . will only reflect the good gifts of who our Creator made us to be."[69]

If creational finitude constitutes a violation of the integrity of being human, if it is inconsistent with human being as God designed and created us, if it is a result of the fall, it would be done away with or overcome or healed in eschatological redemption. But this is not to be the case. The transformed, glorified future of those who are in Christ is the future of finite creatures who will be blessed by beholding their Creator "face to face" (1 Cor 13:12).

BOTH-AND: CHALLENGES AND GIFTS OF FINITUDE

We have sought above to rescue finitude from the misperception that all finitude, that finitude per se, is evil. Correspondingly, we have looked at the present and future of God's salvific work and observed that creational finitudes are part of God's good designs and are thereby not in

---

[67]Bauckham, *Revelation*, 48. While Bauckham's statements are about creation in general, the context (e.g., reference to "the resurrection of individuals" on page 49) makes it clear that the bodily resurrection of human beings is included.

[68]Michael Horton, *The Christian Faith: A Systematic Theology for Pilgrims on the Way* (Grand Rapids, MI: Zondervan, 2011), 692-93, emphasis original.

[69]Treier, "Finitude," 319a.

need of redemptive address. This affirmation of creational finitude as characteristic of God's good design of human beings and their world does not entail a denial that life on earth includes challenges, difficulties, and struggles. In taking a more complete, nuanced, and affirmative view of finitude, we are not suggesting that life and work within limits is without challenges or difficulties or frustrations.

A person may want to be in two places at once—both on a getaway with her husband and at her daughter's soccer championship—but she is not able to be so. A person might desire to turn back the clock or redo a business meeting or social engagement, but they cannot. A weather researcher might wish that he could guarantee a clear and sunny day for his wedding, but he cannot. The finitude of the world and our lives will not always be as we might desire. Limitations are sometimes inconvenient. Boundaries can be challenges, and finitude frustrating. We may want to stay awake a few more hours tonight either to finish the great novel that we're reading or to be more fully prepared for the presentation that we will be giving tomorrow. We may wish that we had more information before making our decision about medical treatment. Veli-Matti Kärkkäinen rightly observes, "It belongs to the nature of finite existence that there are hurdles, riddles, unresolved problems, potential for growth, 'fallings down,' and so forth."[70]

The grain of our consumer-oriented culture seeks to offer us that which is easy, comforting, convenient, effortless, rewarding, but these will not always be the characteristics of living and working within the boundaries of finitude. Hence the culturally pervasive tendency to regard limits as bad. Yet for other reasons—theological reasons—some Christians may have a posture that is fundamentally set in opposition to the limitations of creational finitude, as if they are evil. Treier insightfully observes, "Conservative theologians . . . underscored human sinfulness [and] finitude fell victim to conceptual guilt by association."[71]

---

[70]Kärkkäinen, *Creation and Humanity*, 426.
[71]Daniel J. Treier, "The Gift of Finitude: Wisdom from Ecclesiastes for a Theology of Education," *Christian Scholar's Review* 48, no. 4 (Summer 2019): 378.

This guilt by association is sometimes conscious and sometimes not. It occasionally manifests itself in theological reflection on work but is not limited to that arena. We are often prone to view finitude of any kind as malevolent. That which is disliked or unwanted or simply inconvenient—including but not limited to limitations—is, de facto, regarded as not good, as needing to be exceeded.

However, most, if not all, of the challenges associated with creational finitude are not bad, much less evil. The world as God made it, including its finitude, may not be as we would design it if we were in charge. But we should be very careful in assuming that our finite, creaturely estimate of God's creation design is the best and wisest. Contrary to what might be felt in accord with human hubris and modern affluent sensibilities, limitations in themselves do not necessarily constitute something wrong with the world. This—the distinction between our likes or preferences and that which is bad or evil—is a very important distinction, and one that may be particularly difficult, but all the more important, to embrace for those of us who live in and have been shaped by a cultural context that places a very high priority on and has been extremely successful at minimizing or eliminating so many forms of difficulty and discomfort. But we will here dare to make the claim that challenges, difficulty, and discomfort that accompany creational finitude are not always synonymous with *bad* or *evil* in any meaningful, theological sense of those words.

Recognizing and embracing our limits as good gifts may very well require graced wisdom. Ecclesiastes 3:11 tells us that there is "eternity in the human heart," and Treier rightly recognizes that, as a result, we have "a sense of self-transcendence that creates tension over embracing our limits and discerning the distinction between finitude and fallenness."[72] This does not constitute a denial of the distinction but does acknowledge tension, requiring discernment. We need to think carefully, think theologically, to discern this distinction because discerning this distinction, or not, will manifest itself in how we live and work in response to the limits we

---

[72]Treier, "Finitude," 317b. Also see Treier, *Proverbs and Ecclesiastes*, 196 and 236.

encounter. Discerning this distinction will determine whether we respond to the challenges associated with creational finitude as evils to be rejected and overcome or good gifts to be received and stewarded. This may require us to discipline ourselves to think differently from the ways to which we are personally inclined or culturally conditioned, ways of thinking that associate all circumstances or events that are difficult, painful, inconvenient, hard, or costly with evil or fallenness. Even more, we need to go beyond merely viewing creational finitude as not bad to recognizing, receiving, and stewarding it as part of God's creation design, as good gift.

Taking a step back for a moment, receiving the gifts of creational finitude as gifts is but one expression of receiving creation-life itself, the sheer fact that we exist at all, as a gift, not as our own achievement.[73] Were it not for God freely fashioning us from "dust" and "rib" and breathing the breath of life (Gen 2:7, 18-23), and then continuing to give breath and sustenance, we would "die and return to the dust" (Ps 104:29 NIV). Julie Canlis suggests that the only obligation of Adam and Eve in the garden was "their ordinary existence, offered to their creator with *gratitude* and *dependence*."[74] But we may be prone to feel and think otherwise, particularly when life is "good" by our reckoning, blessed with health and prosperity. Anticipating such good times and knowing of the human propensity to forget, Moses directs God's people to "remember the LORD your God, for it is *he* who *gives you* power"— not infinite power, but *enough* power—"to get wealth" and care for yourself and others (Deut 8:18). Moreover, if life and agency are indeed a gift they should be received with gratitude toward God and generosity toward others. And gratitude for life should include gratitude for the gift and gifts of finitude.

Thus, Katherine Sonderegger celebrates a "strong notion of finitude," noting that human beings can "touch one another . . . respect one

---

[73]Portions of this paragraph were prompted by Andy Crouch, *Playing God: Redeeming the Gift of Power* (Downers Grove, IL: InterVarsity Press, 2013), 263.

[74]Julie Canlis, *A Theology of the Ordinary*, 2nd ed. (Wenatchee, WA: Godspeed, 2018), 20, emphasis added.

another's privacy, indeed form a notion of privacy at all . . . can join together in common cause or enjoy solitude," and that "these common acts of human dignity and joy *rely upon* the notion of finite, individual existence."[75] Sonderegger's observations also illustrate that finitude, like any other good gift, needs to be *properly received* in order for the goodness to be genuinely appreciated. In the case of finitude, we need a twofold response. We need to and can receive our *freedom not* to be everywhere and *not* to be doing all the time and *not* to know everything, while at the same time *taking joy in being* someplace and *doing* some of the time and *knowing* some things.

Furthermore, there are other gifts of creational finitude to which we should keep our theologically discerning minds and hearts open. These can be discerned through the lens of *dependence*—dependence on *God*, dependence on other *people*, and dependence on *the created order*. Julie Canlis writes, "The limitations that are part of us being 'not-God' were intended to keep us close and in relationship with God. Our very limitations *imply the need for relationship*." We did not create ourselves. We do not re-create ourselves. As creations of Another it is only wise to "joyfully accept our limitations." "Wisdom in the Bible," she notes, "is recognizing this relationship between Creator and creature and joyfully submitting to it."[76] Appreciatively embracing finitude from the creature's side—the not-God side—of this relationship is grounded in our dependence on God . . . ultimately for everything. And if we recognize *this* relationship, our dependence on God, as gift, then our reliance on God will flow not from frustration or resentment but from gratitude. This is not to deny that there will be times of frustration or resentment, but rather to suggest that such should not and do not need to be one's baseline, default disposition. We will not regard our limits and dependence as either a divine curse or a moral failing, but part of the good *relational fabric* of which God has woven the creation. Our finitude is

---

[75]Sonderegger, "Finitude and Death," 392, emphasis original.
[76]Canlis, *Theology of the Ordinary*, 15, emphasis original.

the ground from which constancy and intimacy of relationship with our Maker can grow. James K. A. Smith notes that the summons to embrace our finitude may be "an affront" to contemporary notions of autonomy. However, as he goes on to observe, "perhaps it is my autonomy that is the source of my dis-ease, not its solution. What if dependence is a gift because it means I'm not alone? What if the [divine] welcome I experience is how I learn to be human?"[77]

Grounded in the constancy and intimacy of a relationship of dependence on God, finitude also becomes the ground in which our relationships with other people and the natural world can flourish. Recall, for instance, Katherine Sonderegger's celebration of the fact that human beings can "respect one another's privacy, indeed from a notion of privacy at all . . . can join together in common cause or enjoy solitude," and that "these common acts of human dignity and joy *rely upon* the notion of finite, individual existence." In her exhortation to embrace "the ordinary," Canlis wisely submits that "we need to press into what we already have" before we go in pursuit of what is beyond.[78] At the center of what we already have are the people among whom and the places in which we live, and a healthy awareness of our limitations can nurture a richer appreciation for and dependence on these people and places. "Our created finitude means that we need each other," writes Beth Felker Jones, "that we receive the gift of learning to live with and for another, and, above all, that we need God."[79] The first and greatest commandment is to love the Lord our God. But there is a second commandment that is "like it": to love our neighbors (Mt 22:37-40; Mk 12:28-31). We are not able to love our neighbors well if we do not recognize that *we need* our neighbors and that *they need* us. We need each other. Furthermore, as observed earlier in this chapter, starting with air and water we need the created world, and as is the case with our human neighbors, we will not

[77]James K. A. Smith, *On the Road with Saint Augustine: A Real-World Spirituality for Restless Hearts* (Grand Rapids, MI: Brazos, 2019), 44.
[78]Canlis, *Theology of the Ordinary*, 56.
[79]Jones, *Practicing Christian Doctrine*, 99.

care *well* for the created world if we are not mindful of its origin in the work of the Creator and our *inescapable need* for it.

"The Bible places human limits in a set of relational contexts," observes Treier. We have here noted three of these: dependence on God, dependence on other people, and dependence on the created order.[80] We have spoken of the finitudes, the limitations, that constitute these dependencies as gifts. Yet very strictly speaking, the finitudes are not *in and of themselves* the gift. The gifts ultimately reside in the relationships. Were it not for the God on whom we depend, the people by whom we are blessed, and the air that fills our lungs, we would simply be needy and nothing but needy, if we were to exist at all. But in God's creational design, he provides for our needs. We are not left without provision for our finitudes. We are dependent on God, and there is no place or life circumstance that is beyond God's loving presence and providential care (see Ps 139). We need other people and are born into a family, and we can also be reborn into Christ's family, the body of Christ. We need air and water, and God grants the breath of life and sends his rain to fall on the just and the unjust (see Acts 17:25; Mt 5:45). As Treier points out, "Ultimately, in light of Christ's resurrection, the goodness of human finitude is an 'evangelical' theme, promoting devotion to our Creator and dependence upon divine grace along with delight in God's good gifts."[81] In the next chapter we will consider how the gift and gifts of finitude can grace our understanding of and engagement with work.

---

[80]Cf. Treier, "Finitude," 318a-b. He identifies ten "relational spheres": in the created cosmos, in our bodies, in family, in time, in places/spaces, at work, at play, at rest, in Jesus Christ and the church, and in the Holy Spirit.

[81]Treier, "Gift of Finitude," 372.

3

ENOUGH

Work (with)in God's Creation

When you understand that life is a vapor and appreciate
that the seasons of life are both expected and transitory,
you're primed to inhabit them with
the proper expectations . . .

to face such times without the delusion of American
can-do-ism or some cheery, pious spin.

JAMES K. A. SMITH

Do not wear yourself out to get rich; be wise enough to desist.

PROVERBS 23:4

WORK (WITH)IN GOD'S GOOD CREATION[1]

The words *finitude* and *limits* rarely occur in writings on work, whether theological or not. Far more common are words like *potential, possibilities*, and even *limitless*. It is not uncommon in the self-help and business arenas to come across articles with titles like "Your Potential Success Is Limitless, Despite What You've Been Told," and to encounter career coaches who brand themselves with descriptors such as "No

---

[1]The authors gratefully acknowledge collaboration with Don J. Payne on this chapter.

Limits Thinker and Mentor."[2] Nor should it be surprising that this type of boundary-denying posture is appealing. No one can—or should—head into their work, day after day, asking, "How little can I accomplish?" No one wants to ponder a regular pattern of work, whether paid employment or household routines, with the idea that their lifetime of work will have resulted in few if any constructive outcomes.

Literature in the theology of work pervasively emphasizes that work is both necessary and good. Anchored in Genesis 1–2, it is noted that God set human beings to work *prior to the fall*, tilling the ground, keeping the garden, naming the animals (see Gen 2:15, 19-20). The prelapsarian created order included work, both physical labor and cognitive effort, in tending the garden and its creatures. So it is right and good to affirm and uphold the dignity and goodness of work. However, too often the theology of work does not adequately take account of the next chapter of the Bible and the next chapter in the story of God and the world—the fall as presented in Genesis 3. Yet, building on the theology of finitude set forth in the previous chapter, it is the burden of this chapter to say that finitude itself is not part of the fallenness of work east of Eden but rather is a good part of work, including good work done east of Eden. Finitude does not need to be either eliminated or redeemed for work to be good. Good work can be and is done within the conditions of finitude.

A recognition of finitude is a necessary part of theology of work for the real world, because finitude is characteristic of the world that God has created and is an ever-present fact of life and fact of work. Tish Harrison Warren observes, "Employees . . . go to work sick because they don't have enough sick leave, or because their boss comes in sick and they want to measure up. We've created whole HR systems and corporate cultures

---

[2]Grant Cordone, "Your Potential Success Is Limitless, Despite What You've Been Told," *Entrepreneur*, November 18, 2015, www.entrepreneur.com/article/252830, and Chris Schenk, "10 Things You Need To Know to Have a No Limits Mindset," May 22, 2015, Addicted 2 Success, https://addicted2success.com/motivation/10-things-you-need-to-know-to-have-a-no-limits-mindset/.

based on our collective willingness to ignore the limits of our bodies."[3] But failing to acknowledge and name finitude leaves one vulnerable to flawed thinking about it and, correspondingly, unwise responses to it. A failure to recognize finitude as a characteristic of the real world can lead to unhelpful, distracting, and unproductive approaches to work.[4]

Unfortunately, despite considerable emphasis on Genesis 1–2 and creation, faith and work conversations are sometimes marked by their own neglect of an account of creational finitude. Andrew Lynn observes that faith and work explorations of calling "take place *not* at the intersection of overlapping commitments and dependencies but instead within a metaphysical arena with only two relevant actors, the caller (God) and the one called (the worker). The wider culture surrounding work in the United States reinforces this notion of the abstracted, Promethean worker with few limits on their time and energy." Lynn reports the insight of one participant-observer of the faith and work movement, Kate Harris, who suggests that "workers' day-to-day realities often get papered over within the grander creation-to-consummation narrative."[5] When this is the case, creational finitude goes unaccounted for.

By exploring the significance of finitude for work, this chapter can contribute to completing and thereby correcting the contribution of chapter one of the grand narrative to the theology of work. Finitude is characteristic of the created order and of all creatures, including human beings, whose work is always carried out within that created order. Finitude is characteristic of the context, the stage, the setting in which human work, of whatever form, is pursued. One can say that, here on earth and for human beings, finitude is part of the grain of creation and therefore human beings will be

[3]Tish Harrison Warren, *Prayer in the Night: For Those Who Work or Watch or Weep* (Downers Grove, IL: InterVarsity Press, 2021), 96.
[4]Alfred North Whitehead highlights the power of pervasive and, as a result, "unconsciously presuppose[d]" assumptions. "Such assumptions appear so obvious that people do not know what they are assuming because no other way of putting things has ever occurred to them." See Alfred North Whitehead, *Science and the Modern World* (New York: Macmillan, 1925; reprint, New York: Free Press, 1967), 49-50.
[5]Andrew Lynn, *Saving the Protestant Ethic: Creative Class Evangelicalism and the Crisis of Work* (Oxford: Oxford University Press, 2023), 175, emphasis original, and 244.

best served, and serve best, when they work with that grain, within both the external and internal limits discussed in the previous chapter.

In conjunction with this realism, we need to acknowledge again, as we did in the previous chapter, that work can be frustrating or daunting or taxing as a result of finitude. There will be times when we very much want to get around the limits associated with finitude. We will want more time or more resources or more people to share the load of work. We will want *more*. But the desire for more is not necessarily an indication of a circumstance of fallenness or evil. Some lacks are evil, a result of the fall. For example, when a people are driven to starvation because human forces conspire to deprive them of food, this is evil. But not having enough physical and mental energy to write excellent computer code for twenty-four hours straight may be frustrating or disappointing, but it is not evil. The human need for rest is simply part of creaturely, embodied life. Furthermore, because our knowledge is limited, work is often carried out amid ambiguity, without complete information or understanding of its likely outcomes. Even after a task has been completed we may lack knowledge of all its results and outcomes, and as a consequence we may lack a sense of resolution or closure. Additionally, because of finitude, work of virtually any kind requires learning, growing in knowledge and skills.[6] Sometimes the path to work-related competence is relatively brief; other times it is years or decades in the making. However short or long the path, learning is a sequence of progress in response to finitude. We respond to a lack of information or skill by acquiring more information or skill. And very often, when we do acquire more, we find that this yet reveals another lack of information or skill.

Finitude is a fundamental contributor to the necessity of work—the fulfilling of various needs—and the associated reality that work can be, as Brent Waters accurately notes, "monotonous and boring." He observes, "Humans cannot exist for long if they refuse to work. This is the case because we are embodied creatures, and bodies demand a great deal of

---

[6]When viewed developmentally, a task does not have to be complex to require learning. I (David) remember my father teaching me, as a child, how to properly sweep our garage floor.

attention."[7] Furthermore, work is often drudgery, emotionally and psycho-logically exhausting. Again and again, there is the need to change the in-fant's diapers, manage monthly household cash flow, clean bathrooms, do laundry, schedule and drive to medical appointments. Paid employment may entail chronically filling-out forms or looking into hundreds of peo-ple's throats and ears or digging in the dirt day after day in ninety-five-degree sunshine or tackling a new project for which you are not yet equipped. As Waters says, "Meeting the needs of embodied life necessarily requires our labor" and much of that labor is monotonous or boring.[8]

Thus, due in no small part to finitude, work can be a challenge, un-pleasant, and it can require us to do things that we don't want to do. But contrary to modern sensibilities, none of this is inherently synonymous with evil. None of this means that either work or finitude are in themselves bad.[9] Work done within the bounds of finitude "remains," as Waters says, "a crucial feature of human identity and an essential means of human flour-ishing. Consequently, most work is never devoid of dignity and is at least somewhat ennobling."[10] Whether we *experience* any given instance of work in a way that inclines us to associate it with evil or in a way that enables us to at least glimpse that which is ennobling will depend in part on the *expec-tations and desires* we carry into that work—expectations and desires that need to be calibrated in accord with the realities of finitude.

As many Christian writers over the centuries have taught, one of the keys to wise and good living is the cultivation of rightly ordered expecta-tions and desires.[11] As James K. A. Smith observes, we "live toward what

---

[7]Brent Waters, *Common Callings and Ordinary Virtues: Christian Ethics for Everyday Life* (Grand Rapids, MI: Baker Academic, 2022), 165 and 164.

[8]Waters, *Common Callings*, 165.

[9]As will be seen in the following two chapters, the fallen condition of the world and of human beings can result in evil distortion of the finite conditions in which work is done and offense against the finite creatures—that is, human beings—who are workers.

[10]Waters, *Common Callings*, 165.

[11]Augustine of Hippo provides historically foundational theological reflection along this line. See, for example, his *Confessions*. In our own day, James K. A. Smith, drawing on Augustine and others, is writing on these themes. See, for example, his three-volume *Cultural Liturgies* (Grand Rapids, MI: Baker Academic, 2009-2017), or the more accessible *You Are What You Love: The Spiritual Power of Habit* (Grand Rapids, MI: Brazos, 2016).

we *want*."[12] Work is part of living, and the experience of work is significantly informed by the expectations and desires carried into it. Thus, wise and good working requires that we cultivate and order expectations and desires in ways that acknowledge and correspond to, among other things, the realities of finitudes. What we generally want—and in conjunction with various technological advances perhaps increasingly expect—is more. More opportunities, more money, more time, more resources, more recognition. Generally speaking, we don't like limits. But to deny or attempt to reject limits is to go against the grain of creation, to go against the fact that creation and human beings, who are creatures within creation, are finite. Our expectations and desires regarding work thus need to be calibrated by a realistic recognition of finitude.

Finitude is universal. It qualifies and informs everyone's work. It is, thus, a *condition* of work. At the same time, we need to acknowledge that there are varying *circumstances* in which work is carried out. For example, workers have varying degrees of agency to respond to the demands of work, including the demands occasioned by finitude. Different workers in different forms of work have differing degrees of authority or control over their work and how to undertake it. It is important to recognize that no one, including the president of the United States and the highest-paid CEO of the largest Fortune 500 company and the most elite professional athlete, has absolute, 100 percent freedom and control with respect to their paid employment. However, people in such roles do have more latitude and options with respect to the kinds of work open to them and the way they go about their work than the average hotel housecleaner or framing carpenter or fast-food worker. Generally speaking, people with more formal education have more potential options with regard to the kinds of paid employment they can pursue than people with less formal education. And many of the kinds of employment obtained by people with higher degrees of education provide them with more control than the employment obtained by people with less education. People who embody a culturally

---

[12]Smith, *You Are What You Love*, 13, emphasis original.

favored demographic profile related to gender or skin color or age have more options open to them, and many of those options afford them more agency than people who embody a less culturally favored profile. Finitude is a universal condition of all work, but the ability to manage its effects varies with the circumstances of the worker and the work.[13]

Before we next consider work in relation to three facets of finitude, there is one more fundamentally important observation to make regarding work and life. *Work itself is finite.* Work is necessary, but there is more to life than work. Human beings are made to be workers, but *not only* workers. While work fulfills various human needs, it is not in itself a sufficient basis for human well-being. Although work constitutes an inescapably important exercise of human agency, there is more to persons and to personal identity than work. As we now consider work in relation to three specific facets of finitude—space, time, and human capacities—we will not only learn about work but also glean insights about workers as human beings and life beyond work.

HERE, NOT THERE: WORK AND SPACE

Of the three facets of finitude that we are considering here, in recent years the relationship of work to space has likely undergone, and continues to undergo, more dramatic changes than the relationship to time or human capacities. Articles with titles like "Offices Around America Hit a New Vacancy Record" and "Big Tech Is Downsizing Workspace in Another Blow to Office Real Estate" are easy to find in business-oriented publications.[14] These types of changes in

---

[13]Without minimizing the significance of varying degrees of agency among various workers and types of work, it is worth acknowledging the potential significance of phrases such as "the working class" and "working men and women." This rhetoric, common in political and socio-economic discourse, understandably arose and is used to give due acknowledgment and respect to "blue-collar" and related forms of work, often involving considerable physical labor. We would simply note here that it not-so-implicitly suggests that, for example, "white-collar" or "creative class" work is not work.

[14]Konrad Putzier, "Offices Around America Hit a New Vacancy Record," *The Wall Street Journal*, January 8, 2024, www.wsj.com/real-estate/commercial/offices-around-america-hit-a-new-vacancy-record-166d98a5; and Konrad Putzier, "Big Tech Is Downsizing Workspace in Another Blow to Office Real Estate," *The Wall Street Journal*, April 16, 2024, www.wsj.com/real

workers' relationship to brick-and-mortar spaces are manifest in Christian ministries, with numbers of evangelical organizations "giving up their buildings and developing models for remote work."[15] Commenting on this shift, the president of one ministry said, "It's just the new work rhythm." Recent years have seen a significant rise in remote work, telecommuting, hybrid work, and work from home (aka WFH). Technological advances have made these forms of work more readily possible, and the Covid-19 pandemic of 2020 forced many workers into a remote mode.[16] While traditional, in-person modes of work are, according to *Forbes*, "far from obsolete," *Forbes* nonetheless reported on the increasing and "rapid *normalization* of remote work environments."[17] Whatever one thinks of these developments, they serve to highlight the significance and evolving configurations of the relationship between work and space . . . between work and place.

Work occurs within space and takes up space. Historically, work has not been conducted simply in space but very often in a specific, identifiable place. A combination of technological advancements, a worldwide pandemic, changing priorities among workers, and evolving strategies among employers has unsettled the relationship of work and workers to space and place. To an unprecedented degree, many workers no longer must be bodily present in a particular place in order to work. The very term *workplace* is in search of new meaning.

-estate/commercial/big-tech-is-downsizing-work-space-in-another-blow-to-office-real-estate -67b4685c. As these articles indicate, while overbuilding is a factor contributing to office vacancies, changing work patterns are at least as significant and were underway prior to the Covid-19 pandemic of 2020.

[15]Daniel Silliman, "For Sale: Christian Ministry Headquarters," *Christianity Today*, June 3, 2024, www.christianitytoday.com/news/2024/june/remote-work-evangelical-office-headquarters -for-sale.html.

[16]While the seminary at which we teach was already offering some online education, we both witnessed and participated in an aggressive and industry-wide movement in seminary education into various remote delivery formats.

[17]Katherine Haan, "Top Remote Work Statistics and Trends in 2023," *Forbes*, last updated June 12, 2023, www.forbes.com/advisor/business/remote-work-statistics/#key_remote_work_statistics _section, emphasis added.

A worker cannot be both here and there at the same time.[18] We are, as noted in the previous chapter, emplaced beings.[19] As embodied creatures, human beings are located beings. Through the marvels of technology, our mind and senses can receive and comprehend signals from other places, and the exercise of actions such as oral speech and physical gesture can be mediated and thereby virtually extended to other places. But our embodied selves remain located in one place at any given time, and the *direct and immediate,* the *actually embodied*, employment of our mind, our senses, and our capacities in work is limited to that place, wherever it is. Despite the occasional use of language such as being "nowhere," in fact human beings are always somewhere. And by virtue of our finitude with regard to space, being somewhere means *not* being somewhere else. We can be in different places at different times, but we cannot be in different places at the same time. Space *and* time *together* constitute the context in which embodied human beings work.

By nature and character human beings are created to be, are meant to be, in a place, emplaced. Karina Kreminski notes, "Adam and Eve's story becomes particular by the fact that they are placed in Eden." Thus, "When we read Genesis, we see that to be human means to be placed."[20] This is a large part of the tragedy of homelessness. As Helmut Thielicke says, "Home and place are part of human identity. . . . We have our being in that which sustains us, in the times and places that shape us."[21] Whether or not people consciously think in pseudo-philosophical terms about the nature and character of human beings, there is a keen and

---

[18]Key to this statement is "at the same time." As previously noted, in the real world of life and work the facets of finitude are often interrelated and overlapping. This is clearly and always the case with space and time.

[19]Craig G. Bartholomew, *Where Mortals Dwell: A Christian View of Place for Today* (Grand Rapids, MI: Baker Academic, 2011), xi.

[20]Karina Kreminski, "Embodying Christ in the Neighborhood: A Reflection on Place, Home, and Mission," in *Grounded in the Body, in Time and Place, in Scripture*, ed. Jill Firth and Denise Cooper-Clark (Eugene, OR: Wipf and Stock, 2021), 64.

[21]Helmut Thielicke, *Being Human . . . Becoming Human: An Essay in Christian Anthropology*, trans. Geoffrey W. Bromiley (New York: Doubleday, 1984), 46.

ready awareness that it is not good to be without a home, to be without a place.[22]

The term *place* inevitably arises in the discussion of the human relationship to space. As noted in the previous chapter, place is constituted by particularized finitude within space. Craig Bartholomew observes, "Place is ubiquitous and yet always particular."[23] This is why it is true and wise to say that a person cannot be in two *places* at once. "It is time and place," writes Brent Waters, "that situate finite and mortal creatures within a temporal and material creation," and he astutely notes that "unlike temporary space, the significance or value of place is not derived from its utility. Rather, people bestow meaning and value," including meaning and value related to work, "on a place over time."[24] Bartholomew rightly observes that "although space and place are inseparable, place must be distinguished from space. . . . place is part of our lived, everyday experience," including all experience of work, "whereas space, especially in our modern world, is a theoretical concept and as such an abstraction *from* the lived experience of place."[25] Unlike mere space, a place becomes "a landmark demarcating important events."[26] And, while not everything that occurs in the course of work constitutes an "important event," this bestowal of significance by embodied presence and action over time is a fundamental part of what can be known as a *workplace*.[27] Thus, place is a significant contributing factor to the creation and maintenance of organizational culture.

The importance, in some instances the necessity, of a physical workplace is greater for some workers and some forms of work than for

---

[22]See Steven Bouma-Prediger and Brian J. Walsh, *Beyond Homelessness: Christian Faith in a Culture of Displacement* (Grand Rapids, MI: Eerdmans, 2008), and Stephen Eide, *Homelessness in America: The History and Tragedy of an Intractable Social Problem* (Lanham, MD: Rowman and Littlefield, 2022).

[23]Bartholomew, *Where Mortals Dwell*, 1.

[24]Waters, *Common Callings*, 62 and 176.

[25]Bartholomew, *Where Mortals Dwell*, 3, emphasis original.

[26]Waters, *Common Callings*, 176.

[27]When the relationships and events that occur are chronically evil, the significance and meaning of a particular workplace are, obviously, not good—not to be either desired or treasured. This does not, however, deny the equally significant potential for a workplace to accrue positive and life-affirming significance.

others. There are forms of work that simply cannot be carried out remotely.[28] The most obvious among these are forms of work that require
physically touching another person or animal or material object. For
example, people who drill and fill dental cavities or who style hair or
who care for people with physical disabilities need to have contact with
the bodies of the people they serve, as well as, in some instances, non-
mobile equipment.[29] People who cook food and wash dishes for restaurants need to be physically present in the restaurants to do their jobs.
People who change the linens and clean the rooms in hotels need to be
bodily present at a hotel to do their work, while people who care for
children or those confined to home need to be at home to provide care.
This list could be expanded, not least with "essential workers," the overwhelming majority of whose jobs are not candidates for remote work,[30]
but these examples are sufficient to illustrate the abiding reality of the
intersection between work, workers, and embodied spatial finitude.

These intersections of work and finitude with respect to space are not
cited to make a case against all remote and other emerging modalities
of work. However, in an era characterized by "a crisis of place," an era
in which abstract space has significantly triumphed over humanized
place, we do want to helpfully complicate discussions of work by recognizing that new work-enabling technologies and new models of working

---

[28]We focus on types of work that cannot currently be carried out remotely. Technological advances of various kinds are always unfolding, and in the future some of these will render some
forms of work that cannot now be done online or at a distance capable of being carried out
remotely.

[29]The technological possibilities with respect to some of these endeavors are astounding. For
example, while remote robotic surgery is currently far from routine, it is currently practiced
and will assuredly continue to be advanced. (See "New Research into Remote Robotic Surgery,"
King's College London, News Centre, January 21, 2022, www.kcl.ac.uk/news/new-research
-into-remote-robotic-surgery.) It needs also to be acknowledged that even if the surgeon is not
physically present, other medical professionals are, for example, preparing the patient, setting
up the computer and robotic systems, and caring for the patient after the surgery.

[30]See, for example, "Essential Workers, Essential Protections," United States Department of
Labor, Wage and Hour Division, www.dol.gov/sites/dolgov/files/WHD/ewep/EWEP_Initiative
.pdf, accessed December 7, 2023; and the report "COVID-19: Essential Workers in the States,"
National Conference of State Legislatures, updated January 11, 2021, www.ncsl.org/labor-and
-employment/covid-19-essential-workers-in-the-states.

are themselves finite. They are, for example, not applicable to everyone or to every form of work, and in some instances they may prove to be unhealthy for workers.

Some of the new models of work enabled by emerging technologies simply do not apply to workers whose work demands embodied presence, and it is important to remember that this need for physical presence is not bad. It is a function of embodied, finite human existence, not an evil to be defeated. Therefore, instead of, for example, only trying to figure out how to technologically overcome this need for physical presence, perhaps more energy and creative attention needs to be given to enabling and supporting workers whose work requires physical presence. Thoughtful and creative attention could be given to factors such as transportation to and from work, the best forms of equipment needed, the schedule and pace of work, and the adequacy and pattern of breaks and time off.

In addition to the needs associated with sheer physicality, embodiment in space is significant for the relational and communications-related dimensions of work. Digitally convened meetings and digitally supervised work on projects can have some advantages with regard to financial costs and aspects of efficiency. For example, these forms of work save the time and money—both of which are finite—associated with people traveling to meet. In part because of these savings of time and money, people who might otherwise not be able to work together in person are able to do so, and in some instances more and shorter meetings among people who are at a distance can more readily be convened. Thus, it is easy to see why, as Waters states, "there is a growing preference for space over place," such as digitally mediated remote conduct of work.[31] However, when workers are not bodily in the same place, the relational and communicational dimensions of work are, at the least, more challenging, and these challenges affect both workers

---

[31]Waters, *Common Callings*, 176. While this is a "growing preference," Waters provides extended analysis and expresses this as a concern, not something to be celebrated.

and the companies or organizations for which they work. Acquiring and sharing information can be more difficult[32] and, more subtly but every bit as important, it can be more difficult to cultivate and share organizational culture.[33] This is often of particular significance for people who are new to an organization or a particular field of work. In an article titled "What Young Workers Miss Without the 'Power of Proximity,'" Emma Goldberg and Ben Casselman note that in-person mentoring relationships are of particular importance for young workers and for women and persons of demographic groups who may lack experiential background in a particular field of endeavor or a particular kind of work culture.[34]

There is no one correct modality of work for all work and all workers. However, all workers—whether onsite or remote—are embodied workers, finite with regard to space and located at any given time in a particular place. This reality should not be treated as evil but simply as a reality of embodied human beings that should inform the

---

[32]In the *Harvard Business Review*, Mark Mortenson reports that "one of the early findings in research on the effects of technology-mediated communication was that people become more disinhibited and exhibit less self-monitoring and self-control when communicating through technology." See Mark Mortenson, "Why Hybrid Work Can Become Toxic," *Harvard Business Review*, July 28, 2023, https://hbr.org/2023/07/why-hybrid-work-can-become-toxic. While "information workers" can be expected to function as well or better than anyone in a technologically mediated work environment because it is their home turf, a study of over 60,000 Microsoft employees found that "remote work caused the collaboration network of workers to become more static and siloed, with fewer bridges between disparate parts." This study also found that "there was a decrease in synchronous communication and an increase in asynchronous communication. Together, these effects may make it harder for employees to acquire and share new information across the network." See Longqi Yang et al., "The Effects of Remote Work on Collaboration Among Information Workers," *Nature Human Behaviour*, September 9, 2021, https://doi.org/10.1038/s41562-021-01196-4, accessed June 11, 2024.

[33]Mortenson notes that the "lack of close contact reduces connection and trust, which are key elements of a healthy culture" (Mortenson, "Hybrid Work"). For both of us (the authors), the enterprise of seminary education is the context of our paid work. A few years ago, before remote teaching reached its current prevalence, a seminary president indicated that his greatest concern with respect to remote work was maintaining a shared and healthy institutional culture.

[34]Emma Goldberg and Ben Casselman, "What Young Workers Miss Without the 'Power of Proximity,'" *The New York Times* (April 24, 2023), www.nytimes.com/2023/04/24/business/remote-work-feedback.html?searchResultPosition=4 (accessed March 6, 2025). As we reflect on our own entry years ago into our work as professors, we both can testify to many benefits of in-person mentoring from experienced scholar-teachers.

configuration of any given form of work and any particular worker. Seeing workers not as objects that work within amorphous space but as human beings who are emplaced should help to guide the vision of work and workers. Brent Waters helps point the way. He writes, "People require places where they belong together. The mobility afforded by space needs to be counterbalanced by the constraints of place." Indeed, he asks, "If humans are to flourish, is space an adequate substitute that can displace place entirely? No. Human flourishing requires physical places where embodied humans congregate to collectively undertake certain tasks and establish relationships over time."[35]

The process of transforming space into place requires drawing on the resources of the nonhuman created order, either directly or indirectly. Land, water, air, plants, animals. As humans occupy space they use creation resources of whatever particular place, including the workplace, they occupy. Drawing on these resources is not a sin—indeed, it is necessary—so long as it is done with proper stewardship. In God's creation design, human beings are intended to use, and have no choice but to use, these resources, including using them in the process of creating workplaces. We walk and rest on land.[36] We must take in water and air simply to survive. We need to be nourished by plants and animals. We draw on creation's resources to meet basic needs such as clothing and shelter. For human beings, to live and work on earth is to live and work from the earth. This is God's good design.

Work, of whatever kind, cannot help but draw on the resources of the created order. The specific resources on which work draws and the quantity of resources used varies with the form of work. There is, however, no form of work that makes no demands on the resources of the created world. There has been and will be only one instance of work

---

[35]Waters, *Common Callings*, 176-77.

[36]Dietrich Bonhoeffer says, "Man's origin is in a piece of earth. His bond with the earth belongs to his essential being. . . . From it he has his body. His body belongs to his essential being. Man's body is not his prison, his shell, his exterior, but man himself." See Dietrich Bonhoeffer, *Creation and Fall—Temptation: Two Biblical Studies*, trans. John C. Flether, revised by SCM Press (New York: MacMillan, 1959), 46.

ex nihilo and it was the direct work of God himself.[37] For human beings, drawing on and using the resources of the created order in the course of working is inevitable, and this does not catch God off guard. He designed the creation and humans as creatures within it.

Furthermore, the finitude of creation is not a flaw. It is not a consequence of the fall. The finitude of the earth, its resources and its creatures is a characteristic of creaturehood. It is creation, not Creator. While there is a long and rich history of interest in and respect for the natural world, it is largely over the course of the twentieth century, particularly the second half of the twentieth century, that there is clear evidence of *concern* specifically over the *finitude* of the natural world. Historically speaking, it is only relatively recently that concerted attention has been given to *the question of whether there are enough natural resources, globally, to sustain human life.* Whatever one's views are of the varying responses to that question, a properly Christian view will include, without being limited to, three fundamental affirmations. First and most fundamentally, God is the Creator, and the creation and its creatures are his. Second, human beings have been uniquely gifted by God with the privilege of caring for and respectfully using his creation. Third, guided by the fact that the created world is ultimately God's, care for creation— including care for creation in the course of any and all work—needs to respect the finitude of the resources of creation. There is not limitless land, and the resources of the land are not limitless. So whether the work is that of farming or urban and suburban planning or a form of work that is based on mineral extraction, an attentive eye needs to be kept on the finitude of land. "All of us who are living owe our lives directly to our

---

[37]For a brief but learned and substantive introduction to creation ex nihilo see John Webster, "Creation Out of Nothing," in *Christian Dogmatics: Reformed Theology for the Church Catholic,* ed. Michael Allen and Scott R. Swain (Grand Rapids, MI: Baker Academic, 2016), 126-47. God the Creator created ex nihilo, which can thereby be regarded as first-order creating. All creation by human beings is derivative thereof and thus can properly be regarded as second-order creating. Andy Crouch appropriates, in a way that we would not readily endorse, and applies the language of "ex nihilo" to human creative work (Crouch, *Culture Making: Recovering Our Creative Calling* [Downers Grove, IL: InterVarsity Press, 2008], 23).

connection to the land," writes Wendell Berry, "the connection that we make economically, by work, by living, by making a living."[38] Douglas Moo and Jonathan Moo commend the work of a group of scientists known as the "planetary boundaries" group who constructively grapple with the fact that there is a finite amount of land that can "safely be brought under cultivation or intensively used in other ways without jeopardizing the healthy functioning of the planet."[39] There is a finite amount of water. So whether the work is that of regulating suburban housing development or a form of work that requires water for a secondary purpose (e.g., water to cool electric power generators), the design and conduct of the work needs to take into account that water is a finite resource. The air to which we have access needs to be breathable. Whether the work is that of legislating laws that guide the Environmental Protection Agency or designing landfills, to the degree possible (an acknowledgment of finitude) these tasks need to be carried out in ways that minimize negative impacts on the air future generations breathe. Plants and animals are capable of being used to the point of extinction . . . which is, rather, abuse and misuse. Whether the work is the production of lumber or commercial fishing, it is important that it be guided by the reality that plants and animals, even if in some sense renewable, are finite. Within the boundaries of responsibility and agency, each worker—particularly those who have the agency to design the work of other workers—needs to care for creation.[40]

---

[38]Wendell Berry, *Our Only World: Ten Essays* (Berkeley, CA: Counterpoint, 2015), 42-43. With both cultural and economic interests in view, Berry writes, "If we want to save the land, we must save the people who belong to the land. If we want to save the people, we must save the land the people belong to."

[39]Douglas J. Moo and Jonathan A. Moo, *Creation Care: A Biblical Theology of the Natural World* (Grand Rapids, MI: Zondervan, 2018), 217-18. One organization doing very fine work in advancing wise and effective stewardship of the land is Plant with Purpose (see https://plantwith purpose.org/).

[40]The issues raised in the preceding paragraphs are large, long-term, complex, and often emotionally charged, thus a few words of elaboration are merited. First, all forms of work mentioned above are important, in some instances necessary, and are capable of being done in ways that are respectful of creation. Second, as noted above, these and other forms of work are large and very complex. Doing work in ways that honor the finitude of creation is possible, but doing so is often complex, difficult, and costly. Third, some workers have more responsibility and

NOW, NOT THEN: WORK AND TIME

As we transition into consideration of work and time, it is worth noting that the preceding section, on work and space, includes numerous references to time. For human beings, space and time are inextricably interconnected. At any given moment we are both "here" *and* "*now.*" Yet James K. A. Smith suggests that we currently suffer from "*temporal* dislocation," leading to "the delusion of being 'nowhen,' unconditioned by time."[41] Just as limitations and particularity are associated with embodied existence in space, so too there are limitations and particularity associated with time. All work occurs within time and all work "takes up" time. There is no alternative to this. Nor does there need to be.

However, at least in the modern West, many people frequently feel that they do not have enough time. In *Redeeming the Time*, Leland Ryken captures this sentiment with his opinion that "the only people who have enough time to do what they want to do are retired people. . . . until we retire we will never feel that we have enough time to accomplish all our goals in work and leisure. The problem then is how to find satisfaction in both work and leisure within a daily and weekly schedule that provides less time than we need."[42] In recent years, the susceptibility to this experience has increased rather markedly with the increasing presence of portable digital technology. Theologian Kelly Kapic speaks for more than himself when he says, "even if we don't 'work' more actual hours than we used to, we still don't feel that we ever rest, because work never begins or ends, and because digital technology fosters in us the belief that we can and should be doing something every moment we are awake."[43]

---

more agency than others with regard to the design and conduct of work in relation to the use of the resources of creation. Each worker is responsible to do what they can . . . itself an acknowledgment of finitude.

[41]James K. A. Smith, *How to Inhabit Time: Understanding the Past, Facing the Future, Living Faithfully Now* (Grand Rapids, MI: Brazos, 2022), 4, emphasis original.

[42]Leland Ryken, *Redeeming the Time: A Christian Approach to Work and Leisure* (Grand Rapids, MI: Baker Books, 1995), 269.

[43]Kelly Kapic, *You're Only Human: How Your Limits Reflect God's Design and Why That's Good News* (Grand Rapids, MI: Brazos, 2022), 106. Later in this chapter we will consider the experience of time as reflected in words like *enough* and *want, feel* and *need*.

Discernment and decisions regarding the relative amount of time for work and the rest of life are necessitated by *the fact of finitude*. Whatever the work and whomever the worker, work and the rest of life occupy a single and finite time continuum. Kiara Jorgenson observes, "To express one's self in work is also to set personal parameters around time."[44] Work, time with family, vacation, caring for household chores, engagement with church or community—these are "not separate elements of our lives but rather complementary aspects of a single whole. . . . We can increase one segment of the continuum only by subtracting something else."[45] Thus, to put it simply, "To be more engaged at home means having less time for work."[46] There is no single correct answer or objective standard delineating how much time anyone should spend engaged in work vis-à-vis the rest of life. This will vary with life circumstances, relational world (i.e., family and friends), and the form of work undertaken. It will also vary from one season of life to the next. However, amid this variety there is the universal constant that work is finite. Work is a necessary part of life, but only a part. Human beings are created to be workers, but not only workers. Thus, the book of Proverbs wisely instructs, "Do not wear yourself out to get rich; be wise enough to desist" (Prov 23:4).

Furthermore, because work occurs within temporal finitude, *when* we work matters. The finitude of time is such that for human beings we always work now—neither then in the past nor then in the future. When we are engaged in some form of work we cannot simultaneously—key word here—be engaged in another form of work or another activity.[47] A

---

[44]Kiara A. Jorgenson, *Ecology of Vocation: Recasting Calling in a New Planetary Era* (Lanham, MD: Lexington/Fortress, 2020), 135.

[45]Ryken, *Redeeming the Time*, 43.

[46]Kapic, *You're Only Human*, 156. Obviously, Kapic has in view someone whose primary workplace is outside the home. For someone who works at home the message is clearly that to be more engaged in personal matters at home means having less time for work.

[47]In recent years, particularly with the advances and expansion of digital technologies, one often hears references to multitasking. This is one type of attempt to override or bypass human finitude in relation to time. In fact, multitasking entails moving back and forth, however quickly or frequently, between two or more tasks. While this may give the impression of doing more

person cannot both mow their lawn and manage a store at the same time. A physician cannot perform surgery while coaching her child's softball team. A plumber cannot coach his child's little league team while repairing a leaking pipe. While this type of limitation is at times frustrating or challenging, it is not a function of evil or fallenness—it is simply a function of creational finitude. Furthermore, there is a particular goodness—a distinctive beauty and satisfaction, particularly in our "distracted" age—that can accompany being singularly focused on, entirely devoted to, a given task. Work should be managed accordingly.[48]

In addition to the importance of when we work, because time is finite the *amount of time* we devote to work matters. Implications of this unfold over both the course of a day and the course of a lifetime, and decisions regarding how much to work in a given day and over the course of one's lifetime need to be informed by realistically accounting for the finitude of time. As noted above, we live and work in an unfolding now and can meaningfully devote our attentions and energies to only one activity at a time. Thus, because the time available to us is not unlimited, the amount of time we devote to work inescapably determines how much time we have available for the rest of life.

Human beings have a daily need for rest, and the amount of work undertaken in any twenty-four-hour period must take this into account. Some people have greater capacities, whether physical or cognitive or social, than other people. Some forms of work are particularly taxing mentally while other forms of work are more taxing cognitively and yet others more demanding interpersonally or emotionally. What all people in all forms of work have in common is a need for rest from work each day. What constitutes rest varies among people and among types of work.

---

than one thing at once, it is in fact switching between tasks, and often creates stress, accelerates fatigue, and decreases performance. See, for example, Kevin P. Madore and Anthony D. Wagner, "Multicosts of Multitasking," *Cerebrum* (March-April 2019), www.ncbi.nlm.nih.gov/pmc/articles/PMC7075496/.

[48]The cultural reality of distractedness and its impact on work are reflected in the dozens of books attempting to address this problem, such as Cal Newport, *Deep Work: Rules for Focused Success in a Distracted World* (New York: Grand Central, 2016).

Some people find it restful to take a walk, others to sit in the break room and casually chat with coworkers, others to sit in silence, others to putz in their garden. People whose work is cognitively taxing will likely need a break from or significant change in mental activity, while people whose work is physically demanding will need to stop exerting themselves physically. But the finitude of time and of human capacities means that work needs to be accompanied by daily rest, and a measure of rest during waking hours contributes to human health and flourishing.

In addition to rest during waking hours, the amount of work undertaken in a given twenty-four-hour period should leave adequate time for sleep. Some people pride themselves on needing very little sleep and celebrate a correspondingly large agenda for work and productivity each day. To be sure, there is variation among people as to how much sleep is needed to be adequately rested and energized. However, it is widely recognized that as a matter of routine, in order to sustain physical and emotional health, and effectiveness in work, over time, most everyone needs seven to eight hours of sleep on a daily basis.[49] Including adequate time for sleep is not a problem to be solved but rather part of the rhythm that God wove into temporal human life, and attempting to deny it is detrimental to both work and workers. In his theological exploration of restfulness, Euntaek David Shin expounds and commends the wisdom of *daily portion*. "Quotidian activities that engage with finite good," and do so within the limits of daily time, "are our *portion* in life," he writes. "God has demarcated human desires and ends in his provision of *portions*. And such demarcations are the limitations that make contentment and joy possible each day."[50]

---

[49]For just one example of the connection between sleep and a particular form of work, see Christopher M. Barnes, "Sleep Well, Lead Better," *Harvard Business Review* (Spring 2024): 32-36. Also see Andrew Davison, "Waking from Our Slumbers Concerning Sleep," *Theology and Science* 18 no. 4 (2020): 521, https://doi.org/10.1080/14746700.2020.1825186. For a longer yet accessible treatment, see Matthew Walker, *Why We Sleep: Unlocking the Power of Sleep and Dreams* (New York: Scribner, 2017).

[50]Euntaek David Shin, *Rest: A Theological Account* (Waco, TX: Baylor University Press, 2024), 87, emphasis original, and 74-75, emphasis original. For further exploration of *portion*, see chap. 3, "Eat, Drink, Enjoy."

Moving beyond the twenty-four-hour day, historically the Christian tradition commends a particular form of weekly rest, sabbath. There is a variety of views within Christianity regarding sabbath.[51] However, whatever one's particular view is of specific biblical prescriptions, or lack thereof, with regard to sabbath, the practice of weekly sabbath is a wise recognition of finitude—human finitude, temporal finitude, and the finitude of work. It is one lifegiving way of creating what Abraham Joshua Heschel refers to as an "architecture of time."[52] It is one way of "saying no to the culture of now"[53] and embodying the fact that in addition to time being finite work is finite.[54] Jeff Haanen observes that in order for work to "stay good, it needs limits." He goes on to testify, "After years of trial and error, I believe that practicing sabbath is the central practice in healing our relationship with work."[55]

As noted earlier, it is not uncommon for people in our cultural context to be frustrated by feeling that they "do not have enough time." Thus, it is worth pondering the *experience of* time against the backdrop of *temporal finitude*. *Objectively*, the quantity of time within which everyone lives and works is the same. Regardless of who we are, where we live, and what kind of work we do, we each have twenty-four hours in each day, seven days in each week. *Subjectively*, there is a variety of factors—both individual and cultural—that inform the *perception and experience of* time, not least with respect to time spent working. And the perception and experience of time significantly influence our sense of whether or not we have enough time.

Scientists Marc Wittman and Virginie van Wassenhove observe that "many factors including attention, memory, arousal and emotional

[51]For a comparative survey of four of these views, see Christopher John Donato, ed., *Perspectives on the Sabbath: Four Views* (Nashville: B&H Academic, 2011).

[52]Abraham Joshua Heschel, *The Sabbath: Its Meaning for Modern Man*, intro. by Susannah Heschel (New York: Farrar, Strauss, and Giroux, 2005), 8.

[53]Walter Brueggemann, *Sabbath as Resistance: Saying No to the Culture of Now,* new ed. (Louisville, KY: Westminster John Knox, 2017).

[54]Jeff Haanen, *Working from the Inside Out: A Brief Guide to Inner Work That Transforms Our Outer World* (Downers Grove, IL: InterVarsity Press, 2023), 82.

[55]Haanen, *Working from the Inside Out*, 82.

states are all potential modulators of time perception" in *individual people.*[56] They note that "subjective" factors "strongly [influence] how time is being experienced." For example, "time flies during pleasant activities but drags during periods of mental distress." Time flies, so to speak, during work that we enjoy but drags when we are required to do work that is distasteful or painfully challenging. Time is more likely to fly when we are rested and have the physical and mental energy required by our work than if we undertake the same task when physically or mentally depleted. While other modulators of time perception could be noted,[57] these instances suffice to highlight the fact that the *experience of* time, not least time when working, is subjectively individual.

The perception of and response to time is also *culturally conditioned.* Some cultures are informed by a cyclical or circular view of time while others by a strongly linear view of time. Linear views of time more readily lend themselves to optimistic views of the future and notions of progress, which in turn can be positively motivating forces with respect to work.[58] Cultural differences regarding the respective value placed on efficiency and on relationships inform the management of certain forms of work in relationship to time. For example, in cultures in which efficiency or productivity is a very high priority and substantive relationships less so, one attempts to make the sale or sign the contract quickly, whereas in

---

[56]See Marc Wittmann and Virginie van Wassenhove, "The Experience of Time: Neural Mechanisms and the Interplay of Emotion, Cognition and Embodiment," *Philosophical Transactions of the Royal Society B: Biological Sciences* (July 12, 2009), www.ncbi.nlm.nih.gov/pmc/articles /PMC2685824. For an introduction to the psychological dimensions of the perception of time, see William J. Matthews and Warren H. Meck, "Time Perception: The Bad News and the Good," *WIREs Cognitive Science* 5, no. 4 (June 26, 2014): 429-46.

[57]For example, for many people the experience of time seems to change over the course of a lifetime. While there is still considerable mystery surrounding the causes and mechanisms underlying this phenomenon, there is widespread agreement among researchers that the sense of time "speeding up" in older age is a common one. See Clifford N. Lazarus, "Why Time Goes By Faster as We Age," *Psychology Today* (November 29, 2020), www.psychologytoday.com/us /blog/think-well/202011/why-time-goes-faster-we-age; and James M. Broadway and Brittiney Sandoval, "Why Does Time Seem to Speed Up with Age?," *Scientific American* (July 1, 2016), www.scientificamerican.com/article/why-does-time-seem-to-speed-up-with-age/.

[58]For an analysis of cyclical and linear views of the passage of time in history see David W. Bebbington, *Patterns in History: A Christian Perspective on Historical Thought*, 4th ed. (Waco, TX: Baylor University Press, 2018), 21-41 and 67-89.

cultures that place a higher priority on relationships, a period of
relationship-building must precede the completion of any deal.[59] There
are also varying cultural values regarding the proportionate relationship
between paid work and the rest of life. For example, policies, or lack
thereof, with respect to everything from vacation to maternity/paternity
leaves to PTO (i.e., paid time off or personal time off) to retirement reflect value judgments regarding the proportionate amount of time spent
in paid work in relation to the rest of life. These types of cultural understandings and postures significantly shape *the experience of* time and
work, and correspondingly significantly influence the sense of whether
there is "enough" time for work or for life beyond work.

The reality of temporal finitude is ultimately the reason that questions
related to having enough time for work or rest, or any other activity, *are
even questions.* If there were no limit to the time available to us we would
not have strong feelings about or ask questions about enough time. But
there are limits, so there are feelings and there are questions. That said,
there is no objective or universal mathematical equation for determining
whether one has enough time for work or for any other part of life. It is
essentially a judgment call, an assessment. In addition to being mindful
of the types of subjective individual and cultural factors observed above,
a distinctively Christian approach to questions about enough time need
to be informed by distinctively theological understanding.

Time is a dimension of creation, created by God. Time is not a
product of the fall. It is not evil. It is an integral dimension of God's good
creation. Whether or not we always understand or enjoy that which
unfolds in time, such as work, stewardship of time is simply part of our
stewardship of creation.[60] Our relationship to time is one of finitude. By
God's design, we live within time and cannot escape it (nor do we need

[59]See the Program on Negotiation, "The Importance of Relationship Building in China," *Harvard Law School: Program on Negotiation,* August 29, 2024, www.pon.harvard.edu/daily
/international-negotiation-daily/negotiation-in-china-the-importance-of-guanxi/.

[60]I (David) recall my father, a Christian and a hard-working businessperson, describing to me
as a child how he made a concerted effort to manage his work in a way that sought specifically
to honor the precious value of time.

to). As long as we are alive on earth we have twenty-four hours for each day and seven days in each week, no more (and no less). We need to allow these facts about time to inform both our thinking about and our experience of time, including our thinking about and use of time in relation to work.

Books, seminars, tools, and conferences on time management abound. Yet perhaps time management is not the best way to approach thinking about work in relation to the rest of life, and whether we have enough time. After all, time is. Time is and there is nothing we can do to either stop it or increase it, so strictly speaking there is nothing we can (or need) to do to manage it. Perhaps the management that is needed is management of our *work* and management of our *view of and expectations with respect to* time.

It is important for workers who have some measure of control over the what and when of their work to include a realistic estimate of time available for and, correspondingly, time needed to complete the work. Such assessment is an important but sometimes neglected accompaniment to other considerations such as impressing clients or reaching a desired financial target. For those who are responsible for configuring and leading the work of others, it is important to resist the temptation to let all other factors except realistic estimates with respect to time determine the timelines for projects and to be realistic about the finitude of time and our inability to control it. Joanna Meyer notes that for many women, recognizing the "limits" associated with having multiple roles and providing "flexibility" in the scheduling of work are particularly important.[61]

No strategy will eliminate all challenges and frustrations in calibrating the relationship between work and the rest of life. However, one

[61]Joanna Meyer, interview by David Buschart, November 13, 2023, Denver, Colorado. For further perspective on the reality of limits in relation to women and work, see Firth and Cooper-Clark, *Grounded in the Body*; Joanna Meyer, *Women, Work and Calling* (Downers Grove, IL: InterVarsity Press, 2023); Kate Harris, *Wonder Women: Navigating the Challenges of Motherhood, Career and Identity* (Grand Rapids, MI: Zondervan, 2014); and Katelyn Beaty, *A Woman's Place: A Christian Vision for Your Calling in the Office, Home, and Work* (New York: Howard Books, 2007).

can respond to those challenges and frustrations by recognizing that time is part of God's good creation design and that, in that design, it is finite. One can better respond when time is received as a God-given gift within which we live and work. We can view and receive time as a gift of creation and not blame it (or the Creator) for frustrations we may have in relation to time. We can view and receive finite time as a good gift and do what we can (again, an acknowledgment of finitude) to manage our work—rather than attempting to manage time—accordingly. In the absence of conscious, explicit attention to creational temporal finitude, it is easy to regard time itself as something wrong with the world in which we are called to work. If this is our view of time it will misshape our responses to working within time and likely lead to the feeling that we don't have enough time.

Properly understood, whatever frustration or stress we might feel related to time, the fact is that this is not caused by time itself but rather the understanding of and approach to *the relationship between workers and work and time*. At this three-way intersection, human beings have a measure of control over only two components: the worker and the work. We have no control over time, either the quantity available to us or the speed at which it moves. We do not have a limitless amount of time, and it may not always *feel like* we have enough. But in God's good creation, properly stewarded, we do.

CREATURE, NOT CREATOR: WORK AND HUMAN CAPACITIES

Myk Habets and Peter McGhee astutely observe that what is needed is "not only a theology of work but a theology of workers."[62] For example, the important recognition that work itself is finite is grounded in the

---

[62]Myk Habets and Peter McGhee, "TGIF! A Theology of Workers and Their Work," in *Evangelical Review of Theology* 41 no. 1 (2017): 35, quoted in Joshua R. Farris, *Introduction to Theological Anthropology* (Grand Rapids, MI: Baker Academic, 2020), 194. Habets and McGhee are not here reducing human beings to being only workers. They are simply, and rightly, highlighting the fact that any adequate theology of work will include a theology of workers.

fact that we, the workers, are finite.[63] Thus far in this chapter we have examined two defining realities external to workers, realities of the context in which all work is carried out: space and time. The finite space-time reality of earth is the stage on which all human work is conducted. We turn now to the *workers* whom God commissioned to till and keep this earth (Gen 2:15).

Corresponding to the previous chapter, we will explore here the physical, intellectual and cognitive, psychological and emotional, and social or relational dimensions of human beings in relation to work. The distinctions among these dimensions are largely heuristic, for in embodied human life they are inescapably interrelated. Furthermore, it is not possible to identify with precision the specific ways and degrees to which each dimension is interrelated with each of the other dimensions in any given work-related scenario. However, as we consider various forms of work and various worker scenarios, we can offer suggestive observations about the significance of the finitude of one or more of these four dimensions. Furthermore, while all four of these dimensions are always present for all workers, there is variation in how various types of work affect workers. For example, roofing a house is more physically demanding than conducting a sales meeting, and creating a research-based national sales strategy is more cognitively demanding than painting a fence. Providing follow-up care for high school students following an in-school shooting episode is more taxing psychologically and emotionally than copyediting a book, and facilitating a networking event is more relationally and socially demanding than roofing a house.

Two important notes accompany these illustrations. First, these comparisons are not evaluative. They are not intended to suggest a relative importance or value among the various types of work. Rather, these are descriptive comparisons, suggestively illustrating the fact that differing forms of work have differing kinds of impacts on workers. Second,

---

[63]Douglas Wilson, *Ploductivity: A Practical Theology of Work and Wealth*, foreword by Rebekah Merkle (Moscow, ID: Canon Press, 2020), 71.

human beings are wholistically integrated beings. As James Beck and Bruce Demarest correctly observe, Scripture "depicts the human person operationally as a unified whole."[64] Because of how intimately and inescapably integrated the human person is, none of these examples are intended to suggest that the identified dimension of human being is the only dimension affected. Indeed, because each human being is "a unified whole," all forms of work make demands on more than one dimension of the worker.[65] With this holistic perspective in mind, the observations we will offer along the way are simply suggestive of the relationships between work and the finitude of various human capacities.

Too much and too little are extremes encountered in many areas of life, and it is possible to encounter both in the realm of work, whether paid employment or personally necessary tasks. Because the focus of our attention here is human workers and human finitude, too much work is of greater relevance to the present discussion. However, we need also to acknowledge that too little work carries its own costs, its own demands on the capacities of human beings. Because work is an integral part of God's creation design and intention for human beings, not working, within the limits of whatever capacities one has, is not good. In the case of paid employment, the lack of such constitutes the lack of basic financial and material provision. In the case of either paid employment or personal and domestic tasks, not working can lead to "a sense of uselessness or even of being a nuisance." It can "destroy . . . human self-respect."[66] Not working can be the result of either an individual's choice or circumstances beyond one's control.[67] (Note that the

[64]James R. Beck and Bruce Demarest, *The Human Person in Theology and Psychology: A Biblical Anthropology for the Twenty-First Century* (Grand Rapids, MI: Kregel, 2005), 137.
[65]While this cannot be documented, we would venture the suggestion that, looked at closely enough and with attention to the broader context of work, virtually all forms of work draw on all dimensions of human being.
[66]Miroslav Volf, *Work in the Spirit: Toward a Theology of Work* (Oxford: Oxford University Press, 1991; reprint ed., Eugene, OR: Wipf and Stock, 2001), 156.
[67]In keeping with the fact that work is not confined to paid employment, Miroslav Volf suggests that "Since an unemployed person has not been deprived of all charisms, in a pneumatological understanding of work he is not left without a divinely appointed, significant activity. . . . To

latter is itself a manifestation of human finitude.) In either case, it is not good for human beings to be without work.[68] Work is, as Darrell Cosden says, "embedded into the fabric of both this world and the one to come."[69] And because the One who wove this fabric is both wise and good, "intrinsically work is good for us, good for the world and good for God."[70]

With this said, it is possible to have too much of a good thing. In *Working from the Inside Out*, Jeff Haanen recounts an employee of a nonprofit organization saying, "I can't give everything at work and then even more to my wife and kids at home. I'm empty. I have nothing more to give—I'm on the edge of addiction. I don't want it all to come crashing down."[71] A person may work beyond the healthy limits of their finitude either by their own doing or, again, as the result of circumstances essentially beyond their control. Enough people struggle with working too much as a result of their own choices that there is an organization analogous to Alcoholics Anonymous, complete with meetings, publications, and an annual conference, devoted to helping people "recover from workaholism." The primary purpose of Workaholics Anonymous is to help its participants "stop working compulsively."[72] People may work compulsively, excessively, for a variety of reasons. Some people are motivated by the drive to "succeed" or to "accomplish something great." Some are motivated to work more than they should because they fear for their employment—they hope to attain job security by demonstrating

---

be unemployed need not mean being without work, but can mean being free for other significant kinds of work" (Volf, *Work in the Spirit*, 156).

[68]See, for example, Christian van Scheve, Frederike Esche, and Jürgen Schupp, "The Emotional Timeline of Unemployment: Anticipation, Reaction, and Adaptation," *Journal of Happiness Studies* 18 (2017): 1231. While this study focuses on unemployment, many of the psychological and emotional dynamics analyzed are relevant to the absence of work beyond paid employment.

[69]Darrell Cosden, *A Theology of Work: Work and the New Creation*, foreword by Jürgen Moltmann (Milton Keynes: Paternoster, 2004), 186.

[70]R. Paul Stevens, *The Other Six Days: Vocation, Work, and Ministry in Biblical Perspective* (Grand Rapids, MI: Eerdmans, 1999), 124.

[71]Haanen, *Working from the Inside Out*, 105.

[72]See their website at https://workaholics-anonymous.org/. In chap. 5 we will consider the suggestion that we have moved on from workaholism to what journalist Derek Thompson describes as "workism."

their value and commitment. Some hope to find their worth or their identity fulfilled through a form of work. Some people are simply perfectionists, and hope that "more" will bring them closer to their elusive goal. Whatever the reasons might be for the choices made, they all flow from and/or lead to an unhealthy, and often counterproductive, denial of human finitude. "Workaholics convince themselves," observes Arthur Brooks, "that that fourteenth hour of work is vital to their success, when, in reality, their productivity is likely severely diminished at that point. Economists consistently find that our marginal productivity tanks with hours beyond eight or ten per day."[73]

Not everyone who works beyond the healthy limits of finitude does so of their own choosing. Many people who work beyond healthy limits do so because of circumstances or demands beyond their control. The first who must be recognized in this regard are the tens of millions of women, men, and children around the globe who currently are, literally, enslaved.[74] The indignity and violence of the work done in slavery consists in the *nature* of the work itself *and* the *conditions* under which it is done *and* the sheer *amount* of work that is enforced. While it might initially appear unfitting to introduce a seemingly esoteric notion such as finitude into a few words about slavery, one way to try to begin to grasp the evil of slavery is to recognize that it mocks and violates all the limits of God-given human finitude—physical, cognitive, psychological and emotional, and relational. These people are dragged beyond proper human limits. There are good organizations doing incredibly important, and often dangerous, work to educate about and obtain freedom for people who are enslaved.[75] And there is much more of this work to be done.

---

[73]Arthur Brooks, *From Strength to Strength: Finding Success, Happiness, and Deep Purpose in the Second Half of Life* (New York: Penguin Random House, 2022), 49.

[74]Depending on the definition of slavery that is used, global estimates range from twenty million to fifty million women, men, and children.

[75]The organizations doing this good and extremely important work include International Justice Mission (www.ijm.org), National Underground Railroad Freedom Center (www.freedomcenter .org), Anti-Slavery International (www.antislavery.org), and Walk Free (www.walkfree.org).

Too many people who are not enslaved nonetheless find themselves having to work beyond healthy limits. Some people must work multiple jobs to adequately—not luxuriously, just adequately—provide for themselves and their household.[76] Other people care at home for a family member who is disabled or in declining health, and in some instances this care requires being on call twenty-four hours per day, seven days per week. (And some people must both work multiple paying jobs and provide special care for someone at home.) Other people work for a company, an organization, or a supervisor that demands excessively long hours as a condition of employment, even if not explicitly stated as such.

When such demands are made, the problem is not human finitude. The problem is not that people need seven or so hours of sleep each night. The problem is not that people need non-working time each day and a day off with some regularity. The problem is not that people need appropriate opportunities, amid their work, for cognitive and relational refreshment. These are nothing other than *basic creaturely, human needs.* (Perhaps much of the economic and efficiency-based appeal of robots is that while they do require upgrading, they do not have the need for genuinely creaturely kinds of and degrees of rest.) While there may be variations, creaturely human needs are not characteristic of just one gender or one age group or one ethnic or cultural subgroup. They are universal. They are human.

Earlier in this chapter in our discussion of the experience of time, we noted factors, both subjective and external, that shape differing *experiences of* time. Somewhat analogously, those same kinds of factors can influence differing formulations of healthy or reasonable limits on work in order to appropriately provide for human needs. But *legitimate human needs these are,* and those responsible for designing and

---

[76]Whatever one thinks of the principles and strategies behind specific laws and policies related to a minimum wage, the increasing amount of attention being given to this is a reflection that something is wrong with "the math" of pay for full-time employment that is not sufficient, in some contexts not even remotely sufficient, to provide for the basic necessities of life.

overseeing the work of people have a responsibility to respect and do everything possible (an acknowledgment of finitude) to recognize these human limitations and to structure work accordingly.[77] Furthermore, when this is not done, it is not only the workers but the enterprise and the work itself that can suffer.[78] Lee Hardy reports that "when human limits are transgressed in the name of profits, productivity often goes down. What appears on paper to be the most efficient way to run a business may not be the most effective, once human beings are plugged into formulas."[79] When natural human limits are ignored, ultimately no one wins.

Yet the acknowledgment of human finitude occasions not only guidance regarding what should *not* be done in the management of work, whether this be self-management, managing others, or being managed as an employee. A proper acknowledgment of human limits *constructively points the way toward collaboration with and reliance on others.*[80] A proper acknowledgment of human limits makes it clear that all workers need other workers. No worker is an island. Since the original creation, no worker accomplishes her or his work entirely alone, of their own devices and their own resources only. No human work is accomplished utterly alone. "The Craftsman's Code" is a resource

---

[77]For one approach to structuring work in accord with human limitations, including limitations related to time, see Cal Newport, *Slow Productivity: The Lost Art of Accomplishment Without Burnout* (New York: Portfolio, 2024).

[78]Diane Fassel offers the following observation about employers and supervisors who fail to acknowledge legitimate human limitations: "One of the reasons workaholic managers do poorly with employees is that they do not understand the concept of limits from their own experience. Their workaholism is rampant in their own lives. They are unable to tune into their own bodies and psyches. Because they can't monitor their own needs, they have no respect for others' needs. They don't know what is realistic to expect and what is not. They are loose cannons in the organization. The problem is, they are in charge." See Diane Fassel, *Working Ourselves to Death: The High Cost of Workaholism and the Rewards of Recovery* (New York: HarperCollins, 1990), 87.

[79]Lee Hardy, *The Fabric of This World: Inquiries into Calling, Career Choice, and the Design of Human Work* (Grand Rapids, MI: Eerdmans, 1990), 177. Also see Fassel's description of workaholic companies and organizations in her book *Working Ourselves to Death*.

[80]For a poignant illustration of this from popular culture, enjoy the movie *The Boys in the Boat*, directed by George Clooney (2023, Amazon MGM Studios) or the documentary film *The Boys of '36* (Elastic String Productions, for American Experience, 2016).

employed in the training of trades people and is grounded in wisdom about finitude. Its first two affirmations are "I am not the center of the universe. The trades stand on the shoulders of those who have come before us," and "I do not know everything, nor nearly as much as I think I do," so "I'm always learning."[81] No human work is accomplished *ex nihilo*. Acknowledged or not, all work is reliant on the work of others.[82]

This is most clearly evident in endeavors where teamwork is the mantra, though it is not limited to such endeavors. "As much as we admire solo achievement, the truth is that no lone individual has done anything of value. The belief that one person can do something great is a myth." So says an influential leader in leadership thought and practice, John C. Maxwell. Like most leadership coaches, Maxwell is not one to focus on finitude or limits. Problems and challenges—potential limitations—are identified and engaged, but the emphasis is on moving beyond them. The emphasis is on realizing possibilities. Nonetheless, the very first "law" of Maxwell's "17 indisputable laws of teamwork" is, "*One is too small a number to achieve greatness*."[83] This, the foundational "law," is nothing less than an acknowledgment of human finitude. No one worker can know or do everything related to the vast majority of forms of work. "We fulfill our vocations in partnership with others," writes Gordon Smith, and "the most obvious form or expression of this is found in the organizations in which we work and through which we invest our lives and our energies."[84] All significant undertakings require the combined efforts of numbers of people, whether or not they are identified as a team. (Every quotation and

[81] Dave Hataj, *Good Work: How Blue Collar Business Can Change Lives, Communities, and the World* (Chicago: Moody, 2020), 242.

[82] Not only is the conduct of work reliant on others but the motives and telos of work should include an orientation toward others. See Volf, *Work in the Spirit*, 131 and 186-95; Robert C. Roberts and W. Jay Wood, *Intellectual Virtues: An Essay in Regulative Epistemology* (Oxford: Oxford University Press, 2007), 286-304, on "generosity."

[83] John C. Maxwell, *The 17 Indisputable Laws of Teamwork: Embrace Them and Empower Your Team* (Nashville: Thomas Nelson, 2001), 2, 4, emphasis original.

[84] Gordon T. Smith, *Courage and Calling: Embracing Your God-Given Potential* (Downers Grove, IL: InterVarsity Press, 1999), 228.

citation in this book constitutes an instance of us learning from and drawing on the work of others.) Furthermore, the larger and more complex the task the more obvious become the limitations of individual workers.[85] This type of acknowledgment of human limitations does not constitute an assault on the dignity and identity of workers, but rather honors them by being realistic, by respecting and treating them as they actually are. They are finite. "To be oneself," says Brent Waters, "is to serve and depend on others."[86] Workers need other workers.

In addition to appropriately assessing one's own work in the light of finitude, each worker needs to correspondingly and charitably recognize the finitude of other workers. The reality of finitude applies to everyone, including one's coworkers and others on whose work one relies. In a cultural context where postures of assertiveness and self-reliance are celebrated, it is both wise and good to recognize that "No one who achieves success does so without acknowledging the help of others. The wise and confident acknowledge this help with gratitude."[87] Maxwell notes, "In America, we value independence highly because it is often accompanied by innovation, hard work, and a willingness to stand for what's right. But *independence taken too far* is a characteristic of selfishness, especially if it begins to harm or hinder others."[88] Indeed, to be either unable or unwilling to acknowledge indebtedness to the

---

[85]The second of Maxwell's laws of teamwork is, "As the challenge escalates, the need for teamwork elevates" (Maxwell, *17 Indisputable Laws*, 42). With an eye on the longer and bigger societal picture and developments in industry and technology, Miroslav Volf observes, "With growing division of labor and complexity of goods and services in modern societies, individuals became increasingly unable to satisfy their increasing needs by themselves and more dependent on the work of others" (Volf, *Work in the Spirit*, 187).

[86]Waters, *Common Callings*, 166.

[87]This quotation is widely attributed, though without citation, to the philosopher and mathematician Alfred North Whitehead.

[88]John C. Maxwell, *17 Essential Qualities of a Team Player: Becoming the Kind of Person Every Team Wants* (Nashville: Thomas Nelson, 2002), 131, emphasis added. "Taken too far" is indicative of another instance of too much of a good thing. The realism and wisdom of collaboration with others is not true only of individual people but also of entire organizations. See Gordon T. Smith, "Strategic Partnerships: The Synergy of Collaboration," in his book *Institutional Intelligence: How to Build an Effective Organization* (Downers Grove, IL: InterVarsity Press, 2017), 174-91.

work of others may well be nothing less than vainglory. To "drop the act" and express gratitude is no heroic deed—it is simply an act of realism, an expression of humility, a recognition of finitude. If we actually see the work of others and genuinely express gratitude often enough, it may have the ennobling effect of making us a little less vainglorious.[89]

We conclude this chapter by considering the penultimate and ultimate limits on the work span of workers: retirement and death. The term *retirement* has come to be associated with an individual worker's full-time or primary form of paid employment, and that is the intended reference here.

In both principle and practice there is tremendous variety in the timing of and lifestyles associated with retirement. Our interest here is focused on the ways in which a proper understanding and appreciation of human finitude can inform principles and practices associated with retirement.[90] First, the very notion of retirement is itself an acknowledgment of finitude. Whenever it occurs and however it is envisioned, retirement is a recognition of limits: no one's capacities persist *undiminished forever*. In this respect retirement is like any other stage of adult life—one is able to do some things and, correspondingly, not able to do other things. "The work of varied seasons and thresholds of life," notes theologian Kiara Jorgenson, "make for different needs around time, some more intensive and some less."[91] Retirement constitutes a stage in which full-time paid work occupies less, if any, time and energy, thereby leaving time and energy for other endeavors.

---

[89]See Ryan Tafilowski, *Virtue and Vice at Work: Ancient Wisdom for a Modern Age* (Denver, CO: Denver Institute for Faith and Work, 2022), 57-67.

[90]There is an abundance of resources, both Christian and non-religious, on financial planning and strategies related to retirement. Thoughtful writing from a Christian perspective on the meanings and substance of retirement are harder to come by. Here are several books and portions of books worth reading: Jeff Haanen, *An Uncommon Guide to Retirement: Finding God's Purpose for the Next Season of Life* (Chicago: Moody, 2019); Smith, *Courage and Calling*, 92-108; Alice Freyling, *Aging Faithfully: The Holy Invitation to Growing Older* (Colorado Springs, CO: NavPress, 2021); and Paul C. Clayton, *Called for Life: Finding Meaning in Retirement* (Lanham, MD: Rowman and Littlefield, 2008).

[91]Jorgenson, *Ecology of Vocation*, 135.

Second, in principle, there is nothing morally wrong with retirement. Indeed, properly stewarded it is a good gift to both the person who retires and those whose life she touches. While it may seem odd to explicitly affirm the goodness of retirement, this needs to be said because there are Christians who bluster that "the Bible knows nothing of retirement," and they therefore assert that it is unbiblical, morally wrong. In his book *Rethinking Retirement*, John Piper approvingly quotes missiologist Ralph Winter making this very point, with Winter rhetorically asking, "Did Moses retire? Did Paul retire? Peter? John?"[92] As an alternative to this thinking, without presuming to prescribe a specific path of retirement, Jeff Haanen helpfully suggests two "prohibitions," two guardrails if you will, related to work in later life.[93] One guardrail is willful, chosen "idleness." Proverbs 19:15 warns of the consequences of laziness and idleness, and the apostle Paul does not merely warn against avoidance of work but commands, exhorts, the Christians at Thessalonica to do as he has done, to "do their work quietly and to earn their own living" (2 Thess 3:11-12; also Eph 4:28 and 1 Pet 4:10). The other boundary is "self-focused pleasure." The apostle Paul teaches Timothy that Christians are not to be consumed with concern about "the uncertainty of riches" (riches are perhaps *the* most frequent theme in publications about retirement) but instead are to "do good, to be rich in good works, generous, and ready to share" (1 Tim 6:17-18; also Titus 2:14; 3:8, 14). In the power of the Holy Spirit, Christ-followers are to "not grow weary in doing what is right," and as long as there is "opportunity . . . work for the good of all" (Gal 6:9-10; also Mk 10:45). Paul was not addressing would-be retirees. He was instructing and exhorting Christians how to live and work, in general. However, the basic values and principles of his teaching are relevant to retirement because they are applicable to all Christians in all

---

[92]John Piper, *Rethinking Retirement: Finishing Life for the Glory of Christ* (Wheaton, IL: Crossway, 2008), 24. On the surface, there is some rhetorical appeal here. However, in our contemporary context the word *retirement* is used with reference to paid employment, one's job . . . not to Christians' witness for or service to God in the world.

[93]Haanen, *Uncommon Guide to Retirement*, 49.

phases of life. Their specific incarnation will likely vary from person to person and across the narrative of an individual's life, but they are relevant to all stages of life, including retirement.[94]

One of the characteristics of human finitude is that the already finite capacities with which we enter adulthood eventually begin to decline.[95] Veli-Matti Kärkkäinen accurately states, "To creaturely, finite life belong physical limitations, the most dramatic of which is the ultimate disintegration of our lives over the years."[96] If one is granted long life various capacities decline, whether suddenly or gradually. The poet Robert Frost gives poignant acknowledgment to this reality at the conclusion of his poem "The Oven Bird," in which a singer plaintively puts the question of "what to make of a diminished thing."[97] A diminished thing. Somewhere between idleness and self-indulgent pleasure, retirement can be a God-honoring period of stewarding well the life that God sustains. It may be in some respects "diminished," but it is life, life sustained and called by God.

Gordon Smith astutely observes that unhealthy views of retirement are often the result of having "confused calling or vocation with career."[98] For the Christian, being called by God and living for him and his work in the world is a lifelong vocation. A career, important as it is, is not our *raison d'être*. A career can end but life with and for God continues. Again, work itself is finite—there is more to life than work. Leland Ryken

---

[94]Some people are said to retire early, meaning they retire from paid work at a younger age than is customary in a given cultural context, an age when most people are still capable—physically, cognitively, psychologically, relationally—of and are employed in full-time paid work.

[95]Arthur Brooks observes that "like resistance to death, resistance to decline in your abilities is futile. And futile resistance brings unhappiness and frustration" (Brooks, *From Strength to Strength*, 107).

[96]Veli-Matti Kärkkäinen, *Creation and Humanity*, A Constructive Theology for the Pluralistic World, vol. 3 (Grand Rapids, MI: Eerdmans, 2015), 426.

[97]Robert Frost, "The Oven Bird," www.poetryfoundation.org/poems/44269/the-oven-bird (accessed June 26, 2024). This poignant reminder of human finitude was first brought to our attention by Vernon Grounds, who in his eighties periodically quoted it as expressive of his own musings on growing older.

[98]Smith, *Courage and Calling*, 92. Also see William W. Klein and Daniel J. Steiner, *What Is My Calling? A Biblical and Theological Exploration of Christian Identity* (Grand Rapids, MI: Baker Academic, 2022).

observes, "At a certain point we have to let ourselves be mastered by the nonacquisitive and nonutilitarian."[99] So retirement may indeed mean the conclusion of a career, but that is not synonymous with the end of being called by God to live with and serve him. While for most people retirement will be accompanied by a variety of challenges associated with older age—physical, cognitive, emotional, relational—rightly understood and rightly engaged, it is (simply) the continuation of a life given to us by our Creator, a life that is limited and good because it is life.

In concluding our consideration of retirement, we offer two brief but important observations. As we have periodically noted, life, simply living, entails work in addition to whatever one does to "make a living." There is more to life than paid work, so retiring from paid employment does not constitute retiring from life. At the same time, for most people retirement from paid full-time work is a very significant life event, usually leading to changes, often very significant ones, in, for example, lifestyle, patterns of relationships, recreation, and community engagement, as well as being of psychological and emotional significance. While paid employment is not the only form of work, it, along with other work, is inextricably bound up with the fabric of *life*. Second, we need to acknowledge that not everyone *can* retire. Whether due to personal choices made along the way or a lack of adequate financial remuneration from work over the years, some people must continue in paid employment simply to pay the bills. For those who can retire and choose to, there is certainly nothing for which to apologize. The point here is simply that if you can retire, receive this with gratitude and joy . . . not everyone can retire.

Finally, the ultimate manifestation of the earthly finitude of human beings and the definitive conclusion of work on earth is bodily death.[100] Todd Billings, a theologian who is living in the midst of a years-long

---

[99]Ryken, *Redeeming the Time*, 278. This reflection is prompted by Ecclesiastes 3:1-8.

[100]We here include the qualifiers "earth" and "earthly" because, as David Kelsey observes with regard to the ultimate state of those whom God redeems, "Death as a sign of finitude may be gone, but transfigured human creatures nonetheless remain finite in their ongoing radical dependence on God's creativity" (David H. Kelsey, *Eccentric Existence: A Theological Anthropology* [Louisville, KY: Westminster John Knox, 2009], 1:508).

struggle with cancer, writes, "Strange as it seems, coming to terms with our limits as dying creatures is a life-giving path."[101] As Billings himself exemplifies, work is an important part of this life-giving path,[102] and so coming to terms with our limits as dying creatures is also a path of wisdom with respect to work. Against the backdrop of Ecclesiastes 3:13, James K. A. Smith wisely observes that "our finitude—our lack of Godhood—is not something to resent or lament. . . . Our being subject to conditions of temporality is not a prison but a focus. Gifted with boundaries, we are given room to be happy, to find joy, to enjoy time and—perhaps?—even toil."[103] As described in the *Theology of Work Bible Commentary*, in contrast to "the tidy prescriptions for doing business God's way so commonly encountered in Christian circles," the book of Ecclesiastes provides an "honest, unvarnished look at the reality of work," including work in the light of death.[104] Yet the inescapable reality of bodily death does not constitute a reason to despair with regard to work. "So I commend enjoyment," says the author, "for there is nothing better for people under the sun than to eat, and drink, and enjoy themselves, for this will go with them in their toil through the days of life that God gives them under the sun" (Eccles 8:15; also Eccles 9:7-10).

The author of Ecclesiastes did not have the benefit of the hope-giving divine revelation of God in the death, resurrection, and ascension of Christ.[105] Yet in passages such as Ecclesiastes 9:10-12; 10:18–11:6 he

---

[101]J. Todd Billings, *The End of the Christian Life: How Embracing Our Mortality Frees Us to Truly Live* (Grand Rapids, MI: Brazos, 2020), 11.

[102]Billings is, among other things, a professional theologian, professor, and author, and he has continued these forms of work amid his struggle with cancer. In addition to his book cited earlier, *The End of the Christian Life*, Billings has also done the work of insightfully and poignantly writing about life and death in *Rejoicing in Lament: Wrestling with Incurable Cancer and Life in Christ* (Grand Rapids, MI: Brazos, 2015).

[103]Smith, *How to Inhabit Time*, 23.

[104]William Messenger, gen. ed., *Theology of Work Bible Commentary*, vol. 2, *Joshua through Song of Songs* (Peabody, MA: Hendrickson, 2015), 201.

[105]As Craig Bartholomew notes in commenting on Ecclesiastes 9:1-12, "In the light of the fuller revelation in Christ . . . death, we now know, has no sting for the believer but is the stepping stone into God's presence." See Craig G. Bartholomew, *Ecclesiastes*, Baker Commentary on the Old Testament (Grand Rapids, MI: Baker Academic, 2009), 311. Earlier in his commentary (on Eccles 2:12-23), Bartholomew suggests that "because Qoheleth lacks a NT perspective on

nonetheless affirms that there are things that are good to do while we are alive on earth. According to Ecclesiastes 9:10 those good things include work: "Whatever your hand finds to do, do with your might; for there is no work or thought or knowledge or wisdom in Sheol, to which you are going." With respect to the fruits of work, Ecclesiastes 9:7 exhorts us to "eat your bread with enjoyment and drink your wine with a merry heart; for God has long ago approved what you do."[106] As the authors of the *Theology of Work Bible Commentary* observe, without in any way denying or minimizing the significance of death the author of Ecclesiastes says to the worker, "Throw yourself into your work wholeheartedly" and "Work diligently."[107]

In the previous chapter, one of the observations we made about the eschatological future, both individual and cosmic, is that that future entails a combination of continuity and change. In recent years, some writings in the theology of work and the related topic of "culture making" have given a greatly increased degree of emphasis to eschatological continuity as it relates to the fruit of human labor. For example, in *Culture Making*, Andy Crouch writes, "The city at the heart of the new creation preserves much in continuity with the past."[108] To be sure, there is a recognition that there will also be much change. Crouch clearly states that "every cultural artifact will have to undergo a radical transformation of some sort."[109] However, the overall arc of the book is clearly proposing a much greater emphasis on continuity than has often been the case in evangelical eschatological thought.[110] Drawing on the imagery of Genesis and Revelation, Crouch writes that "The city does not pave over the garden—the garden is at the city's heart, lush and green with life." He even expects to find such cultural goods as an America's Cup yacht and a

---

the coming and consummation of the kingdom, one needs to have some sympathy for his struggle with history and the problem of death. On this side of the Christ event there is less room for sympathy as regards this struggle" (145).

[106]Messenger, *Joshua*, 211-12.

[107]Messenger, *Joshua*, 212 and 213, reflecting on Ecclesiastes 9:10; 10:18.

[108]Crouch, *Culture Making*, 164.

[109]Crouch, *Culture Making*, 169; also see 163, 165, 170.

[110]Historically, perhaps the most influential eschatological view, particularly in evangelical circles, with an emphasis on change rather than continuity, has been dispensational thought.

birchbark canoe, Bach's *Mass in B Minor* and Miles Davis's *Kind of Blue*, fish tacos and bulgogi, an iPod and a Mini Cooper—each having been "suitably purified and redeemed"—in the new Jerusalem.[111] The appeal of this eschatological speculation is that it reinforces the importance and value of the work—all sorts of work—that humans do now. However, one need not embrace an overrealized eschatology to affirm the value of all legitimate forms of work done now. Whatever one's eschatological vision is, the fundamental goodness of work begins with and continues to be grounded in God's creation design, which includes embodied human life and work, which has an earthly beginning and an earthly end.

Whether one shares a Crouch-like robust view of eschatological continuity between the present and the eschatological future or has a view of that future that does not include some sort of eternal perseverance for the fruit of mundane human labors, the fact is that this side of the eschaton bodily death brings earthly work to an end. The psalmist tells us that we may "gain a wise heart" by "count[ing] our days" (Ps 90:12), always keeping before us the reality of our God-given creatureliness.[112] When that end comes for a Christian the most significant continuity is not their identity as a worker but as a child of God, and their continuation in life with God is not determined by having done enough or good enough work but by resting on the uniquely salvific work of Christ. Death brings earthly work to an end, but for the Christian it does not bring life with God to an end.

---

[111]Crouch, *Culture Making*, 170.

[112]For a book-length exploration of "counting our days," see Ephraim Radner, *A Time to Keep: Theology, Mortality, and the Shape of a Human Life* (Waco, TX: Baylor University Press, 2016).

4

THE VIEW FROM THE MIDDLE

Life East of Eden

But humans are born to trouble just as sparks fly upward.

JOB 5:7

There is no other story.

JOHN STEINBECK, *EAST OF EDEN*

TOWARD A PHENOMENOLOGY OF SIN

The Bible begins at the beginning—but not really. Narratively, Genesis starts at the beginning, but existentially, we receive it *in medias res*, in the middle of the story. Whatever we know about how things were in the garden we know only indirectly; whoever described creation in its Edenic state did not do so from memory. The Bible's opening "in the beginning" has a "once upon a time" quality about it. Indeed, some theologians, particularly Christian existentialists such as Paul Tillich, have taken Genesis 1–2 to describe a time that never was, a nostalgic state of "dreaming innocence."[1] Even if we stop short of Tillich's conclusion, which is to deny the historicity of the creation account altogether, the salient point remains: none of us *knows* firsthand what life in the garden was like; we have only heard stories, echoes of a rumor.

---

[1]Paul Tillich, *Systematic Theology*, vol. 2 (Chicago: University of Chicago Press, 1957), 33.

That is to say, even though we can read about the world's origin story, humanity has "lost the beginning," as Dietrich Bonhoeffer puts it. "[Humankind] now finds itself in the middle, knowing neither the end nor the beginning, and yet knowing that it is in the middle."[2]

There is no going back. "He drove out the man; and at the east of the garden of Eden he placed the cherubim, and a sword flaming and turning to guard the way to the tree of life" (Gen 3:24 NRSVA). "Paradise is locked and barred," writes poet Heinrich von Kleist, "and the cherub is behind us; we must make our way through all the world, looking to see whether it may possibly be open again somewhere in the rear."[3] Whatever else the cherub with the flaming sword signifies, it surely communicates that humans will not be able to devise a means back to the garden through any amount of ingenuity or technique. Humanity thus finds itself situated between creation and new creation. The biblical narrative itself refuses any sentimental vision of repristination. The story is always pulling the action forward, not backward; the promise of redemption lies ahead, in God's future, not behind, in vain attempts to re-create the conditions of Eden. Nostalgic questions—"Why were the former days better than these?" (Eccles 7:10)—prove frustrating at best and fruitless at worst. Like it or not, starting with Cain, every generation is born and bred east of Eden.

This has important implications for theological method, because theological method is concerned, principally, with starting point. Paradise is plainly not accessible to us existentially, and it is only marginally accessible to us in terms of theological method. While it is of course true that we can, and should, look to Genesis 1–2 in constructing a theology of work, we ought to be cognizant that the resplendent goodness of the original creation is now refracted through the jagged prism of sin, which

---

[2]Dietrich Bonhoeffer, *Creation and Fall: A Theological Exposition of Genesis 1–3*, ed. John W. de Gruchy, trans. Douglas Stephen Bax, *Dietrich Bonhoeffer Works*, vol. 3 (Minneapolis: Fortress, 2004), 28.

[3]Quoted in Helmut Thielicke, *Theological Ethics*, ed. William H. Lazareth (Grand Rapids, MI: Eerdmans, 1979), 1:284.

complicates any appeal to life "in the beginning" to inform life "in the middle." In light of this, we shall argue that the proper place to situate a theology of work is not in chapter one of the grand narrative (protology) nor chapter four (eschatology), but chapter two, since no one works in the garden, and we are still awaiting the redeemed commerce of the new Jerusalem. In terms of method, therefore, our starting point is not the beginning, but the middle. This, in turn, means that we are concerned primarily with a *phenomenology* of sin rather than a *genealogy* of sin. Here we use the term *phenomenology* in a broad sense to describe a method that emphasizes the experience of phenomena over the essence of phenomena. Stated crudely, we are more interested in what it is like to live under the conditions wrought by sin than we are in isolating the ontological nature of sin. Put another way, a realistic theology of work will be less interested in *what sin is*, where it came from and how it is transmitted, than in *what sin does*, how it warps and distorts both the systems and structures of world and the agents who live and work within them, and what it is like to live and labor "in the long, melancholy aftermath of a primordial catastrophe."[4] For our purposes, the doctrine of sin will serve a cartological function, mapping the topography of "the land of Nod, east of Eden" (Gen 4:16) to which Cain and we, his descendants, are exiled.

A sound theology of work, the sort that can reckon seriously with sin's impact on every aspect of human labor, will therefore seek to cope with the world as it is, not just as it once was and will be again. To supplement a faith and work literature that, quite rightly, emphasizes protology and eschatology, what we offer here is a theology for the middle. With such an aim in view, we will seek not to present a comprehensive overview of the doctrine of sin, much less an exhaustive history of Christian thinking on the subject, so much as to sketch the contours of sin with particular attention to its distorting effect on work. For our purposes, then, classical, genealogical accounts of the doctrine of original sin, which have typically

---

[4]David Bentley Hart, *The Doors of the Sea: Where Was God in the Tsunami?* (Grand Rapids, MI: Eerdmans, 2005), 62.

grappled with the ontology and transmission of sin, are less helpful than descriptions of the manifold manifestations and consequences of sin as real people experience them in the real world.

In any case, from the beginning, the doctrine that has come to be called "original sin" has been a bedeviling challenge for Christian theologians, namely because the doctrine is trying to articulate a profound and mysterious paradox: that "sin is at bottom a matter of being rather than doing, such that *we are not sinners because we commit sins; rather, we commit sins because we are already sinners.*"[5] The matter is further complicated by the notion that the Scriptures generally, and the Old Testament specifically, never explicitly thematize a universal "fall" into sin, and that language is never actually used by any biblical author. But at the same time, this primal fissure between God and his human creatures is the background of the entire biblical drama. Indeed, it represents the fundamental crisis from which not just humans, but all of creation, needs to be rescued. The dominion of death, which has spread to all, as Paul explains, began when "sin came into the world through one man" (Rom 5:12).

But what is it, if it is indeed some *thing*, that "came into the world"? What is it to which we are bound and for which we are yet responsible, and where did it come from? In his description of the human predicament in Romans 5:12-21, what does Paul take Genesis 3 to mean? Historically, Christian accounts of original sin have been focused primarily on sin's ontology, wrangling with various metaphysical models to conceptualize the nature and character of sin and the mechanics of its transmission. Early Christian theologians, East and West, almost universally understood the whole of humanity to be somehow implicated in Adam's sin. Eastern writers, such as Cyril of Jerusalem, Gregory of Nyssa, and Gregory of Nazianzus, thought of humans as being mystically present in Adam. In the West, writers like Tertullian interpreted the transmission of sin along the lines of Roman legal conventions, with humans

---

[5]Ian A. MacFarland, "Original Sin," in *T&T Clark Companion to the Doctrine of Sin*, ed. Keith L. Johnson and David Lauber (London: Bloomsbury T&T Clark, 2016), 303, emphasis original.

inheriting Adam's guilt in the way that heirs inherit the property of their ancestors.[6]

Without question, however, it was Augustine who introduced the most influential model for the origins and dissemination of sin. For Augustine, all humans were literally, if proleptically, complicit in the fall into sin by virtue of being present seminally in Adam's loins. "For we were all in that one man," Augustine explains, "since we were all that one man, who fell into sin by the woman who was made from him before the sin. For not yet was the particular form created and distributed to us, in which we as individuals were to live, but already the seminal nature was there from which we were to be propagated."[7] But at this point perhaps the paradox threatens to unravel into contradiction. To begin with, Augustine is at pains to emphasize that God is not the author of sin. Evil, he therefore concludes, has no positive, independent existence at all, but subsists only as a parasite that siphons its perverse vitality from its host organism, God's good creation. As a result, Augustine frames evil as a *privatio boni* ("a privation of the good")—that is, quite literally, a *no thing*, since "evil has no positive nature; but the loss of good has received the name 'evil.'"[8] However, if this is the case, then what, exactly, did we receive from Adam's loins, and what is it, exactly, that we continue to transmit from generation to generation? This, it seems to us, is a tension that Augustine cannot quite resolve. Indeed, as Rowan Williams has argued so persuasively, in the end, for Augustine "talking about evil is not like talking about things, about what makes the constituents of the world the sorts of things they are; it is talking about a *process*, about something that happens to the things that there are in the universe."[9] Thus, even if we do take a genealogical starting

---

[6]For an excellent discussion of the ideas summarized quite briefly here, see Marguerite Shuster, *The Fall and Sin: What We Have Become as Sinners* (Grand Rapids, MI: Eerdmans), 159-60.

[7]Augustine, *The City of God* XIII.14 (NPNF 1/2:251). While this notion is perhaps Augustine's signature contribution to Christian teaching on sin, his hamartiology is quite dynamic. For a robust and thorough overview of the contours and evolution of Augustine's thinking on original sin across his lifetime, see Hans Schwarz, *The Human Being: A Theological Anthropology* (Grand Rapids, MI: Eerdmans, 2013), 178-83 and 187-201.

[8]Augustine, *The City of God* XI.9 (NPNF 1:2:210).

[9]Rowan Williams, *On Augustine* (London: Bloomsbury, 2016), 79, emphasis original.

point, we still eventually come full circle to phenomenology. The origin, transmission, and mechanics of sin will always remain mystifying, simply by virtue of the nefarious and confounding nature of sin itself. Even if we were to collate these factors into a totally coherent system, speculative excursions into the ontology of genealogy of sin are of little value for workers who toil east of Eden. Instead, "the burden of original sin," as David Kelsey has written, is to describe the "dynamic impurity before God that is internal to the objective status of those born into proximate situations" that we did not personally create but must nevertheless endure and in which we are nevertheless complicit.[10]

In terms of theological method, then, this project's phenomenological approach will take seriously the confounding character of sin, since "only he who understands that sin is inexplicable knows what it is."[11] Sin, as the biblical writers present it, is a kind of malignant intelligence: it devises schemes and hatches plans, like a predator crouching in wait for its prey (Gen 4:7). Sin is therefore in some important sense undomesticatable, cunning, and elusive.[12] This is why one of Martin Luther's more vivid metaphors for sin continues to resonate. Sin, says Luther, never takes any one permanent expression, but has an uncanny ability to mutate and regenerate. "This sin is Hydra, that extremely stubborn monster with many heads with which we fight in the Lerna of this life until death."[13] What makes sin so pernicious is precisely the fact that it is not mechanical but organic: cut off one head and two grow in its place. Sin, in other words, does not always follow predictable patterns or principles that can be observed and anticipated. As we will see when we explore sin's impact on

---

[10]David H. Kelsey, *Eccentric Existence: A Theological Anthropology*, vol. 1 (Louisville, KY: Westminster John Knox, 2009), 437. Dorothee Sölle phrases a similar point somewhat differently: "I am also responsible for the house which I did not build but in which I live." See Dorothee Sölle, *Thinking About God: An Introduction to Theology* (1964; repr., Eugene, OR: Wipf and Stock, 1990), 55.

[11]Emil Brunner, *Man in Revolt: A Christian Anthropology*, trans. Olive Wyon (Philadelphia: Westminster, 1947), 132.

[12]So Marguerite Shuster: "Sin is inexplicable. Every time a causal explanation fully succeeds, we are no longer dealing with sin." See *The Fall and Sin*, 126.

[13]Martin Luther, *Lectures on Romans*, ed. and trans. Wilhelm Pauck, Library of Christian Classics (Philadelphia: Westminster, 1961), 168.

work specifically, sin can manifest its dark purposes even when—perhaps especially when—humans are intending to create something good or beautiful. To translate it into a pastoral idiom, "All that can go wrong with a car is mechanical. . . . There are only a certain number of ways that problems can occur and be fixed. But sin is exponential. You can't imagine all the ways that sin can destroy a life."[14] Stated methodologically, while it is possible to have an underdeveloped theology of sin, we doubt whether it is possible to have an overdeveloped theology of sin.

It is our contention that, for all its strengths, which are many, the preponderance of existing faith and work literature has "not yet considered how heavy the weight of sin is," especially when it comes to matters of theological method.[15] Almost without exception, theological accounts of work, most of them produced by thinkers within the evangelical tradition broadly defined, situate work in chapter one of the grand narrative, appealing to Genesis 1–2 as the blueprint for human work, a point we shall explore in depth in due course. To be sure, the most sophisticated studies within this literature do attend seriously to sin, but few focus on sin as methodologically central. However, as we shall argue at length in what follows, work, like every other aspect of creaturely existence, is caught in sin's gravitational pull—to adapt Anselm's phrase—and therefore cannot be repristinated simply by pointing to God's original design for work. All workers are contending against the *centrifugal deathward momentum* of sin, which seeks to unravel God's world in a kind of de-creation: from *creatio ex nihilo* ("creation out of nothing") to *corruptio in nihilum* ("corruption into nothing"). The pull of sin is centrifugal in that it has a subjective element also, deluding human creatures, the only ones made in God's image, into fleeing the very source and center of their own life. Yet sin is an objective momentum as well, in that, to adapt Anselm's notion of the weight of sin further still, it has a gravity, sucking individuals,

---

[14]Marva Dawn and Eugene Peterson, *The Unnecessary Pastor: Rediscovering the Call* (Grand Rapids, MI: Eerdmans, 2000), viii-ix.

[15]Anselm of Canterbury, *Why God Became Man*, I.21, in *Anselm of Canterbury: The Major Works*, ed. Brian Davies and G. R. Evans (Oxford: Oxford University Press, 2008), 305.

systems, and structures into its vortex. And, ultimately, sin's teleology is deathward, with designs on total disintegration, what Athanasius described as a kind of corruption into nothing, a reversing of God's primal act of creation.[16] In other words, sin is an agent of anti-creation, hellbent on dragging a world ordered for the flourishing of creatures back into the chaotic abyss out of which God originally summoned it. "But one is tempted by his own desire, being lured and enticed by it," writes James. "Then, when desire has conceived, it engenders sin, and sin, when it is fully grown, gives birth to death" (Jas 1:14-15).

In the end, sin is as sin does. To repurpose a common phrase, sin is like pornography: you know it when you see it. It is thus, as we have seen, relatively difficult to define but relatively easy to describe. In the analysis to follow, we shall concentrate on three phenomenological manifestations of sin and its effects—enmity, absurdity, and tragedy—as the interpretive framework in which to situate a realistic theology of work. Accordingly, we make no pretension of offering a comprehensive and exhaustive account of sin. Rather, we concentrate on these three basic expressions of sin because they illuminate the view from the middle, between creation and new creation. Moreover, enmity, absurdity, and tragedy are the three heads of the Hydra that tend to sprout wherever humans undertake their work. A young professional grinding himself to dust out of a relentless ambition to make partner at his firm, which inevitably involves bitter competition with his peers, knows from experience how a wrongly ordered view of work thwarts his own flourishing, even if he cannot acknowledge it fully. A low-level employee entering data into a spreadsheet that literally no one else will ever see or use knows from experience how absurd work can be. An advertising executive who feels pangs of conscience while crafting a marketing strategy for a global corporation that exploits cheap, unregulated labor does not need to read Augustine to sense her tragic implication in this state of affairs.

---

[16]Athanasius, *On the Incarnation of the Word* 4, in *Contra Gentes and De Incarnatione*, ed. and trans. Robert W. Thomson (Oxford: Clarendon, 1971), 143-45.

Within the context of a theology of work, then, commonsensical descriptions of original sin actually come closer to describing the situation
on the ground than abstract, highly philosophical speculations. For example, writing from the ruins of two catastrophic world wars, German
theologian Dorothee Sölle captures both the stuckness of fallen existence that we all feel intuitively—"People are somehow wrong all the
way through"—and the haunting sense that we are somehow also partially responsible for it: "We are aliens, alienated, not only as those who
have been carried off by sin, but also in the sense that we have gone
along with it, that we have organized ourselves in it."[17] Philosopher Hud
Hudson sums up our predicament with a bit of gallows humor most
anyone who has worked east of Eden can appreciate: "We live in an
exceedingly rough neighborhood in very trying times."[18]

PROMETHEAN EMANCIPATION: ENMITY

Whatever the exact character of our first parents' primal act of rebellion
against their Creator, there is something pitiable about it. Adam and Eve
are undone by what Wolfhart Pannenberg has termed the "deceitful character of sin," which continues to dupe their descendants. As Pannenberg
has observed, the serpent's tactics have not changed all that much since
the garden. Sin still deludes: "Human beings regard as good what is objectively bad for them and therefore choose it."[19] Although there is perhaps
a passive dimension to the fall, behind this fateful act there is a posture of
rebellion. As John Calvin has suggested in characterizing the fall as a
"revolt," Adam and Eve are not merely guilty of naiveté, they are guilty of
"hold[ing] the Word of God in contempt." Hence, says Calvin, "it is clear
that disobedience was at the beginning of the Fall."[20] Accordingly, the

---

[17]Sölle, *Thinking About God*, 56, 64.

[18]Hud Hudson, *Fallenness and Flourishing*, Oxford Studies in Analytic Theology (Oxford: Oxford
    University Press, 2021), 21.

[19]Wolfhart Pannenberg, *Anthropology in Theological Perspective*, trans. Matthew J. O'Connell
    (Philadelphia: Westminster, 1985), 118.

[20]John Calvin, *Institutes of the Christian Religion*, II.1.4, ed. John T. McNeill, trans. Ford Lewis
    Battles, Library of Christian Classics XX (Louisville, KY: Westminster John Knox, 1960), 245.

majority of classical accounts of the fall emphasize the contemptuous "against-ness" of human sin, in both horizontal and vertical dimensions. That is to say, in our fallen state, our ruptured relationship to God manifests in our ruptured relationships with one another.

Following from humanity's flight from God and the introduction of the toxic passions of shame and guilt, the curse narrative of Genesis 3:14-19 describes an unfolding of cascading alienation with *enmity* at its heart: the sons and daughters of Eve will be in perennial struggle with the serpent's offspring (Gen 3:14-15), the curse will haunt childbirth and childrearing while it also corrodes the intimacy of marital relations (Gen 3:16-17), humanity will be estranged from the earth and, subsequently, from work (Gen 3:18-19). Genesis depicts a cosmos marred by a multifaceted ruin, with sin distorting each dimension of human existence concentrically: psychological, interpersonal, social, and ecological. Most basically, though, at the root of all this estrangement is a *theological* rupture, namely the fatal breach between God and humans. As the biblical writers see it, in their enslavement to sin, humans do not just function suboptimally or fail to fulfill the cultural mandate as efficiently as they otherwise would have. The crisis is more profound than that; in the fall, humans become enemies of God (Rom 5:10).

As we have seen, there is a certain inscrutability to sin; there lurks in us something with which we are complicit and yet which we do not fully understand. To put the problem in Pauline terms, sin scrambled human mental and cognitive faculties so that those under its dominion became "futile in their thinking, and their senseless hearts were darkened" (Rom 1:21). For this reason can the psalmist plead with God to be cleansed of "hidden faults," for "who can detect one's own errors?" (Ps 19:12). It is not a rhetorical question. The problem of self-knowledge has occupied Christian theologians, not least Augustine, for centuries. The noetic effects of sin notwithstanding, the biblical writers are sober about human capacity for sins of open defiance against God, which the Law of Moses distinguishes from unintentional or hidden faults with the category of "high-handed" sin (Num 15:27-31). While it is central to any theological account of work that humans can conspire with grave evils solely as a function of our moral finitude (more on that below), it is important to emphasize that, first and foremost, sin is active rebellion against God and God's ways. To sin is to undertake an act of malice, an affront to God made "with willful intent."[21] This is why David confesses his manifold sins, including sins against others, as sins committed, in the end, solely against God: "Against you, you alone, have I sinned and done what is evil in your sight" (Ps 51:4). At first blush, this confession is puzzling, seeing as this psalm was composed in the grisly aftermath of David's illicit affair with Bathsheba, in which his sins claimed a great many victims, not least Bathsheba herself as well as her murdered husband, Uriah.

With that said, David's confession does reflect the logic of Genesis 3, where all manner of alienation between people, including husband and wife, is downstream from alienation between creatures and God. In the final analysis,

> All sin has first and finally a Godward force. Let us say that *a* sin is any act—any thought, desire, emotion, word, or deed—or its particular absence, that displeases God and deserves blame. Let us add that the disposition to commit sins also displeases God and deserves blame, and let us therefore use the word *sin* to refer to such instances of both act and disposition. Sin is a culpable and personal affront to a personal God.[22]

In light of the "Godward force" of sin, we ought to resist the impulse to trivialize sin through euphemisms or therapeutic vocabulary. Sin is not "baggage" or "junk" or "issues" or "brokenness," although these may well result from sin. Sin is "culpable shalom-breaking."[23] Any realistic theology of work will need to emphasize both the sinister ways in which work can deform us into vandals of God's designs and the shalom-breaking

---

[21]See David L. Smith, *With Willful Intent: A Theology of Sin* (Wheaton, IL: BridgePoint, 1994).

[22]Cornelius Plantinga Jr., *Not the Way It's Supposed to Be: A Breviary of Sin* (Grand Rapids, MI: Eerdmans, 1995), 13, emphasis original.

[23]Plantinga, *Breviary of Sin*, 14.

purposes to which we so often direct our labor and energies. No approach to anthropology, theological or no, will get very far in describing the human predicament with any degree of accuracy without coming to terms with enmity, understood as the human propensity for against-ness. Indeed, most classical Christian accounts of sin focus intently on enmity, the notion that, though created in the image of God, "[man] has set himself in opposition to his origin, and that it is this opposition that determines the contradiction in his nature, the conflict between his true nature and his actual, empirical nature."[24]

The conviction that humans, in an unredeemed state, are attempting to live out of concert with our true nature, "engaged in an attack on the One who is [our] life and being,"[25] undergirds the approach we take in this book. With that said, on this point it is critical to recognize and dispel a common theological misconception. It is sometimes supposed that the wretchedness we call sin is "just human nature." While we understand the sentiment, we nonetheless need to clarify that sinfulness is *not* human nature, it is a distortion of human nature. To put it colloquially, enmity is a bug, not a feature, of our operating system. In fact, as Dietrich Bonhoeffer has argued, sin consists in an unwillingness to accept our original nature and simply be what we are: creatures who reflect the *imago Dei* but are not the image itself, who is none other than Jesus Christ (Col 1:15). In a tragic irony, humans, who already bear the divine image, opt instead to try to usurp God's authority and thereby become *sicut deus* ("like a god")—a bizarro version of the *imago Dei* characterized by a perverse aseity, a cognizance of the realities of good and evil but with the inability to attain the good or to resist evil.[26] The fall, on Bonhoeffer's reading, is simultaneously a mutinous rebellion against the Creator and a "defection, a falling away from being safely

---

[24]Brunner, *Man in Revolt*, 114.

[25]The phrase is H. Richard Niebuhr's. See H. Richard Niebuhr, *Christ and Culture*, 50th anniversary expanded ed. (1951; New York: HarperOne, 2001), 154.

[26]See Bonhoeffer, *Creation and Fall*, 111-14. Ray S. Anderson has likewise described sin as an "inversion" of the *imago Dei*. See Anderson, *On Being Human: Essays in Theological Anthropology* (Grand Rapids, MI: Eerdmans, 1982), 98-102.

held as a creature."[27] Enmity not only defies the source of our life and
being, but also diminishes our own humanity by refusing to come to
terms with our creational finitude, which, as we have already seen, is a
genuinely good gift of God. A sound Christian anthropology, then, is
not misanthropic—it does not imagine that humans are irredeemable
scum—but in fact properly philanthropic, offering a vision of the renewal of human nature through the redeeming work of Christ.

Apart from this redemption, however, humans are concave rather than
convex creatures, trapped in a self-referential feedback loop of enmity:
enmity toward God producing enmity toward self, which in turn begets
enmity toward others. Bonhoeffer's analysis of Genesis 3 is picking up on
a theme developed at length by Luther, who phrases it memorably:

> Due to original sin, our nature is so curved in upon itself [*incurvatus in
> se*] at its deepest levels that it not only bends the best gifts of God toward
> itself in order to enjoy them . . . nay, rather, "uses" God in order to obtain
> them, but it does not even know that, in this wicked, twisted, crooked
> way, it seeks everything, including God, only for itself.[28]

For Luther, sin is no mere brokenness; it is something that should always
be stated in the active voice. Enslavement to sin, the state of being *in-
curvatus in se*, turns humans *malicious*. East of Eden, we are all beset by
"the tendency to use for evil purposes all the goods [we have] received
from God or [others]," including, we would add, the good gift of work.[29]

In sum, for the purposes of our project, the language of enmity functions to articulate sin as rebellion and overreach; it is a way of describing
the chaos and devastation that ensue when humans seek to go beyond
creaturehood and finitude in a vain attempt to make gods of ourselves.
Hudson states the logic of enmity clearly: "Where my will conflicts with
God's, I will nevertheless pursue my own desires and my own independence, even to the contempt of God and to the (earthly) ruin of my fellow

---

[27]Bonhoeffer, *Creation and Fall*, 120.
[28]Luther, *Lectures on Romans*, 159.
[29]Luther, *Lectures on Romans*, 35.

creatures; thus, shall I seek my own good."[30] The implications of enmity for a theology of work will come into sharper relief in our next chapter, but for now we will anticipate the direction of the argument by alluding to Helmut Thielicke's concept of "promethean emancipation." For Thielicke, the fall is not just the loss of some good thing—it is not merely a *privatio boni*—but an insurrection: "The fall means quite simply that we want to break out of the role of creatureliness and usurp the throne of God."[31] Thielicke judges that "promethean emancipation" comes to expression above all through technology, understood in its broadest sense: not just particular artifacts like iPhones or excavators or computer processors, but *technē* more generally, the powerful-yet-dangerous techniques by which humans devise methods to engage the world and build culture. East of Eden, *technē* is a profoundly ambiguous proposition: it is the means by which we solve complex problems, promote economic flourishing, invent chemotherapy and insect repellant and symphonies. But, enslaved to sin and distorted by enmity, it is also at the root of idolatrous work by which we defy our Creator and dehumanize our neighbors. It is likewise at the root of absurd work, tragic work, and grotesque work. In short, as active rebellion, humanity's "promethean emancipation" can unleash forces that we are not competent to control or predict, which poses serious challenges for any theological interpretation of human work.

THE DISTRESS OF INCONGRUENCE: ABSURDITY

"Utterly absurd, said Qoheleth, utterly absurd. It's all absurd."[32] Antoon Schoors offers an unconventional rendering of the Hebrew *hebel*, though the term's polyvalence also serves to illustrate the elusiveness of ultimate

---

[30]Hudson, *Fallenness and Flourishing*, 92.

[31]Helmut Thielicke, *Being Human . . . Becoming Human: An Essay in Christian Anthropology*, trans. Geoffrey W. Bromiley (New York: Doubleday, 1984), 298. Reinhold Niebuhr has likewise developed the theme of human overreach as a fatally flawed human means of coping with the insecurity of creaturehood. See Reinhold Niebuhr, *The Nature and Destiny of Man* (Upper Saddle River, NJ: Prentice Hall, 1964), 1:178-81.

[32]Antoon Schoors, *Ecclesiastes*, Historical Commentary on the Old Testament (Leuven: Peeters, 2013), 38.

meaning and purpose east of Eden. *Hebel* has a wide semantic range, from the abstract, such as vanity, futility, or transience, to the concrete, such as smoke, haze, or vapor—the fullness of which, argues the sociologist and lay theologian Jacques Ellul, is required to capture Qoheleth's meaning throughout Ecclesiastes.[33] Although Qoheleth's remarks are cryptic and enigmatic by design, Schoors, among others, identifies absurdity as the key motif of the book. "Absurd," as Qoheleth uses the idea,

> is to be understood in the sense this word has in existentialist philosophy: it refers to a disparity between two phenomena that are thought to be linked by a bond of harmony or causality but are actually disjunct or even conflicting. Absurdity arises from a contradiction between two undeniable realities. Absurdity means that one sees that ideas, visions, convictions often do not tally with reality as it is expected.[34]

Put another way, the language of the absurd is a way of naming the experience of having our logics break, riven apart by unmanageable circumstances; it is the perception of a rupture in the assumed relationship between cause and effect, desire and fulfillment. On Matthew V. Fox's reading, Ecclesiastes amounts to a protest against the irrationality of divine behavior, since the order of things does not in fact operate according to a coherent moral logic despite the appearance that it does (or ought to). "The absurd is an affront to reason, in the broad sense of the human faculty that looks for order in the world about us."[35] This notion of disparity or disjunction will be key in our interpretation of the fallenness of work, as the curse of sin has warped reality so that absurd things—awful things but also pointless things and darkly comic things—beset every son and daughter of Eve, not least in their labors. With respect to the human condition, there is "a sense of terrible misalliance, a

---

[33]For an extended discussion on the translation of *hebel*, see Jacques Ellul, *Reason for Being: A Meditation on Ecclesiastes*, trans. Joyce Main Hanks (1987; repr., Eugene, OR: Wipf & Stock, 2021), 52-56.

[34]Schoors, *Ecclesiastes*, 43.

[35]Matthew V. Fox, "The Meaning of Hebel for Qoheleth," *Journal of Biblical Literature* 105, no. 3 (1986): 409.

failure of fit between the deepest needs of human beings and the world in which they reside—an Absurdity."[36]

According to Qoheleth, to be a human being is to be the kind of creature who is subject to *hebel*, to futility, profitlessness, and absurdity. It is to be the kind of creature whose fundamental existence and life trajectories are, in some important sense, inscrutable. As Qoheleth shows, this absurdity can manifest in any number of ways: we may not live to enjoy the fruits of our labor (Eccles 2:18-19); the more we have, the less satisfied we are (Eccles 5:10-12); we leave the world in the same condition we came despite our efforts and accomplishments (Eccles 5:13-17); we are all subject to "time and chance," as "the race is not to the swift, nor the battle to the strong" (Eccles 9:11); and sometimes we accomplish our aims (such as breaking down a wall) only to be bitten by a serpent (Eccles 10:8). These various expressions of the absurd point to the great Absurd haunting every page of the book: "There is a vanity that takes place on earth, that there are righteous people who are treated according to the conduct of the wicked and wicked people who are treated according to the conduct of the righteous. I said that this also is vanity" (Eccles 8:14).

The Bible's wisdom literature, not least the book of Job, makes clear that the Hebrew-Christian worldview does not supply a tidy, karmic framework capable of rendering intelligible every experience we encounter in the middle. An honest and realistic theological anthropology, including an honest and realistic theology of work, must acknowledge that the very nature of our existence poses situations that defy a manageable moral calculus and will not yield to an entirely cogent framework of meaning. This is the common lot of Adam's descendants, and not even the incarnate Logos was spared from the absurd conditions of human life east of Eden. When asked what the victims of a collapsed tower had done to deserve their fate, Jesus supplied no explanation at all. Sometimes towers collapse (Lk 13:1-5) and sometimes people are born blind (Jn 9:3). That is not the way it is supposed to be, but that is the way it is.

---

[36]Hudson, *Fallenness and Flourishing*, 129.

So then, concludes Fox, "the absurd is humanity's condition of existence."[37] But what shape does the absurd take? Mirroring the polyvalence of the term *hebel* itself, absurdity has a shape-shifting quality to it. But for our purposes, we will identify one overarching manifestation of the absurd that has particular salience for a theology of work: the incongruence or disparity between desire and fulfillment. To put it colloquially, every single one of us, in one dimension of our lives or another, has felt the inchoate disappointment of things just not working out as we hoped they would. We might articulate this vague heartsickness of disappointment by borrowing a phrase from theologian Edward Farley. When we suffer unresolved longing, we are experiencing the "timbre of discontent," the "emotional tone life takes on when it is a mixture of satisfaction and suffering."[38] This is not to say that human beings are, or must be, fundamentally unhappy or cynical, only that to be human is to be in a perpetual state of partial satisfaction or fulfillment. One aspect of our lives may be full and rich, while another is in disrepair; seldom, if ever, do all our desires come to total fruition. This state of affairs, says Farley, may also involve "benign alienation," by which he means the inevitable damage that human beings do to one another, often unwittingly, simply as a function of the absurd character of existence. To put it crudely, sometimes people get hurt, but it is no one's "fault." Rather, it is simply the case that the "aims and agendas [of some living things] do not coincide with those of others."[39] As we shall see, benign alienation proves a useful category for a realistic theology of work, since the marketplace by its very nature breeds conditions in which not everyone can thrive in equal measure.

There are yet other shades to the absurdity of discontentment. In the voice of Qoheleth we can detect an unfulfilled longing that is perhaps best summarized in the concept of boredom. Boredom is a paradoxical state in that its listlessness simultaneously attests both to the agony of

---

[37]Fox, "Meaning of *Hebel*," 410.
[38]Edward Farley, *Good and Evil: Interpreting a Human Condition* (Minneapolis: Fortress, 1990), 123-24.
[39]Farley, *Good and Evil*, 122.

pining for something insatiable and the emptiness that can ensue even when we get what (we think) we want. On the one hand, boredom is indexed by what the nineteenth-century existentialist Nicolas Berdyaev has called "anguish," which arises under the conditions of the "dull and the commonplace." Anguish, he says, "implies *yearning*, striving upwards and pain from being down below."[40] As we see it, Berdyaev's description of anguish may also serve as a vivid description of what it is like to experience bad work, to be stuck, as many workers are, in "jobs that are too small for our spirit. Jobs that are not big enough for people."[41]

Boredom, then, can present as a symptom of heartsickness at the inability to fulfill one's potential, but on the other hand it can also be an expression of the world-weariness of high achievers, such as Qoheleth himself, who are nevertheless left cold by their accomplishments (Eccles 2:1-8). The Christian tradition has historically described this expression of boredom as *acedia*, typically rendered as "sloth," which is a misleading translation. *Acedia* does not usually manifest as physical torpor; rather, it is best thought of as a kind of "metaphysical boredom" that cannot muster any zest or vigor to engage the color and beauty of God's world.[42] In this respect, the notion of laziness does not quite capture what *acedia* is aiming to describe. Indeed, the monk Evagrius of Pontus identified the demon of *acedia* with a riotous restlessness of ambition in remarks that, although dating to the fourth century, have proven uncannily prescient in our culture of overwork: "This demon drives him along to desire other sites where he can more easily procure life's necessities, more readily find work and make a real success of himself."[43] In fact, as Catholic theologian Josef Pieper has

---

[40]Nicolas Berdyaev, *The Destiny of Man*, trans. Natalie Duddington (London: Geoffrey Bles, 1937), 175, emphasis original.

[41]Nora Watson as quoted in Studs Terkel, *Working: People Talk About What They Do All Day and How They Feel About What They Do* (New York: The New Press, 1972), xxiv.

[42]The term "metaphysical boredom" is R. J. Snell's. See Snell, *Acedia and Its Discontents: Metaphysical Boredom in an Empire of Desire* (Kettering, OH: Angelico, 2015).

[43]Evagrius Ponticus, *The Praktikos and Chapters on Prayer*, trans. John Eudes Bamberger (Kalamazoo, MI: Cistercian Publications, 1972), 19. Catholic theologian Jean-Charles Nault has argued that

shown, frantic hyperactivity is actually the terminal stage in the sickness of boredom. "Not only can *acedia* and ordinary diligence exist very well together," he explains, "it is even true that the senselessly exaggerated workaholism of our age is directly traceable to *acedia*."[44] In other words, overwork is very likely a means by which humans seek, in vain, to anesthetize themselves from the absurdity of existence, a point to which we will return in due course.

Although it is no one's fault, the absurd character of human existence generates distress. While it is true that there is no one moral agent responsible for the absurd distortion of the structures of human existence, sin is still at the root of the problem. In other words, absurdity is a function of fallenness, not an original feature of reality. The distress we feel as we negotiate the world, our eyes watering as we squint through the *hebel* that clouds all our endeavors, is born of that primal rupture of sin, a "contradiction which exists at the level of human existence."[45] However, what distinguishes absurdity from enmity (and from tragedy) is an element of passivity. To put it crudely, while enmity is something we *do*, something we commit, absurdity is something that *happens to us*. It is the experience of being "complexly overwhelmed," to use a phrase from David Ford, overcome not only by the anguish of discontentment or the boredom of *acedia*, but also by the many demands made on our labors and energies that we cannot meet in full.[46]

In the end, the language of the absurd attempts to articulate the sense of incongruity, disparity, and disjunction between desire and fulfillment, ambition and accomplishment, which all humans endure because sin has warped the structure of reality itself, often to tragicomic effect, which helps to account for the sometimes whimsical tone of Qoheleth. As

---

acedia is the signature vice of the modern period. See Jean-Charles Nault, *The Noonday Devil: Acedia, the Unnamed Evil of Our Times*, trans. Michael J. Miller (San Francisco: Ignatius, 2015).

[44]Josef Pieper, *On Hope*, trans. Mary Frances McCarthy, S.N.D. (San Francisco: Ignatius, 1986), 54-55.

[45]Anderson, *On Being Human*, 93.

[46]David F. Ford, *The Shape of Living: Spiritual Directions for Everyday Life* (Grand Rapids, MI: Baker, 1997), 15.

Ishmael, the protagonist of Melville's *Moby-Dick*, muses, there are moments when it is hard not to wonder whether we are the butt of some cosmic joke: "There are certain queer times and occasions in this strange mixed affair we call life when a man takes this whole universe for a vast practical joke, though the wit thereof he but dimly discerns, and more than suspects that the joke is at nobody's expense but his own."[47] In terms of a theological anthropology, the category of the absurd gives us additional vocabulary—beyond good and bad or sinful and not sinful—to approach the subject of work, suspended as it is between creation and new creation. As we shall argue, the concept of absurdity gives us some of the language we need to speak honestly and truthfully about both the promise and limits of work. Acknowledging absurdity can help us come to grips with work that results in discontentment, work that results in boredom (both anguish and *acedia*), and work that results in distress.

FAUSTIAN BARGAIN: TRAGEDY

In laying the foundation for a realistic theology of work, we have offered an account of fallenness that emphasizes enmity, by which human beings actively rebel against God in an attempt to defy our creatureliness and usurp God's authority, resulting in the fracturing of all manner of relationships—psychological, interpersonal, social, and ecological. We have argued also for the necessity of the category of the absurd, which describes the futility, pointlessness, and distress that attend human existence east of Eden. Supposing these categories exist on a continuum ranging from active to passive, enmity identifies the active pole of human resistance to God's designs while absurdity speaks to the other pole, the passive dimension of fallen existence. We now introduce the mediating category of the tragic, which involves both enmity and absurdity and yet is to be distinguished from those concepts on two fronts. With the language of the tragic, we aim to communicate *both* the freedom of human

---

[47]Herman Melville, *Moby-Dick*, ed. Hershel Parker, 3rd Norton Critical Edition (New York: W. W. Norton, 2018), 179.

agents *and* their inevitable and inescapable entanglement with and complicity in sinful systems and structures. "Existence is rooted both in ethical freedom and in tragic destiny," writes Paul Tillich. "If the one or the other side is denied, the human situation becomes incomprehensible. Their unity is the great problem in the doctrine of man. . . . [Theology] must simultaneously acknowledge the tragic universality of estrangement and man's personal responsibility for it."[48] In other words, tragedy implies (distorted and incomplete) agency, for which we are responsible, and conditions wrought by sin, for which we are not responsible but in which we nevertheless participate, often unwittingly. Tragedy, in short, is both something we do and something that happens to us.

The New Testament speaks to these realities with reference to the powers and principalities (Rom 8:38-39; Eph 6:10-18; 1 Pet 3:22), understood as structures and institutions intended by God to serve human flourishing but which have been commandeered by sin and now function to advance the dominion of darkness (Col 1:13). Paul develops these themes at length especially in his epistle to the Romans, where he personifies sin as both a human creation and an enslaving cosmic power capable of bending human will into alignment with its perverse designs (Rom 7:7-25). Recently, Matthew Croasmun has offered an "emergent" reading of Romans that depicts sin as a "superorganism" that is, paradoxically, both the product of human actions and a force against which humans are rendered powerless:

> The dominion of Sin [sic] is established through the rebellion of human beings, the nature consequences of which are permitted by God. This is a picture of the power, Sin, emerging from the sinful rebellion of human beings. This rebellion provides the base on which the cosmic power, Sin, supervenes. Human beings then ironically experience the real dominion of this creation of their own hands.[49]

---

[48]Tillich, *Systematic Theology*, 38-39.
[49]Matthew Croasmun, *The Emergence of Sin: The Cosmic Tyrant in Romans* (Oxford: Oxford University Press, 2017), 108. Fleming Rutledge has mounted a similar argument across the entirety of *The Crucifixion: Understanding the Death of Jesus Christ* (Grand Rapids, MI: Eerdmans, 2015), but especially in chap. 4.

On Croasmun's reading of Romans, sin is not just personified, but "person-ized"; sin (as person, as "superorganism") emerges through sins (as concrete acts of rebellion by humans) and takes on a life of its own. Hence the tragedy, and not merely the absurdity, of the human predicament. Idolatry, as Paul argues across Romans 1, creates a real thing that becomes a tyrant, extracting human worship while depleting human vitality and freedom, steadily corrupting humans into tragic image bearers—reflecting the character not of the one true God, but of the idols themselves (Ps 115:4-8). Croasmun also shows that the reign of this tyrant depends on human cooperation: "One lives under a master of one's own selection—or, to take the emergentist language one step further, of one's own *creation*."[50] It may seem like a trivial example, but anyone who has ever felt chained to their desk or enslaved to their calendar knows the reality Croasmun is describing.

Croasmun is not the first to note the Faustian bargain humans have made with sin, which opened a pandora's box of unpredicted, and unpredictable, calamities. Karl Barth, for instance, thematized these concepts through an exploration of the "lordless powers" in a series of dogmatic sketches, published posthumously as *The Christian Life*. By "lordless powers," Barth means products of human culture that, having taken on a life of their own, end up enslaving humans. Interestingly, Barth enumerates among the powers entities that Christians sometimes regard as "neutral": sport, transportation, political philosophies, and, most critically for our purposes, matters concerning industry, economy, and money. These enslaving powers are born of the false promise of autonomy offered by the serpent in the garden: "The 'You will be like God' (Gen 3:5), 'you will be your own lords and masters,' was from the very first the promise [man] thought he should grasp when he started on this path. In fact, however, there has never been, is, or will be any fulfillment of this promise."[51]

---

[50]Croasmun, *Emergence of Sin*, 109, emphasis original.
[51]Karl Barth, *The Christian Life* (London: Bloomsbury T&T Clark, 2017), 300.

In a twist of tragic irony, says Barth, humans employ *technē*, as only image bearers can, to try to domesticate the world through the institutions and artifacts they devise, only to find the tables turned: "In reality, he does not control them but they him. They do not serve him but he must serve them."[52] Others have drawn similar insights from an extra-theological perspective. For instance, the research of the social scientist Hartmut Rosa emphasizes the *Unverfügbarkeit*—the implacability, uncontrollability—of reality, including even those realities humans contrive by industrial technique. It is curious but undeniable, argues Rosa, that the more humans try to manipulate the world, the more elusive the world proves.[53] Examples of this phenomenon are not difficult to produce, not least in the hard sciences. In his recent work on the evolution of physics and its industrial applications in the modern period, the Chilean writer Benjamín Labatut has detected a disturbing ambivalence of major scientific advances that have also produced unforeseen consequences, some of them catastrophic. To take only one (particularly dramatic) example, the same artificial compound, developed by the German chemist Fritz Haber, is the key ingredient in both nitrogen-based fertilizer, which made it possible to feed enormous populations more efficiently, and Zyklon B, the chemical agent used to exterminate millions of Jews in the Holocaust.[54]

The emergence of sin creates conditions of misery that are intractable. This is why anthropologies that assume the essential goodness of human beings and which emphasize the human capacity to solve any problem—anthropologies that Reinhold Niebuhr, chief proponent of the "Christian realism" movement, so gleefully derided as "sentimental," perhaps his

---

[52]Barth, *Christian Life*, 300-301.

[53]See Hartmut Rosa, *The Uncontrollability of the World*, trans. James C. Wagner (Cambridge: Polity, 2020), especially chap. 1.

[54]See Benjamín Labatut, *When We Cease to Understand the World*, trans. Adrian Nathan West (New York: New York Review of Books, 2020), 24-33. Although this is a work of historical fiction in which Labatut takes artistic liberties, especially in dramatizing the scientists in question, he makes clear that the technological innovations they devised, as well as the ambiguous uses to which these innovations were put, are a matter of historical fact.

favorite insult[55]—cannot cope with how dire the human situation really is. Reticence to grapple with the category of the tragic is understandable, especially in the optimistic cultures of the West, but must be resisted. As Rowan Williams has shown in his wide-ranging study of tragic literature, both ancient and contemporary, the category of the tragic must retain a vital place in any society's moral vocabulary as "a means of not closing down substantial and deeply difficult areas of our human experience." The function of tragedy, as an art form and as a mode of discourse, "obliges us to pay attention to the sheer *circumstance*, to the different pressures and impulses that are at work on actual agents in the world; it warns us against the fantasy of virtue that has no cost."[56] Simply put, "the tragic" is a category we need to make any sense of our reality, which is not the same thing as saying that everything about our experience or reality is tragic. Rather, it is simply a tool we need to speak honestly about certain aspects of our experience, including work.[57] In some ways, our aim here is a modest one: we invoke the category of the tragic mainly as a means of diagnosing the human situation, a way of admitting the conflict between our original nature and condition and our fallen nature and condition rather than denying it.

In doing so, we are merely acknowledging what the New Testament itself acknowledges, even if only tacitly: that the human situation involves ineluctable complicity with sin, however passive, and intractable moral conundrums, especially in systems with high degrees of complexity (like

---

[55]The deficiencies of sentimentality occupy Niebuhr's thoughts in most of his major works. For some representative examples, see especially Reinhold Niebuhr, *Moral Man and Immoral Society: A Study in Ethics and Politics*, Library of Theological Ethics (1932; repr., Louisville, KY: Westminster John Knox, 2001) and *An Interpretation of Christian Ethics* (1935; repr., New York: Living Age Books, 1956).

[56]Rowan Williams, *The Tragic Imagination*, The Literary Agenda (Oxford: Oxford University Press, 2016), 3, 11, emphasis original.

[57]For these reasons, we must object to Marguerite Shuster's contention that "the Fall and the idea of a tragically structured existence are alternative, essentially incompatible visions of the source of our human dilemma" since "tragedy is the Greek substitute for sin" (*Fall and Sin*, 44-45). We do not claim that tragedy and the fall are identical concepts, only that the fall has created conditions in which tragic entanglement with sin is literally unavoidable. We would also qualify that tragic entanglement does not absolve human agents from responsibility, since human sin is what creates the tragic conditions to which humans are subject in the first place.

economies). For example, the philosopher Gillian Rose has advanced the
provocative thesis that "it is possible to mean well, to be caring and kind,
loving one's neighbor as oneself, yet to be complicit in the corruption and
violence of social institutions. Furthermore, this predicament may not
correspond to, and may not be represented by, *any available politics or
knowledge*."[58] As a case in point, take Jesus' famous dictum to "render unto
Caesar" (Mk 12:17; Mt 22:21; Lk 20:25). While at first blush this may appear
to be a straightforward moral instruction for disciples who would also be
good citizens, Marilyn McCord Adams sees a more disturbing implication. "Insofar as He willy-nilly participated in the benefits of Roman law
and order, roads and information services, taught disciples to render unto
Caesar what is Caesar's (and hence to pay taxes), through His life and
hence long before His crucifixion, He joined every other subject in collective complicity in the horrors wrought by Rome."[59] While McCord
Adams does go on to clarify that Jesus is not a "perpetrator of horrors"—
that is, he did not sin with malignant agency—she nevertheless concludes
that the incarnation by necessity entails the Logos subjecting himself to
the identical conditions in which all humans must undertake moral rea-
soning, deliberation, and action. Karl Barth has mounted a similar argument, but he is careful to qualify that although the Son of God enters
into our fallen existence, he does so by means of a unique kind of consubstantiality with humanity through which he "is the same in quite a different way from us." Namely, the Son must endure the consequences of
the fall but does not occasion them. "Therefore in our state and condition
He does not do what underlies and produces that state and condition, or
what we in that state and condition continually do."[60] It is not a coincidence, moreover, that Jesus' entanglements with evil were economic; as
we shall explore at length in our next chapter, the nature of the

[58]Gillian Rose, *Judaism and Modernity: Philosophical Essays* (Oxford: Blackwell, 1993), 35, emphasis original.
[59]Marilyn McCord Adams, *Christ and Horrors: The Coherence of Christology*, Current Issues in
Theology (Cambridge: Cambridge University Press, 2006), 71.
[60]Karl Barth, *Church Dogmatics* I/2 (Edinburgh: T&T Clark, 1956), 155-56.

marketplace itself, at least in any industrialized and globalized economy, guarantees participation in unjust systems and structures.

What are we to make of this? If we are to take seriously the New Testament's claim that Jesus Christ "in every respect has been tested as we are, yet without sin" (Heb 4:15)—a claim codified in the Creed, which insists on Christ's true and full humanity and consubstantiality with us—then clearly what is needed is a category something like the tragic. To enter fully into (and thereby redeem) our predicament, then, the Logos emptied himself into the form of a slave, "being born in human likeness" (Phil 2:7 NRSVA), subject to all the many ambiguities that attend our situation. David Kelsey's analysis of the "proximate context" of human life (that is, the conditions into which we are born) illuminates these ambiguities of our "ontological finitude" by distinguishing between "intrinsic limits" and "extrinsic limits." "Intrinsic limits" refer to the biological factors that determine our life: energy and matter, natural decay, death. "Extrinsic limits" describe "complex networks of other finite creatures who impinge on and damage one another inevitably."[61] Accordingly, the structure of fallen reality, in combination with the limitations of our finitude (not least our moral finitude), cast the world in hues of "twilight," to use Bonhoeffer's term. All experience, without exception, takes place at the intersection of two ages, this present age of darkness, which is gradually dissipating, and the age to come, the dawning of God's new day, which has been inaugurated in the life, death, and resurrection of Jesus Christ (1 Thess 5:5-6). Given that we are seeking to make our way through the world, as well as our work, at twilight, there will inevitably be circumstances in which we must decide not simply "between right and wrong and between good and evil, but between right and right and between wrong and wrong."[62] Day is breaking, but not everything is illuminated just yet.

---

[61] Kelsey, *Eccentric Existence*, 1:201-2.
[62] Dietrich Bonhoeffer, *Ethics*, trans. Neville Horton Smith (1949; repr., New York: Simon & Schuster, 1995), 245.

BORN TO TROUBLE

You, we, and every other descendant of Adam were born into a story already unfolding. We take up our place in the plot not in chapter one nor in chapter four, but in chapter two. We therefore cannot actually begin at the beginning. As attractive as the prospect is, protology, by itself, is not a suitable methodological starting point for a project of this sort, nor can we jump directly to eschatology. The human lot is to live, toil, and die (should the Lord tarry) in the middle—"born to trouble just as the sparks fly upward" (Job 5:7):

> I believe that there is one story in the world, and only one, that has frightened and inspired us, so that we live in a Pearl White serial of continuing thought and wonder. Humans are caught—in their lives, in their thoughts, in their hungers and ambitions, in their avarice and cruelty, and in their kindness and generosity too—in a net of good and evil. I think this is the only story we have and that it occurs on all levels of feeling and intelligence. Virtue and vice were warp and woof of our first consciousness, and they will be the fabric of our last, and this despite any changes we may impose on field and river and mountain, on economy and manners. There is no other story.[63]

There is no other story—this "sighing for Eden" is the only story of "what really happened, is happening, and will happen."[64] Sigh as we might, none of us knows the way back to the garden. Even if we could find it, we would have to contend with the flaming sword of the cherub. As it stands now, all human efforts are tainted by enmity, beset by absurdity, and entangled in tragedy. Of course, this is not the final word of the story. Chapter three of the grand narrative unfolds even now; the kingdom of God has already broken through into this vale of tears, and the gates of Hades will not prevail against it (Mt 16:18).

None of this is to diminish God's work, launched through the inauguration of the kingdom according to the gospel of Jesus Christ, to

---

[63]John Steinbeck, *East of Eden* (1952; repr., New York: Penguin Books, 2002), 411.
[64]William H. Willimon, *Sighing for Eden: Sin, Evil, and the Christian Faith* (Nashville: Abingdon, 1985), 17.

"reconcile to himself all things" (Col 1:20). Of course, the life, death, and resurrection of Jesus has transfigured human experience, opening up new horizons and vistas in the power of the Spirit, including new horizons and vistas for work. These truths notwithstanding, we do contend, however, that methodology matters. Crudely put, theological accounts of work cannot appeal to Genesis 1–2 as if Genesis 3 did not happen, nor can they appeal to Revelation 21 as if the new Jerusalem—a genuine *novum* that comes *down from* God, not a perfection of human culture that builds *up to* God—were somehow realizable through human technique. Instead, our contention is that the proper place to situate a theology of work is squarely in chapter two. In light of the seismic impact of enmity, absurdity, and tragedy on every human endeavor, the theologian will be hard pressed to construct an interpretation of work that can cast a redemptive vision for labor east of Eden. In our view, then, the faith and work movement ought to be considerably less sanguine about the possibility of redeeming bad work and creating good work, especially on a large scale.

As we remarked at the beginning of the chapter, we have made no attempt to offer a comprehensive account of sin and its effects, nor do we deny that other approaches to sin may prove useful in fashioning a realistic theology of work. In what follows, however, we do intend to supplement—not discard or replace—existing frameworks for interpreting work theologically by emphasizing the various ways, both subtle and explicit, in which enmity, absurdity, and tragedy complicate, distort, and in some cases nullify our attempts to carry out the cultural mandate entrusted to us in the garden (Gen 2:15). As we will seek to show in our next chapter, this will involve naming, diagnosing, and addressing idolatrous or self-aggrandizing work (enmity), futile or pointless work (absurdity), and grotesque, unjust, or alienating work (tragedy). Only after this diagnostic work has been done can we turn our attention to constructive solutions that, consistent with the conditions of finitude and fallenness, will be proximate, partial, and unsatisfactory.

5

TOIL AND TROUBLE

Work in the Middle

What do people gain from all the toil
at which they toil under the sun?

Ecclesiastes 1:3

That's working-class life in a nutshell. You're not following your bliss.
You're not pursuing your calling. You're selling time for money.
The way out of the maze, and the way to get your kids out of the maze,
is to get up every day and do something you'd rather not do.

Doug Muder

WORK IN THE MIDDLE

In our previous chapter, we outlined three expressions of the phenomenology of sin—enmity, absurdity, and tragedy—that characterize the nature of things east of Eden. In what follows, we use these three manifestations of fallenness as a framework for approaching the topic of work specifically. In doing so, we will adopt the method described in chapter four, which situates the human experience, first and foremost, in chapter two of the grand narrative rather than chapter one. The vision of work offered in Genesis 1–2—that is, humans fulfilling the great cultural mandate of cultivating the ground and filling the earth through fruitful multiplication—is, by definition, not directly accessible to humans living on this side of the fall. Human beings, in the words of Dietrich Bonhoeffer, "no matter how much they stretch their imaginations and all their other mental or spiritual powers, are simply unable to transport themselves to this paradise 'beyond good and evil,' 'beyond pleasure and pain'; instead, with all their powers of thinking, they remain tied to this torn-apart world, to antithesis, to contradiction."[1] As we shall argue below, because the dominant theology animating the faith and work movement rests on an overrealized protology, it represents just such a "stretch of the imagination," envisioning a repristination of work by appealing to Genesis 1–2.

Instead, we contend, a realistic theology of work ought to begin not in Genesis 1–2, but in Genesis 3, not least because the experience of the vast majority of workers reflects not the garden, but the land of Nod. And, for many centuries, the land of Nod is precisely where most theologies of work, such as they were, began. There has never been one definitive Christian account of work, but it is clearly true that Christian writers have, on balance, held a higher view of work than, say, ancient Greek or Roman philosophers, for whom work is drudgery that interferes with the contemplative life. Even so, it is nevertheless the case that, until the age of the Reformation, most theologians interpreted work as inextricably bound up with the curse of sin. Ethicist Gilbert Meilaender has summed up the view of work prevalent in much premodern Christian (and Hebraic) thought succinctly: work is "dignified but irksome."[2] There seems to have been a sea change, however, with the emergence of the various Protestant reform movements of the sixteenth century. Ever since the appearance of Max Weber's paradigm-shifting treatise *The Protestant Ethic and the Spirit of Capitalism* in 1904, there

---

[1]Dietrich Bonhoeffer, *Creation and Fall: A Theological Exposition of Genesis 1-3*, ed. John W. de Gruchy, trans. Douglas Stephen Bax, *Dietrich Bonhoeffer Works*, vol. 3 (Minneapolis: Fortress, 2004), 92.

[2]For a helpful overview of the place of work in the Western intellectual tradition, see *Working: Its Meaning and Its Limits*, ed. Gilbert C. Meilaender (Notre Dame, IN: University of Notre Dame Press, 2000), especially part 1.

has been, it is fair to say, a broad consensus that the theologians of the Reformation, and especially their descendants (both Lutheran and Reformed), introduced a significant turn in the theology of work. Namely, by emphasizing the holiness of "ordinary" work (as opposed to "sacred" work) as part of a radical recovery of the priesthood of all believers, these reformers drastically expanded the notion of vocation to include (almost) all manner of human labor.[3]

The contemporary faith and work movement, as well as its ever-expanding literature, is best understood as a mutation within this general theological trajectory, as Andrew Lynn has shown in his meticulous sociological study.[4] This literature, quite rightly, seeks to dignify work and imbue it with profound theological purpose in meaning. It does this through two primary methodological decisions. First, these theologies draw their most fundamental analysis of the meaning of work from protology (and, as we shall see, also from eschatology). As we have already established, virtually all recent evangelical theologies of work situate work in chapter one of the grand narrative.[5] Second, this literature operationalizes—and, in our view, over-activates—a *homo faber* ("man as builder") model of the image of God, almost always identifying the *imago Dei* with the capacity to co-create with God.[6]

---

[3]See Max Weber, *The Protestant Ethic and the Spirit of Capitalism* (New York: Routledge, 2000). For more on the broadening of the theology of vocation in the reformed traditions, see the following: Meilaender, *Working*, 104-26; Gustaf Wingren, *Luther on Vocation*, trans. Carl C. Rasmussen (1957; repr., Eugene, OR: Wipf & Stock, 2004); Gene Edward Veith Jr., *God at Work: Your Christian Vocation in All of Life* (Wheaton, IL: Crossway, 2002) and Veith Jr., *The Spirituality of the Cross: The Way of the First Evangelicals* (St. Louis: Concordia, 1999), chap. 5; and R. Paul Stevens, *The Other Six Days: Vocation, Work, and Ministry in Biblical Perspective* (Grand Rapids, MI: Eerdmans, 1999), chap. 4.

[4]See Andrew Lynn, *Saving the Protestant Ethic: Creative Class Evangelicalism and the Crisis of Work* (Oxford: Oxford University Press, 2023), especially chapters 1–4.

[5]See the introduction.

[6]See here the following: Ross Chapman and Ryan Tafilowski, *Faithful Work: In the Daily Grind with God and for Others* (Downers Grove, IL: InterVarsity Press, 2024), 34-36; John Mark Comer, *Garden City: Work, Rest, and the Art of Being Human* (Nashville: Thomas Nelson, 2017), 175-76; Andy Crouch, *Culture Making: Recovering Our Creative Calling* (Downers Grove, IL: InterVarsity Press, 2008), 21-35; James M. Hamilton Jr., *Work and Our Labor in the Lord* (Wheaton, IL: Crossway, 2017), 19-22; Timothy Keller with Katherine Leary Alsdorf, *Every Good Endeavor: Connecting Your Work to God's Work* (New York: Penguin, 2016), chap. 1; Tom Nelson,

"What does it mean that we are made in the image of God?" asks Andy Crouch. Answer: To reflect a God who is "first of all a source of limitless, extraordinary *creativity*" and therefore to become "creative cultivators."[7] R. Paul Stevens, one of the premier intellectuals of the faith and work movement, echoes the sentiment: "The regency of humankind includes the full range of creational tasks and all kinds of 'world-making': cultural, material, political, aesthetic, artistic, musical, technical, and relational."[8] Without question, this interpretation of the image of God as co-creation or collaboration with God is surely present in the Genesis narrative itself, particularly chapter two, and it has deep roots in the Christian intellectual tradition.[9] However, as we shall argue below, much contemporary faith and work literature has thematized this concept in ways that threaten to alienate workers whose jobs do not entail high degrees of agency or creative freedom.

Undergirding these two methodological decisions is the overarching conviction, accurate enough at face value, that work itself is not a result of the fall. "Work is central in Genesis 1 and 2," writes Amy Sherman. "There it is—right in the midst of paradise, right in the picture of God's intentions for how things ought to be. Work is a gift from God. *Work is something we were built for, something our loving Creator intends for our good.* Work is not evil, nor is it a side effect of sin." If this is the case, then labor has "intrinsic value" because it is the means by which we "participate in God's own work."[10] In general, these theologies stress the

---

Work Matters: Connecting Sunday Worship to Monday Work (Wheaton, IL: Crossway, 2011), 20-22; Stevens, *The Other Six Days*, 97-98; Ben Witherington III, *Work: A Kingdom Perspective on Labor* (Grand Rapids, MI: Eerdmans, 2011), 5-8.

[7]Crouch, *Culture Making*, 21-22, emphasis original. For a sympathetic interpretation of Crouch's concept of culture making, see Witherington, *Work*, chap. 6, where he writes that "what being made in the image of God means is not only that we have the capacity for personal relationship with God in a way that other creatures do not, but also that we, like God, have the capacity to be mini-creators, makers of culture, cultivators of gardens, and equally creators of chaos" (115-16).

[8]Stevens, *Other Six Days*, 98.

[9]See Meilaender, *Working*, 25-46.

[10]Amy Sherman, *Kingdom Calling: Vocational Stewardship for the Common Good* (Downers Grove, IL: InterVarsity Press, 2011), 102, emphasis original.

intrinsic, rather than the instrumental, value of work. To put it another way, by rooting their vision of work in Genesis 1–2, these accounts argue that work is meaningful as an end in and of itself, and should therefore not be regarded merely as a means to some other end (e.g., pay, food, shelter, or funding for the "sacred" work done by the professional clerisy).[11] While it is certainly laudable to encourage workers to see the intrinsic value and dignity of their work, there is a risk of romanticizing here. As Matthew Kaemingk and Cory Willson observe, "in our experience, discussions of faith and work tend to be overly cheery and positive."[12] We likewise contend that this emphasis can be overstated and, in some cases, pastorally unworkable, especially when anchored in a distorted or inadequate understanding of calling. As we will suggest in our final chapter, the Bible does acknowledge the intrinsic value of work, but it also presents an instrumental vision of work, a vision that ought to be restored to supplement, not replace, the agency-dignity-power narrative of Genesis 1–2.

While this agency-dignity-power narrative offered in much contemporary faith and work literature is obviously beautiful and inspiring, it does run into methodological complications. The curse formulas of Genesis 3 clearly indicate that, while humans are still to fulfill the cultural mandate entrusted to them in Genesis 2, the conditions under which they must do so have deteriorated *irreversibly*. The ground will no longer cooperate with human labor. Any sustenance the earth might yield will be extracted only through pain and sweat, with workers' hands constantly pricked by thorns and thistles (Gen 3:17-19). We would add that, as a matter of brute existential fact, these conditions have not been altered by the incarnation of the Word nor by his resurrection and ascension; while the power of the curse has been broken, its effects still

---

[11]See, for example, Chapman and Tafilowski, *Faithful Work*, 23-24. Cf. R. Paul Stevens, *Work Matters: Lessons from Scripture* (Grand Rapids, MI: Eerdmans, 2012), 12, and Witherington, *Work*, 2-5.

[12]Matthew Kaemingk and Cory B. Willson, *Work and Worship: Reconnecting Our Labor and Liturgy* (Grand Rapids, MI: Baker Academic, 2020), 12.

haunt the creation. To put it crassly, Edenic work sounds marvelous, but, as Dorothy says, we're not in Eden anymore.

In its (over)emphasis on protology, some quarters of the faith and work discourse have demoted hamartiology in its theological procedure. We should be clear on this point: there is plenty of faith and work theology that offers a sophisticated and thorough analysis of the manifold ways in which sin distorts human work.[13] Still, even where the impact of sin is reckoned with, seldom is hamartiology methodologically prime or methodologically loadbearing. Even texts that grapple with sin do not always operationalize a paradigm shift laid out clearly in the Scriptures themselves: from *labor* to *toil*. Our contention is more a matter of theological method or procedure than it is, necessarily, about the overall conclusions of the faith and work movement. We do not dispute that work is part and parcel of God's original design for creation, nor do we deny that, in the power of God's Spirit, our work can indeed participate in God's redemptive purposes. We aim to show, rather, that these protological emphases notwithstanding, the brokenness wrought by sin is existentially prime—and therefore methodologically prime—for anyone who labors east of Eden. Many of the themes emphasized in this literature, while true in the abstract, do not resonate with workers who, in the words of journalist Doug Muder, are "selling time for money" by getting up "every day and do[ing] something [they'd] rather not do."[14] Stated differently, much of the current theology of work on offer will struggle to meet the experience of the kinds of workers Muder describes, whose daily grind is bound up in enmity, absurdity, or tragedy.

---

[13]A prime example is Miroslav Volf's *Work in the Spirit: Toward a Theology of Work* (Oxford: Oxford University Press, 1991; reprint ed., Eugene, OR: Wipf & Stock, 2001), which features penetrating insight into alienating and dehumanizing labor (chap. 6). But extended discussions of sin's impact and work can be found elsewhere too: David H. Jensen, *Responsive Labor: A Theology of Work* (Louisville, KY: Westminster John Knox, 2006), chap. 2; Keller and Alsdorf, *Every Good Endeavor* (chaps 5–7); Nelson, *Work Matters* (chap. 2); Stevens, *Work Matters* (chap. 2).

[14]Quoted in Jeff Haanen, "Second Shift," *Christianity Today*, December 2018.

TOIL AND TROUBLE: BAD WORK

Following the primal alienation of human beings from God, the curse of sin hangs over human labor as well, resulting in an ugly "divorce" between work and worship, two overlapping meanings within the semantic range of the Hebrew *'âbad*, rendered "to work" in Genesis 2:15.[15] Clearly, God intended—and intends—for humans to flourish in their work; he wants for his creatures not just toil, but labor, understood in some sense as an act of worship. But, of course, this raises the question: What constitutes good work? The definition of good work will inevitably be subjective, at least to some degree; one worker may find a given type of work satisfying that another would not. It is in the nature of the case, then, that a definition of good work will always be somewhat elusive and difficult to measure. Approached sociologically, however, there are data that have held more or less constant for decades. Here is how the social scientist Robert Kahn synthesized the results of a wide-ranging "quality of employment" survey conducted across the late 1970s:

> "A good job," our composite respondent tells us, "is one in which the work is interesting, I have a chance to develop my own special abilities, and I can see the results of my work. It is a job where I have enough information, enough help and equipment, and enough authority to get the job done. It is a job where the supervisor is competent and my responsibilities are clearly defined. The people I work with are friendly and helpful; the pay is good, and so is the job security."[16]

Even accounting for the idiosyncrasies and predilections of individual workers, to qualify as a good job, employment generally must meet common criteria: a degree of autonomy and authority, an element of challenge, opportunity for professional and personal development, sufficient institutional support, a level of prestige, and a sense of satisfaction in seeing a project through to the end.

---

[15]Kaemingk and Willson, *Work and Worship*, 7.
[16]Robert L. Kahn, *Work and Health*, Wiley Series on Organizational Assessment and Change (New York: Wiley, 1981), 48.

Interestingly, while work cultures, attitudes toward work, and work technologies have shifted significantly over the last half century (and have accelerated dramatically since the Covid-19 pandemic), more recent research yields similar results. For instance, note the following definition of a good job, crafted by the researcher and former Gallup pollster, Marcus Buckingham: "A good job is one where you feel seen for being the best version of yourself; you sense that your colleagues have your back; you don't feel discriminated against based on your gender, race, or sexual orientation; you feel your position is secure; and you have confidence that you'll get help navigating constant changes in the working world."[17] Good work, analyzed sociologically, entails both subjective and objective aspects, but common to most every definition are two foundational elements: personal autonomy and personal fulfillment.[18]

It is also possible to come at the question of good work philosophically. The economist E. F. Schumacher, who advocated across his career for "human-scale" rather than industrial-scale organization of labor, theorized the purpose of good work in a threefold formulation: "First, to provide necessary and useful goods and services. Second, to enable every one of us to use and thereby perfect our gifts like good stewards. Third, to do so in service to, and in cooperation with, others, so as to liberate ourselves from our inborn egocentricity."[19] Schumacher's interpretation of work is clearly theologically inflected—and self-consciously so; he saw work as the arena in which "the Great Headmaster" may help us to "become something more than we are"[20]—but similar themes

---

[17]Marcus Buckingham, "What Is a Good Job?," *Harvard Business Review*, September 19, 2022, https://hbr.org/2022/09/what-is-a-good-job.

[18]Business ethicist and management theorist Al Gini summarizes: "In sum, a meaningful job is one that the employee enjoys and excels in, often feeling in control of the work activity. It is a job that fits the individual worker's talents and personality. It is a job in which the incentive to work is not fear or compulsion but rather a search for fulfillment. Most important . . . meaningful jobs require that one has information about one's work; without it, job decisions cannot be intelligently made." See Al Gini, *My Job, My Self: Work and the Creation of the Modern Individual* (London: Routledge, 2012), 53.

[19]E. F. Schumacher, *Good Work* (New York: Harper Colophon Books, 1980), 3-4.

[20]Schumacher, *Good Work*, 23.

emerge in the writings of philosopher Amy Veltman, who takes a somewhat different tack in her book, *Meaningful Work*. Work, Veltman argues, is central to human flourishing and an indispensable ingredient to *eudemonia*—a happy life in the classical, rather than superficial, sense of that term. By drawing on principles of eudemonistic philosophy, Veltman seeks to develop objective criteria for defining good work, beyond subjective and vague self-reporting on job satisfaction. Meaningful work, she concludes, must involve the following (though not necessarily all at once):

1. developing and exercising the worker's human capacities, especially insofar as this expression meets with recognition and esteem;

2. supporting virtues including self-respect, honor, integrity, dignity, or pride;

3. providing a personal purpose or serving a genuinely useful purpose for others, and especially producing something of enduring value; or

4. integrating elements of the worker's life, such as by building or reflecting personal relationships and values or connecting a worker to an environmental or relational context with which she deeply identifies.[21]

This is, without question, a compelling vision for work. While these definitions of good work are not explicitly theological, they do cohere with the kind of labor envisioned in Genesis 1–2, where humans are tasked with work characterized by autonomy, agency, dignity, power, and esteem. The trouble is, east of Eden virtually no jobs—even stimulating, prestigious, and fulfilling jobs—meet all these criteria due to the intrinsic limitations of finitude and the devastating impacts of fallenness.

It is for this reason, we contend, that the faith and work movement, broadly speaking, has had difficulty breaking into not only blue- and no-collar sectors but also the experience of many workers in the

---

[21]Amy Veltman, *Meaningful Work* (Oxford: Oxford University Press, 2016), 117.

corporate class, as both its proponents and critics have observed.[22] What we have called the agency-dignity-power narrative of human work resonates mainly, perhaps exclusively, with a small segment of the global workforce: namely, upwardly mobile professionals with high degrees of autonomy and influence. In a recent study, Andrew Lynn has argued that the contemporary faith and work movement, while not monolithic, is basically animated by one purpose, no matter its particular expression: to outfit evangelicals, who for most of the twentieth century were culturally marginalized, with a theology by which to interpret their unexpected and dramatic windfall of cultural, institutional, and financial capital beginning in the 1980s. To summarize this thesis somewhat bluntly, much faith and work theology was devised to sacralize the professional accomplishments and prestige of what Lynn terms "Creative Class Evangelicals."[23] At the risk of cynicism, it is not difficult to see why the concept of "culture making" resonates with "Creative Class Evangelicals" or with the many skilled tradesmen and tradeswomen who find profound satisfaction in the kind of blue- or no-collar work that entails high degrees of creativity, agency, and expertise.[24] It is much less clear

---

[22]For a diagnosis of this problem from a faith and work insider, see Haanen, "Second Shift." Haanen is the founder and former CEO of Denver Institute for Faith and Work, one of the nation's leading marketplace theology organizations.

[23]See Lynn, *Saving the Protestant Ethic*, 23-27, 117-18. If Lynn's interpretation is a bit cynical, writers considerably more sympathetic to evangelical marketplace theology movements have also acknowledged their white-collar tendencies. For example, David Miller, whose interpretation of these trends differs substantially from Lynn's, acknowledges that at least some expressions of what he calls the "faith at work" movement (rather than the "faith and work" movement) emerged as baby boomers sought to construct a theology of work that could simultaneously satisfy a quest for deeper meaning at work while also leaving room for "successful careers and material pleasures." See David W. Miller, *God at Work: The History and Promise of the Faith at Work Movement* (Oxford: Oxford University Press, 2007), 65-74.

[24]For instance, drawing on his experience as a motorcycle mechanic, Matthew Crawford makes a compelling case for the dignity and reward of blue-collar and no-collar work in *Shop Class as Soulcraft: An Inquiry into the Value of Work* (New York: Penguin, 2009). For another account of the contributions of the trades, see Dave Hataj, *Good Work: How Blue Collar Business Can Change Lives, Communities, and the World* (Chicago: Moody, 2020). Both Crawford and Hataj rightly reject the notion of "unskilled" labor. With that said, the kind of work these authors describe—challenging, fulfilling, and productive of useful artifacts—does not meet the criteria for bad work as described here, which entails boredom, monotony, and lack of challenge.

what, if anything, such a notion might possibly mean to a cashier or a truck driver or a middle manager at a huge corporation.

The ugly truth, and the great challenge for any theological account of work, is that many workers report that they simply do not find their work good or meaningful.[25] Here is how Al Gini summarized the research on the state of job satisfaction two decades ago:

> However we choose to calculate the elusive goal of job satisfaction, one thing is certain: A substantial and ever-increasing portion of the workforce is not satisfied or happy with their work. More and more workers report that although their job absorbs and consumes their time and energy, it doesn't give them what they need. . . . In effect, what many workers are now saying is that work is not enjoyable or satisfying in itself. More and more workers feel that their jobs lack any meaning and value beyond the utilitarian function of providing them with a paycheck.[26]

Matters have not improved. Gallup's 2023 *State of the Global Workplace* report found that, in North America, an astonishing share of workers—no less than 52 percent—describe themselves as "quiet quitters," technically on the clock but totally disengaged from their work. Only one in three workers says they are thriving at work.[27] What is more, these studies do not only reflect the attitudes of workers in what we might think of as undesirable jobs. Since at least the days of Karl Marx, critical theorists, philosophers, and economists have decried the ways in which industrialization—the assembly lines of Fordism, say, or the hypersurveillance of Taylorism—degrades and dehumanizes workers, particularly workers who physically fabricate tangible goods.[28]

---

[25]Of course, many workers find meaning and enjoyment from difficult or taxing work. Our analysis does not intend to deny that reality; we do, however, intend to emphasize the realities workers themselves report, many of which are quite dismal.

[26]Gini, *My Job, My Self*, 48-49.

[27]*State of the Global Workplace 2023 Report* (Gallup, 2024), www.gallup.com/workplace/349484/state-of-the-global-workplace.aspx?thank-you-report-form=1, accessed May 2, 2024.

[28]On these themes, see Carl Cederström and Peter Fleming, *Dead Man Working* (Winchester, UK: Zero Books, 2012), 39-41; Crawford, *Shop Class as Soulcraft*, chap. 2; Miya Tokumitsu, *Do What You Love: And Other Lies About Success and Happiness* (New York: Regan Arts, 2015), 65-66; Veltman, *Meaningful Work*, 73-74; Volf, *Work in the Spirit*, 173-74.

However, these trends have continued apace into the age of the "digital" or "information economy," where more and more workers, particularly office workers, are physically present but existentially absent, a phenomenon that organizational theorists Carl Cederström and Peter Fleming have termed not absenteeism, but "presenteeism."[29]

In his provocative book, *Bullshit Jobs*, anthropologist David Graeber summarizes this state of affairs in a grim syllogism:

1. Most people's sense of dignity and self-worth is caught up in working for a living.

2. Most people hate their jobs.

Graeber adds that, according to his extensive body of quantitative data, this conclusion "appears to hold true, with only minor variations, for both blue- and white-collar workers virtually anywhere in the world."[30] Graeber's contemporary sociological research therefore arrives at more or less the same conclusion reached by the journalist Studs Terkel half a century ago. In his seminal oral history of what it is like to work in America—not just as a mechanic or farm hand, but also as a bank teller or shoeshine or surgeon—Terkel paints a similar picture. His expansive interviews give voice to "the walking wounded" who endure "daily humiliations" in their work, "in search . . . for daily meaning as well as daily bread, for recognition as well as cash, for astonishment rather than torpor; in short, for a sort of life rather than a Monday through Friday sort of dying."[31] This suggests that the problem of bad work is perennial, intrinsic to the givenness of things east of Eden; indeed, it is as old as Genesis 3. Any realistic theology of work will have to reckon seriously with *this* brand of despair and existential resignation—with widespread discontentment and disillusionment, with the pernicious ways in which work degrades and alienates rather than enlivens and enriches.

---

[29]Cederström and Fleming, *Dead Man Working*, 6.
[30]David Graeber, *Bullshit Jobs: A Theory* (New York: Simon and Schuster, 2018), 241.
[31]Studs Terkel, *Working: People Talk About What They Do All Day and How They Feel About What They Do* (New York: The New Press, 1972), xi. More recently, Cederström and Fleming have written that many workers describe their work as a "living death" (*Dead Man Working*, 4).

This is nothing Qoheleth did not know: "What do people gain from all the toil at which they toil under the sun?" (Eccles 1:3). Does Christian theology have the resources to address such a question? Is there a theology of work for "the walking wounded"? Any theology with at least a chance of speaking to this situation will first need to look unflinchingly at the problem—the enmity, absurdity, and tragedy of work—before hazarding any constructive solutions, however provisional.

BRICK AND BITUMEN: ENMITOUS WORK

Humanity's primal act of rebellion—their "promethean emancipation," to return to Helmut Thielicke's phrase—sparked a chain reaction of cascading alienation. As we saw with the curse formulas of Genesis 3, every dimension of human existence, from the interpersonal to the ecological, is subjected to the dominion of sin, which brings forth death. The narrative of Genesis, specifically the "primeval history" chronicled in Genesis 1–11, depicts not just a static fall, but a continual falling away. This is an *in medias res* theology: we are both fallen and falling. It is not a coincidence that, in Genesis 11, the primeval history culminates in an act of *technē*. Humans undertake a massive building project, as only image bearers can, (mis)directing their vast culture-making powers to produce a monument to "their valiant self-reliance" in a high-handed spirit of "Titanism."[32] The narrative reveals, both subtly and not, the ways in which enmity has also poisoned human work, and on several levels. The first thing to note is that these builders plan their project in direct defiance of the cultural mandate issued in Genesis 1:28; rather than multiplying to "fill the earth," the engineers of Babel concentrate in one place, "otherwise we shall be scattered abroad upon the face of the whole earth" (Gen 11:4). Most important for our purposes, though,

---

[32]The language is Gerhard von Rad's. See Gerhard von Rad, *Genesis: A Commentary*, trans. John H. Marks (Philadelphia: Westminster, 1972), 149. Cf. also the comments of R. Paul Stevens, with the reference to Cain's construction of a city in Genesis, which represents an ironic misuse of human capacities "to manipulate their environment to satisfy their own greed, or contrarily, to worship the created order" (*Other Six Days*, 99).

are two details in the narrative: first, the mal-use of human technical capacities in service of a self-aggrandizing and idolatrous vision of human work that reveals, second, a more basic contempt for creaturehood and, by extension, contempt for the Word of God.

In the first place, the Babel account goes out of its way to emphasize that human rebellion against God takes the explicit form of corrupted work, the perversion of *technē*. "And they had brick for stone and bitumen for mortar" (Gen 11:3). This is not an incidental detail or bit of literary flourish to supply a sense of realism; it is a reference to cutting-edge advances in engineering, the fabrication of materials that make possible the construction of "the equivalent of a modern skyscraper."[33] Although, if John Goldingay is right that Genesis 11 is intended to lampoon and parody ancient Mesopotamian building projects, we should sense the comedic irony of this scene, in which God has to stoop and squint to see humanity's titanic achievement. Then, as now, all human attempts to ascend to God through industry will falter due to the "makeshift" quality of mortals' workmanship, which in this passage is the object of Yahweh's derision.[34] Already, then, the Genesis account is gesturing toward the limits of human work.

In the second place, the narrator also supplies the engineers' motives: "let us make a name for ourselves" (Gen 11:4). This is consistent with the practices of ancient monarchs, who erected monuments as an attempt at immortality.[35] In this respect, nothing has changed. As sociologist Robert Wuthnow has written, work continues to be the means by which humans attempt "to give a legitimate account of themselves."[36] Is it true that work is the best means of justifying our existence? A Christian

---

[33]Victor P. Hamilton, *The Book of Genesis: Chapters 1–17*, The New International Commentary on the Old Testament (Grand Rapids, MI: Eerdmans, 1990), 352.

[34]John Goldingay, *Genesis*, Baker Commentary on the Old Testament (Grand Rapids, MI: Baker Academic, 2020), 187.

[35]John E. Hartley, *Genesis*, Understanding the Bible Commentary Series (Grand Rapids, MI: Baker Books, 1995), 124-25.

[36]Robert Wuthnow, *Poor Richard's Principle: Recovering the American Dream through the Moral Dimensions of Work, Business and Money* (Princeton, NJ: Princeton University Press, 1996), 225.

anthropology must subject such a claim to scrutiny, as we will in our next chapter. For now, it is sufficient to note that the name-making of the tower builders of Genesis 11 is contrasted deliberately with the name-giving of Genesis 12, where God promises to "make [Abram's] name great" (Gen 12:2). This is our first clue that, in theological perspective, identities are not generated, they are conferred.

Despite any theological objections we might raise, it is nonetheless the case that, certainly in developed economies, work continues to serve as the primary means of defining one's identity. Anyone who has been to a cocktail party knows this: "So, what do you do?" is the first question we ask upon meeting a new acquaintance. Work has become not something we *do*, but something we *are*. This thesis has been taken up at length in the writings of Al Gini, who has argued that, in the modern period, work has become nearly the sole source of human identity, particularly in Western, individualist cultures. "Work is not just about earning a livelihood. . . . Work is also one of the most significant contributing factors to one's inner life and development. Beyond mere survival, we create ourselves in work. . . . what we do is what we become."[37] Such an anthropology—which, to be clear, Gini does not commend, but simply describes—is a manifestation of enmity, as we shall argue below, and is therefore at odds with a Christian vision of human purpose and flourishing. So long as we equate our selves and our work, we will be susceptible to "losing ourselves" in our work, either by "making a name for ourselves" through idolatrous work or by using work as a drug to anesthetize ourselves from reality, devolving into nothing more than "a cog in the great machine of work and pleasure."[38]

This isn't just an ancient Babylonian problem. In recent years, Americans have increasingly looked to work as a source of ultimate transcendence, loading it with existential weight it simply cannot bear. The writings of journalist Derek Thompson, who has chronicled evolving

---

[37]Gini, *My Job, My Self*, 2, 12.
[38]Paul Tillich, *Systematic Theology*, vol. 2 (Chicago: University of Chicago Press, 1957), 74.

attitudes toward work over the modern period, are especially illuminating here. "In the past century," says Thompson, "the American conception of work has shifted from jobs to careers to callings—from necessity to status to meaning."[39] This is something beyond workaholism, which is a terminal condition we, as a society, have left untreated for decades. The fatal propensity toward frantic overwork, what Diane Fassel once called "the cleanest of all addictions," is alive and well, and shows no signs of abating.[40] In highly developed economies, deaths due to sheer exhaustion remain alarmingly common. Death by overwork is so prevalent in Japan, for example, that this phenomenon has its own distinct nomenclature, *karōshi*. Closer to home, thousands of Americans die from overwork every year, and the trend is accelerating.[41] One could hardly think of a more destructive consequence of sin's impact on human work. This is because workaholism is, at root, an expression both of enmity toward God and of idolatry—and idols consume their subjects.

These deaths by overwork are a sacrifice on the altar of a false god. To put it another way, we have moved from workaholism to what Thompson calls "workism," a quasi-religion organized around "the gospel of labor." Workism, he explains, is three things:

> First, it is the belief that, in a time when religion is in decline, more people, especially the elite, are turning to work to provide everything we have historically expected from organized religions. Second, it is the irony that, in a time of declining trust in most institutions like politics and religion, we expect more than ever from the companies that employ us; . . . Third, it is a mixed blessing. The gospel of labor creates devoted

---

[39]Derek Thompson, *On Work: Money, Meaning, Identity*, Atlantic Editions (New York: Zando, 2023), 39.

[40]Diane Fassel, *Working Ourselves to Death: The High Cost of Workaholism and the Rewards of Recovery* (New York: HarperCollins, 1990), 2.

[41]See Joshua Hunt, "Are Japan's Part-Time Employees Working Themselves to Death?," *The Atlantic*, August 8, 2018, www.theatlantic.com/business/archive/2018/08/japan-overwork/565991/. See also Matt Schiavenza, "Dying at Work," *The Atlantic*, October 30, 2014, www.theatlantic .com/health/archive/2014/10/dying-at-work/382159/.

workers and extraordinary achievements, giving purpose, building routine, and filling time. But our devotion to work can also leave a wake of anguish, with many of its adherents feeling overextended, exhausted, and empty.[42]

As Western societies continue to secularize, it is likely that humanity's innate religious impulses will be increasingly channeled into workism; "the more secular we become, the more we expect our jobs to answer the ultimate questions of meaning and purpose in our lives."[43] If we were to translate this into an explicitly theological idiom, we would have a good description of idolatry: enslavement to a false god that is indeed immensely generative—it is capable of building towers of Babel—but which ultimately depletes and diminishes the humanity of its worshipers.

Because it is a symptom of humanity's primal rupture with God—the ultimate source of all life, meaning, and purpose—enmitous work is upstream from, and vitally related to, both absurd and tragic work. "One of the reasons work is both fruitless and pointless," observes Timothy Keller, "is the powerful inclination of the human heart to make work, and its attendant benefits, the main basis of one's meaning and identity."[44] Accordingly, to anticipate one constructive proposal we will develop in the conclusion, a realistic theology of work will not only insist that we come to terms with our own finitude and creaturehood, but it must also seek to displace work from the center of human identity and purpose. Or, at the very least, it must avoid reinforcing (even inadvertently) the assumption that work is *the* primary means of finding ultimate meaning.

KILLING TIME: ABSURD WORK

The late 1990s and early 2000s represents something of a golden age for workplace comedies, from *Scrubs* to *The Office*, which moved the

---

[42]Thompson, *On Work*, xi.
[43]Gini, *My Job, My Self*, 193.
[44]Keller and Alsdorf, *Every Good Endeavor*, 108.

dramatic action from the private realm to the shared domain of the job. After all, working is a nearly universal experience, and many people spend the majority of their waking hours not with friends or family, but with coworkers, making the workplace a bottomless goldmine of comedy. But these shows and films also reveal the changing nature of work, especially in white-collar contexts, tapping into an inchoate angst just beneath the surface of the information economy. Perhaps nothing captures the sheer inanity and tedium of a dead-end office job quite like Mike Judge's *Office Space*, released in 1999. The protagonist of the film—if one can call him that—is Peter Gibbons, a disaffected computer programmer who spends his days in his cubicle mindlessly crunching code for a bland corporation called Initech. The film captures the comic absurdities that can beset our work: patronizing workshops intended to boost morale, managerial ineptitude, pointless reports that no one reads yet employees must diligently complete. In one memorable scene, a pair of hapless business consultants, both named Bob, ask Peter to describe his typical workday. Peter struggles to explain what he actually *does* in his job:

> I generally come in at least fifteen minutes late. I use the side door—that way, [my boss] can't see me. After that, I just sort of space out for about an hour. Yeah, I just stare at my desk. But it looks like I'm working. I do that for probably another hour after lunch, too. I'd say in a given week, I probably only do about fifteen minutes of real, actual work.

Later on, Peter openly fantasizes about being lobotomized during work hours—a mundane horror considered at length in the recent (and deeply unsettling) series, *Severance*. The reason? "Ever since I started working," he explains, "every single day of my life has been worse than the day before it. So that means that every single day that you see me— that's on the worst day of my life."[45]

Perhaps we laugh to keep from crying. The fact is, a lot of workers can identify with Peter Gibbons or the office clerks whiling away

---

[45]*Office Space*, directed by Mike Judge (20th Century Fox, 1999).

decades selling paper on *The Office*. To recall Terkel's memorable phrase, many people endure their workweeks as "a Monday through Friday sort of dying." However, this is not just because their jobs are physically demanding or painful, although of course many jobs are. Rather, it is because the kind of work parodied in *Office Space* is an expression of the absurd, an incongruence between ambition and opportunity, between desire and fulfillment, between expectations and reality. Absurd work does "spiritual violence" to workers because "it's not just an attack on the person's sense of self-importance, but also a direct attack on the very sense that one even *is* a self."[46] Graeber's sociological analysis thus takes on existential tones, evoking that great champion of the absurd, Søren Kierkegaard. Already in the nineteenth century, Kierkegaard was alert to the manifold symptoms of an underlying illness he called "the despair of weakness": the inability—and unwillingness—to explore the full range and depth of our capacities by engaging the challenges presented by the world.[47] Simply put, when our work does not activate and engage our creative or rational faculties, something inside of us begins to shrink. And yet, because sin has contorted and constricted the givenness of our reality so profoundly, many workers are constrained by jobs "too small for [their] spirits."[48]

Some visions of work offered in contemporary faith and work literature are difficult, if not impossible, to square with the lived experience of workers. To take only one example: suppose we define work as "any necessary and meaningful task that God calls and gifts a person to do and which can be undertaken to the glory of God and for the edification and aid of human beings, being inspired by the Holy Spirit and foreshadowing the realities of the new creation."[49] In principle, there is nothing about this definition of work to which a Christian theologian

---

[46]Graeber, *Bullshit Jobs*, 83-84.
[47]See Søren Kierkegaard, *The Sickness unto Death: A Christian Psychological Exposition for Upbuilding and Awakening*, ed. and trans. Howard V. Hong and Edna H. Hong (Princeton, NJ: Princeton University Press, 1980), 43, 49-67.
[48]Terkel, *Working*, xxiv.
[49]Witherington, *Work*, xii.

can object, at least in the abstract. The difficulty, however, is that ethereal *work* is always instantiated in concrete *jobs*; many people like the idea of work (in theory) but dislike their jobs (in practice). Thus, under even modest scrutiny, this definition starts to fray at the seams. For a start, as we shall explore, many workers report that their work is neither necessary nor meaningful. Moreover, much work does little to foster—and, indeed, may even hinder—the edification and aid of human beings. Not only that, many expressions of human labor are, to put it mildly, not fit for the new creation (nor is it possible to envision how they might be refined to be made so), as we shall argue at length below. Following our analysis of absurdity in the previous chapter—in which we characterized the absurd as a passive, rather than an active, dimension of fallenness—we contend that only a moral vocabulary that includes a category like the absurd can begin to describe the various species of unfulfilling work: "dead-end" jobs, repetitive jobs, jobs that are degrading not so much physically, but existentially—not to mention the experience of unemployment or underemployment. To that end, we now suggest three expressions of the absurd that are especially salient for a realistic theology of work: futility, boredom, and discontentment.

We have already seen that, for Qoheleth, one of the prime ways humans encounter the absurdity of *hebel* is through the futility of work. Qoheleth notes that work is often fruitless, as one's life opus can come to nothing or, worse, fall into the incompetent hands of the next generation (Eccles 2:12-23). This absurdity is thematized throughout the book as a kind of *profitlessness* that plagues every human endeavor, introduced as an organizing refrain in the opening prologue of the book: "What do people gain from all the toil at which they toil under the sun?" (Eccles 1:3). It is not that work is profitless in the sense that its results are not always realized (although that is true), it is that work does not—cannot—supply what we need to give an adequate account of our existence. In other words, Qoheleth does not intend "profit" in a utilitarian way—that is, how many artifacts were produced, how many reports were written, how many units were sold, or what have you. Rather, writes Jacques Ellul, "'What profit for a person?' means 'How can one become more of a person, and how can one answer the questions that are inevitably asked?'"[50] Any time we experience work that makes us feel like less of a person, not more of a person, we are up against absurdity, that fundamental incongruence that generates distress in many forms, namely futility, boredom, and discontent.

An alarming number of workers report that their work is literally pointless—not just that they consider their job unimportant, but that it actually should not exist. This is the disturbing thesis of David Graeber's *Bullshit Jobs*, in which he distinguishes between unpleasant jobs and "bullshit jobs." An unpleasant job is unenjoyable, maybe, but nevertheless unequivocally necessary. A sanitation worker may not relish collecting garbage, perhaps, but even so he fulfills a genuinely vital societal function and thus does productive work. A bullshit job, by contrast, "is a form of paid employment that is so completely pointless, unnecessary, or pernicious that even the employee cannot justify its existence even though, as part of the conditions of employment, the employee feels obligated to pretend that this is not the case."[51] The *pretense* is part of what makes this kind of work absurd: the incongruence, and attendant distress, of knowing that one's work serves no useful purpose but being compelled, usually by financial necessity, to give the appearance of activity or utility: "Quick, here comes the boss! Look busy!"

This kind of work is more prevalent in some contexts (say, low-level clerical work inside a corporation) than in others, but Graeber points out that absurd work can show up in any field or industry and manifests in a wide variety of roles.[52] For instance, some employees function as "flunkies," a last vestige of the Edwardian footman, paid primarily to

---

[50]Jacques Ellul, *Reason for Being: A Meditation on Ecclesiastes*, trans. Joyce Main Hanks (1987; repr., Eugene, OR: Wipf & Stock, 2021), 56.

[51]Graeber, *Bullshit Jobs*, 9-10. Graeber's conclusions are informed by an astonishing body of first-person reports from workers who describe what it is like to have such a job. It makes for harrowing reading.

[52]For the taxonomy of pointless work that follows, see Graeber, *Bullshit Jobs*, 28-58.

make someone else feel important; we might think here of a manager hiring an unnecessarily large support staff when there was already not enough work to go around. Some workers are "duct tapers," employees whose role consists mainly of addressing glitches in the organization that could be remedied easily; in other words, "duct tapers" fix problems that ought not to exist in the first place, like a customer support specialist whose job is to field phone calls about a bug on the company's website. There are "box tickers," employees whose presence allows an organization to fulfill some requirement on a technicality, such as bureaucrats who complete due-diligence reports full of intentionally confounding jargon to satisfy regulatory bodies. And finally, at the top of the pyramid of futility Graeber puts "taskmasters," middle managers whose job is mainly to assign and supervise the pointless work of others. While these jobs are more common in the lower reaches of the managerial and clerical class, even prestigious or coveted jobs have elements of pointlessness. For instance, Benjamin Ginsberg, longtime professor of political science at Johns Hopkins University, offers a scathing insight into the absurd effects of what he calls "make-work" in the academy: "a nightmarish vision of administrative life in which staffers and managers spend much of the day meeting to discuss meetings where other meetings are discussed at which still other meetings have been discussed."[53] To adapt Qoheleth: of the making of meetings there is no end.

In its most pernicious forms, absurd work can be profoundly dehumanizing, not least because it erodes—or, perhaps better, eclipses—the prestige conferred on human beings by virtue of being crafted in the image and likeness of God. What is more, the proliferation of this kind of work is also widening what Jeff Haanen has called the "dignity deficit," which is pulling our society apart as populations silo not just according to economic standing, but also according to (perceived) prestige of

---

[53]Benjamin Ginsberg, *The Fall of the Faculty: The Rise of the All-Administrative University and Why It Matters* (Oxford: Oxford University Press, 2011), 43.

occupation.[54] To frame the matter in a theological idiom attentive to a phenomenology of sin: What does it *feel* like to be mired in absurd work? Studs Terkel relays the heartbreaking account of a washroom attendant at an upscale hotel. "I'm not particularly proud of what I'm doing," he says. So, he hides his occupation from everyone but his innermost family. But the pain of his situation is deeper than that. The most degrading aspect of this job is that the attendant *knows* it would make no real difference whether or not the job exists at all: "The whole thing is obsolete. It's on its way out. This work isn't necessary in the first place. It's so superfluous. It was *never* necessary. It's just a hustle."[55] As it happens, he was right about that; it is rare to find a washroom attendant or an elevator operator these days. While that may seem like progress— and perhaps it is—absurd work has not gone anywhere; it has simply taken a different shape in the so-called information economy. Compare, for instance, the recent comments made by a handsomely paid contractor for the German military, whose job is to handle the transfer of technology and computers whenever a member of the military moves to a new physical office. As he explains, he might drive over 300 miles to pick up the computer, unplug it, fill out a form, carry the computer fifteen feet to the next office, set down the computer, plug it in, and fill out a form. "So instead of the soldier carrying his computer for five meters, two people drive for a combined six to ten hours, fill out around fifteen pages of paperwork, and waste a good four hundred euros of taxpayers' money."[56]

The notion of the bullshit job is sensational in its obvious pointlessness, but absurdity can corrupt work in more subtle ways. Even jobs that do fulfill some genuinely good or essential function can still sap the vitality of workers, above all through *boredom*. Boredom, at least at

---

[54]Haanen, "Second Shift," 9. Economist Guy Standing warns that this "dignity deficit" between what he terms the "salariat" and the "precariat" is fueling a "politics of inferno" characterized by resentment and grievance. See Guy Standing, *The Precariat: The New Dangerous Class*, Special COVID-19 Edition (London: I. B. Tauris, 2021), chap. 6.

[55]Terkel, *Working*, 108-9, emphasis original.

[56]Quoted in Graeber, *Bullshit Jobs*, 2.

the existential level, appears to be a uniquely human experience. Nicolas Berdyaev has observed that, like it or not, we while away most of our waking hours in "the commonplace," which is characterized by "endless repetition and monotony."[57] Indeed, it has long been recognized, of all the many traits that define bad work, monotony is among the most potent. A generation ago, E. F. Schumacher warned that unfettered and thoughtless industrialization would "stunt [the] personality" of workers

> mainly by making most forms of work—manual and white-collared— utterly uninteresting and meaningless. Mechanical, artificial, divorced from nature, utilizing only the smallest part of man's potential capabilities, it sentences the great majority of workers to spending their working lives in a way that contains no worthy challenge, no stimulus to self-perfection, no chance of development, no element of Beauty, Truth, or Goodness.[58]

It is not difficult to see that Schumacher's premonition has come true, for workers both in the blue-collar and white-collar economies. We might think immediately of the interminable assembly lines of Fordism, which alienate workers both from the final product (since they never see the car in its complete form) and from any sense of stimulus, as the work is, by design, highly repetitive and automated. Thus a spot-welder at an automobile assembly plant describes himself precisely as an *automaton*: "[The] repetition is such that if you were to think about the job itself, you'd slowly go out of your mind. . . . You're nothing more than a machine when you hit this type of thing."[59]

But in recent decades Fordism has gradually crept into the information economy too, where jobs that we might not think of as industrial are likewise plagued by monotony and automated repetition. In the 1970s, for example, we have a receptionist lamenting that "a monkey

---

[57]Nicolas Berdyaev, *The Destiny of Man*, trans. Natalie Duddington (London: Geoffrey Bles, 1937), 178.
[58]Schumacher, *Good Work*, 27.
[59]Terkel, *Working*, 160.

could do what I do. It's really unfair to ask someone to do that."[60] As computing technology burst onto the scene in the 1980s, Barbara Garson depicted modern office workers—from bank tellers to airline employees—toiling in which Garson terms "the electronic sweatshop."[61] They describe their work in mechanical terms, reporting that their daily tasks require no meaningful human input and certainly "no worthy challenge." Yet handwringing about how personal computers and fax machines may hinder human autonomy at work seem quaint from the vantage point of the early twenty-first century, where a new permutation of automation—specifically, the advent and widespread mobilization of artificial intelligence across nearly every sector of the economy—has raised fresh anxieties about the future of creative human work.[62] As we have already seen, an increasing share of workers have basically become inured to this state of affairs, negotiating the boredom of work through existential withdrawal, which can take numerous forms. Some workers might make their peace with boring work through "presenteeism": "being present in body with every other part of you being far, far away."[63] Other workers, especially those in demanding-yet-stultifying jobs, might cope through a banal escapism—a kind of anesthesia-by-work—that obscures (or seems to) the "terror of life."[64]

So the absurd can present itself as futile work and as boring work, but it can also manifest as something more inchoate: the unresolved longing of a "dream deferred"—that unfulfilled ambition that "[dries] up like a raisin the sun."[65] We have said, following Edward Farley, that the "timbre

---

[60]Terkel, *Working*, 31.

[61]See Barbara Garson, *The Electronic Sweatshop: How Computers Are Transforming the Office of the Future* (New York: Simon & Schuster, 1988).

[62]See, for instance, Pranshu Verma and Gerrit de Vynck, "ChatGPT took their jobs. Now they walk dogs and fix air conditioners," *The Washington Post*, June 5, 2023.

[63]Cederström and Fleming, *Dead Man Working*, 6.

[64]Berdyaev, *Destiny of Man*, 178. Drawing on the contributions of depth psychology, Ernest Becker has mounted a similar argument—namely that humans sometimes try to cope with the fear of death through hyperactive creativity—though not in a theological register. See Ernest Becker, *The Denial of Death*, 50th Anniversary Edition (New York: The Free Press, 2023), 170-75.

[65]Langston Hughes, "Harlem," in *Hughes: Poems*, ed. David Roessel (New York: Knopf, 1999), 238.

of discontent" characterizes every human life to one degree or another, and in every dimension. However, the world of work is where we have the most exposure to dissatisfaction and discontentment. Running throughout all his many interviews with workers, Terkel discerns a "hardly concealed discontent," which is an element, perhaps, of all occupations, but is compounded when interpreted through the lens of regret or missed opportunity. Many workers, we suspect, can identify with the hotel clerk whose discontentment is especially painful when it intersects with temporal finitude, situated in a constantly flowing passage of time that cannot be reversed: "You look in the mirror and find that you're not twenty-one any more. You're fifty-five. . . . I never really had enough money to get out, more or less."[66] Career trajectories, especially when they fizzle out or never really take off to begin with, are perhaps the most likely context in which we experience what Tillich called "the shock of nonbeing"—that sudden and alarming awareness of finitude and mortality, the moment we come to feel not only that we will die, but also that we will inevitably leave undone that which we had hoped to achieve.[67] Or, to put it less philosophically: the vexing question of whether our lives, most of which we spend at work, really count or whether we are just *killing time* when we're on the clock.

For many workers, professional lives do not turn out as hoped, not least because the exigencies of necessity and finitude may require people to undertake work they would rather not do—"selling time for money," to recall Doug Muder's phrase. In our experience as professors and pastors, we have seen firsthand the restlessness of discontentment in at least two directions. On the one hand, workers near the end of a career in which they spent decades doing unfulfilling work may struggle to make sense of their experience. On the other, people at the beginning of their working life face immense pressures to "find what they are passionate about," with the implication being that they will waste their lives

[66]Terkel, *Working*, 248.
[67]Paul Tillich, *Systematic Theology*, vol. 1 (Chicago: University of Chicago Press, 1951), 186.

if they do not.[68] The ugly truth, however, is that many people undertake their daily labor without a sense of personal vocational fulfillment. As we shall argue in the next chapter, the notion that work must be fulfilling to be meaningful is practically unattainable, theologically suspect, and pastorally unworkable. Regrettably, though, it has been (perhaps unwittingly) reinforced by some Christian interpretations of the concept of calling. Consider, for example, Frederick Buechner's description of "vocation" in *Wishful Thinking*:

> The kind of work God usually calls you to is the kind of work (a) that you need most to do and (b) that the world most needs to have done. If you really get a kick out of your work, you've presumably met requirement (a), but if your work is writing TV deodorant commercials, the chances are you've missed requirement (b). On the other hand, if your work is being a doctor in a leper colony, you have probably met requirement (b), but if most of the time you're bored or depressed by it, the chances are you have not only bypassed (a) but probably aren't helping your patients much either.[69]

Wishful thinking indeed! This interpretation of calling is dubious for exegetical reasons, but it also fails to reckon seriously with the realities of finitude and fallenness.

We shall return to these points in due course. For now, it suffices to name the absurdity—that incongruity between desire and fulfillment, ambition and achievement—that characterizes the phenomenological experience of many workers east of Eden, whose labor is frustrated by futility, sapped by boredom, and beset by discontentment. If sin is a Hydra, as Luther suggested, then we might expect its various heads—enmity, absurdity, and tragedy—not only to co-exist, but to become entangled with one another. It is not surprising, therefore, that workers implicated in absurd work also resort to the language of the tragic to

---

[68] The pernicious effects of this work mythology have been explored at length by Miya Tokumitsu. See *Do What You Love*. We will return to Tokumitsu's critique in the next chapter.

[69] Frederick Buechner, *Wishful Thinking: A Theological ABC* (New York: Harper & Row, 1973), 95.

describe their experience. Graeber relates the case of a social worker who laments not only the pointlessness of her job, but also "the misery of knowing one is doing harm . . . the misery of having to pretend you're providing some kind of benefit to humanity when you know the exact opposite is in fact the case."[70] But work, especially in a highly complex industrial economy, creates intractable situations that strain the logic of some classically Christian approaches to work, in which it is imagined that any work can be made sacred if one does it "heartily, as to the Lord, and not unto men" (Col 3:23 KJV). "God loveth adverbs," wrote the Puritan theologian Joseph Hall, "and cares not how good, but how well."[71] It is a beautiful idea—and doubtless is true in many circumstances—but the conditions of absurdity and tragedy create dilemmas in which adverbs fail.

WHERE ADVERBS FAIL: TRAGIC WORK

If we imagine the phenomenology of sin as a spectrum ranging from the active (enmity) to the passive (absurdity), tragedy should be understood as a mediating category, as it emphasizes both humanity's responsibility for and victimization by sin. Likewise, this taxonomy is a useful heuristic for diagnosing the ways in which sin has twisted the experience of work. Part of what makes absurd work so degrading is that it deprives humans of what German psychologist Karl Groos called "joy in being the cause," the intrinsic delight humans take in having a self-generating effect on objects in their world, particularly through their sensory experience.[72] Put another way, stultifying work is stultifying precisely because workers lack a satisfactory degree of agency to cause anything. This symptom of absurd work must always be kept in view. But what we are calling *tragic* or *grotesque* work is related to, but is to be

---

[70]Graeber, *Bullshit Jobs*, 131.

[71]Joseph Hall, *The Works of Joseph Hall*, vol. 6, ed. Josiah Pratt (London: C. Whittingham, 1808), XIV 85.

[72]Karl Groos, *The Play of Man*, trans. Elizabeth L. Baldwin (New York: D. Appleton and Company, 1901), 385.

distinguished from, absurd work. Specifically, those implicated in tragic work do exercise genuine agency, but it is put to destructive purposes or otherwise produces deleterious effects through the corruption of sin. Tragic work is both something in which we participate and something that happens to us. If this is the case, then there is a kind of work that cannot be remedied by adverbs—jobs where, tragically, the better they are performed, the more harmful they are or jobs that are entangled within intractable structures of injustice or exploitation.

Early Christians, of course, were aware of this. They furnish us with a catalogue of jobs that Christians must not hold: pimps and prostitutes, charioteers and gladiators, actors in pagan theatrical productions, teachers of schoolchildren (since their curricula mandated instruction in the propaganda of Rome), various Roman civic positions, magicians and sorcerers.[73] This ethical teaching surely was not easy for early Christians to enact, but it *was* simple: economies were local, products were generally fashioned under more humane conditions, and work had not been industrialized or (fully) institutionalized. In a globalized economy, though, the means of production, the various component inputs of any given product—as well as the origin and destination of goods—are obscured from us by the inescapable conditions of finitude and fallenness. We do not, as a rule, know where exactly our clothing or food comes from (nor the exact conditions under which they were produced), nor do we know where our mutual fund investment dollars or our taxes go, nor can we fathom the negative impacts our work might have as they reverberate up and down the chain of production. Both the process of working and the products of work, then, are deeply entangled with unjust structures and systems, which are difficult to discern and even more difficult—perhaps impossible—to untangle. So, while it is surely true that "Christians should not work in the sin industries,"[74] such an

---

[73]See, for example, Hippolytus of Rome, *The Apostolic Tradition* XIV.9-25, in *The Treatise on The Apostolic Tradition of St. Hippolytus of Rome*, ed. Gregory Dix (London: Alban, 1992), 25-28, and Tertullian, *The Shows, or De Spectaculis* X-XIII (ANF 3:83-85).

[74]Hamilton, *Work and Our Labor*, 78.

assertion raises the question: What, exactly, is *not* a sin industry? Under the conditions of finitude and fallenness, it is not always obvious what work is redeemable and what is irredeemable.

"Whoever digs a pit will fall into it; and whoever breaks through a wall will be bitten by a snake. Whoever quarries stones will be hurt by them; and whoever splits logs will be endangered by them," writes Qoheleth (Eccles 10:8-9). This is not some bit of inscrutable folk wisdom or a playful tautology. Qoheleth speaks here to the tragic irony involved in work: we are often harmed by the products of our own hands. We dig pits and then fall into them. Sometimes, we are crushed by the rocks we mine, and the trees we chop down fall on us. To extrapolate, we also build work systems and structures that do create flourishing in some respects while creating suffering in others. As the biblical writers see it, these systems—companies, industries, economies—have been subjected to the demonic ends of the powers and principalities, which distort reality, including our institutions. Indeed, as Walter Wink has argued in *Engaging the Powers*, the New Testament authors take *kosmos* to refer both to the world that God created and sustains but also, paradoxically, *"the human sociological realm that exists in estrangement from God,"* producing exploitation, coercion, and above all violence.[75] Sin has therefore warped the structure of reality itself, making it impossible to fulfill our vocation as image bearers as God originally intended. If this is the case, then any realistic theology of work will have to take the theme of the demonic with the utmost seriousness, as all workers, each one of us, must contend with forces to which we are not equal under circumstances we cannot control.[76] Below, we argue that tragic work takes on at least three key manifestations: (1) zero-sum situations, (2) alienation, exploitation, and unintentional harm, and (3) the grotesque.

---

[75]Walter Wink, *Engaging the Powers: Discernment and Resistance in a World of Domination* (Minneapolis: Fortress, 1992), 51, emphasis original.

[76]For an illuminating discussion of work and the demonic, see Stevens, *The Other Six Days*, chap. 9.

In the first place, to be a human being is to be the kind of creature who inhabits a world that is often zero-sum; human persons and communities are often entangled in mutually exclusive conditions for thriving, not least in the world of work. In *The Human Condition*, philosopher Hannah Arendt articulated this tragic element of the givenness of things, in part by distinguishing between labor and work. "Labor" designates those organic processes of subsistence that are required to sustain biological life and are therefore endlessly cyclical and repetitive; "its 'toil and trouble' comes only with the death of [the] organism." "Work," by contrast, produces artifacts, which may be tangible (like a table, say, or a building) or intangible (a concept, for example, or a philosophy). All creatures must labor at least to some extent, but, tragically, the majority of people must labor so that a minority may work.[77] Of course, this is the logic that animates all forms of slavery, ancient or modern, but the same dynamic is at play in all work ecosystems. More recently, Amy Veltman has built on Arendt's work, coming to the depressing conclusion that "meaningful work" for some rests on and is made possible by "the necessity of unfulfilling work" for others.[78]

To put it crassly, even the most just economy is sustained in part because someone cleans the restrooms or recites pre-scripted telephone pitches in corporations where technological breakthroughs are discovered or civic institutions where laws and policies are crafted. By its very nature, the market is inherently competitive, which inevitably means that secure work (salaried, with benefits, regular hours, etc.) comes at the expense of insecure work for others. This has always been so, but the Covid-19 pandemic accelerated this trend with the rise of the so-called gig economy, where workers are eking out a living by piecing together fragments of employment. We may think here of Uber drivers, food service delivery workers, or office employees on temporary or at-will contracts, but also freelance yoga instructors or writers—an

---

[77]See Hannah Arendt, *The Human Condition*, 2nd ed. (Chicago: University of Chicago Press, 1958), 98-101.
[78]Veltman, *Meaningful Work*, 21, 147-48.

emerging class of workers that economist Guy Standing has termed "the precariat." The work situation of the precariat, which is statistically over-represented among migrants and other minoritized communities, is, well, *precarious*: subject to inconsistent hours, little recourse to company-provided benefits or public relief, and chronically overworked yet undercompensated. Tragically, says Standing, the precariat is "at the same time 'underemployed' and 'overemployed.'"[79] The precariat has many faces. The most obvious expressions, perhaps, are the many labor-intensive, low-pay jobs in the service and care sectors: the daily grind of waiters and waitresses, hotel cleaning staff, or retail workers so vividly chronicled in Barbara Ehrenreich's *Nickel and Dimed*.[80] However, precarity shows up even in industries with high levels of prestige, in the form of aspirational labor within tiered employment structures: associate attorneys buried under piles of briefs while earning much less than a living wage or adjunct professors toiling at multiple institutions while striving for an elusive tenure-track position.[81] Simply put, the tragic dimension of human existence often means that there is simply not enough good work to go around.

The tragic, then, creates zero-sum situations in which thriving for some comes at the expense of others, but it can also come to expression through alienation, exploitation, and unintentional harm. In fact, "work is the most immediate way in which human beings dominate and exploit each other."[82] This domination can range from the unambiguously evil, such as slavery or any kind of forced labor, to the more subtle and insidious, such as workplace rhetoric that encourages workers not to pursue fair compensation, for example, by appealing to the intrinsic reward of doing important work. But alienation can also be unwitting, since systems or actors create harm not just from malice but also from inefficiency or

---

[79]Standing, *The Precariat*, 23. Cf. Tokumitsu, *Do What You Love*, 81-82.

[80]Barbara Ehrenreich, *Nickel and Dimed: On (Not) Getting By in America* (New York: Picador, 2011).

[81]Miya Tokumitsu has pursued this line of argumentation at length in *Do What You Love*, 98-105.

[82]Douglas Meeks, *God the Economist: The Doctrine of God and Political Economy* (Minneapolis: Fortress, 1989), 127.

incompetence. Alienation is a complex and multifaceted phenomenon, then, but at base it describes any kind of work that instrumentalizes persons by placing them in systems where they are "used as a means of production."[83] Specifically, as Karl Marx argued in the nineteenth century, work becomes exploitative when it prevents a worker from seeing the fruit of their labor. This is what makes the assembly line so demeaning: workers perform atomized and repetitive tasks on one element of the artifact but never see the finished product.[84] The trouble with alienating labor, though, is that it is ruthlessly efficient; companies that do not adopt at least some alienating practices usually cannot compete in the marketplace. "The problem with alienating work is not what it does to production," as Miroslav Volf puts it, "but in what it does to the worker."[85]

Alienation is perhaps relatively easy to spot in so-called blue-collar settings—the farm hand who reports that he's "treated like a farm implement" or the auto welder who feels he is "nothing more than a machine"[86]—but it also takes deceptive form among white-collar workers, chiefly as the Do What You Love mythology that so extensively pervades American work culture, especially among the creative class. This mythology disguises the toilsome nature of all work behind a veneer of passion, often with pernicious effects. Ideally, of course, everyone would prefer to do work that they find exciting, stimulating, and intrinsically valuable. "But the rhetoric that a job is a passion or a 'labor of love,'" writes Simone Stolzoff, "obfuscates the reality that a job is an economic contract. The assumption that it isn't sets up the conditions for exploitation."[87] By appealing to the abstract concept of passion—the root of which, of course, is the Latin verb *to suffer*—the Do What You

---

[83]Veltman, *Meaningful Work*, 88.

[84]Matthew Crawford details how Fordism drove former craftsmen with broad mechanical knowledge to despair—and to mass walkouts—by confining their contributions to one aspect of production. See *Shop Class as Soulcraft*, chap. 2.

[85]Volf, *Work in the Spirit*, 162.

[86]Terkel, *Working*, 12, 162-63.

[87]Simone Stolzoff, "Please Don't Call My Job a Calling," *The New York Times*, June 5, 2023. See also Tokumitsu, *Do What You Love*, 113.

Love mythology attempts to delude workers into believing that they are not *really* working because they enjoy what they do. In this way, it animates all manner of unjust work structures: aspirational labor (where workers pursue a path to long-term security that is not really there), unfair wages, long hours, and the frenetic despair of the gig economy. On top of all this, there is a patronizing indignity to this ideology, which adds insult to injury: the "command to enjoy work," instilled through morale-boosting seminars and team-building exercises.[88] Theologically, this mythology rests on a problematic premise as well, suggesting that work is meaningful only to the extent that we are aligned with our "calling." As we shall argue in our next chapter, a realistic theology of work will need to dislodge this mythology in part by situating work within a much broader account of human personhood.

The tragic culminates in grotesque work, by which we mean the kind of alienating, corrupting, and ultimately enslaving work that can only be produced, ironically, when humans put profound endowments of the *imago Dei* to misdirected use, wittingly or unwittingly. The language of the grotesque is an attempt to describe labor that is ingenious but destructive. As we have seen, Helmut Thielicke articulates something similar with his concept of "promethean emancipation," by which, through either careless or nefarious use of *technē*, "*homo faber* threatens to become *homo fabricatus*." He puts humanity's relationship with the work of its own hands in Faustian terms:

> The older form of work was, in fact, something that was in our own hands. We had a direct personal relation to what we made. In technology, however, natural forces intervene, such as steam, electricity, electronics, and atomic power. A qualitatively new world of production has come. It is no longer in our own hands. Like Goethe's sorcerer's apprentice, we threaten to be reduced to the role of mere functionaries to whom the law of what we do is dictated by the powers we have unleashed.[89]

---

[88]See Cederström and Fleming, *Dead Man Working*, 41.
[89]Helmut Thielicke, *Being Human . . . Becoming Human: An Essay in Christian Anthropology*, trans. Geoffrey W. Bromiley (New York: Doubleday, 1984), 292. By *homo fabricatus* ("fabricated

Thielicke's remarks are resonant with Barth's exposition of the "lordless powers," institutions and artifacts created by humans that, tragically, now enslave their makers. To Barth's mind, the powers and principalities have commandeered structures intended for human flourishing and put them to destructive purposes. This would include technology, transportation, and sport—but Barth is especially concerned with Mammon, humanity's "very mobile demon." Even though money is, in a literal sense, a fiction—that is, it has no ontological existence at all, but is only a construct signifying theoretical value—it nevertheless takes on a life of its own: "In a thousand ways it can . . . create brutal facts. It can cause the market to rise and then to fall again. It can arrest this crisis and cause another. It can serve peace yet pursue cold war even in the midst of peace. It can make ready for a bloody war and finally bring it about. It can bring provisional paradise here and the corresponding provisional hell there."[90] The entire ecosystem of human work—from individual laborers to companies to industries to economies—is inextricably bound up with and co-opted by the lordless powers, always to some degree intoxicated by the "*mis*enchantment" of the "Gospel of Mammon."[91]

What does the grotesque look like in concrete terms? To pursue only one possible manifestation, the concept of the grotesque captures the cunning of human ingenuity, by which we set into motion processes and produce artifacts that we cannot predict or control. As the only creatures who bear God's image, humans are capable of astounding feats of *technē*, yet in the words of Gilbert Meilaender, "being almost godlike

---

man"), Thielicke alludes to the ironic ways in which the technologies we make as *homo faber* ("man the maker") end up making, or fabricating, us. Likewise, Hannah Arendt judges all promethean activity, including work and technology, to involve violence and the destruction of nature. See *The Human Condition*, 139.

[90]Karl Barth, *The Christian Life* (London: Bloomsbury T&T Clark, 2017), 311, 313-14.

[91]Eugene McCarraher, *The Enchantments of Mammon: How Capitalism Became the Religion of Modernity* (Cambridge, MA: Belknap, 2019), 5, emphasis original. McCarraher's analysis builds on the insights of Thomas Carlyle, who decried the "horrid enchantment" cast by the spellbinding "Gospel of Mammon." The latter term appears to have originated with Carlyle. See Thomas Carlyle, *Past and Present* (1843; repr., Oxford: Oxford University Press, 1915), III.2.

in our creative powers is not an unmixed blessing, however. For we are not godlike in our ability to foresee the full range of consequences that flow from the transformations creative minds bring to the world of work."[92] As an obvious example, smart phones have opened up vast new possibilities for work and culture, but the research is now settled that they also addict us, derange us, and make us anxious.[93] Likewise, complex algorithmic systems, which even their own creators do not fully understand, determine what media content we see online, distorting the way we engage and interpret reality itself. We might also point to the totally unpredictable course of automation powered by artificial intelligence. Automation has been a source of anxiety since at least the industrial revolution, but whereas it was historically assumed that automation would only replace stultifying physical labor, it is now coming for creative work too, which was thought to be the provenance of humans alone. "In every previous automation threat, the automation was about automating the hard, dirty, repetitive jobs," explains business professor Ethan Mollick, "This time, the automation threat is aimed squarely at the highest-earning, most creative jobs that . . . require the most educational background."[94]

In light of the ever-looming threat of grotesque work, we might well ask whether humans really should do all that we are capable of doing: "Might not an unthinking use of all the biological and technical means at our disposal be criminal?"[95] Regardless of how we might choose to answer that question going forward, it is nevertheless the case that, east of Eden, all human work is already implicated in the tragic. We have already misused our vast creative capacities and immense powers as image bearers in a distorted vision of the cultural mandate of Genesis 1–2, illustrated powerfully in Hieronymus Bosch's *The Garden of Earthly*

---

[92]Meilaender, *Working*, 19.

[93]This crisis is particularly acute among Generation Z. See the work of social psychologist Jonathan Haidt in *The Anxious Generation: How the Great Rewiring of Childhood Is Causing an Epidemic of Mental Illness* (New York: Penguin, 2024).

[94]Quoted in Verma and de Vynck, "ChatGPT took their jobs."

[95]Thielicke, *Being Human . . . Becoming Human*, 65.

Delights.[96] Bosch's surreal triptych is of course subject to a wide range of interpretations, but it does evoke a sense of the chaotic, as humans "fulfill" the great cultural mandate in a disordered way—they are fruitful and multiply, filling the whole second panel of the triptych, and they do work the land, to disturbing effect. But as the story unfold across the three panels, the placid harmoniousness of Eden (panel 1) gives way to unregulated sexual desire, bizarre cultural products, and exploitation of humans and animals alike (panel 2), culminating in a hellscape littered with grotesque technological artifacts (panel 3). Whatever else Bosch intends, his work captures a scrambled pursuit of the cultural mandate by which humans have, ironically and tragically, created conditions where not everyone can flourish at once, which is an exact inversion of the original shalom commission given to the only creatures who were meant to reflect the glory of the God in whose image they were made.

BREAD OF TEARS, BREAD OF GRACE

So this is the situation on the ground, which itself no longer cooperates with human labor in the land of Nod. Human work east of Eden is bound up within a threefold paradox: either we ask work to do *too much* for us (enmitous work), the work to which we have access *cannot do enough* for us (absurd work), or we experience work as a combination of ingenuity and alienation (tragic or grotesque work). Any sober approach to work—philosophical, social-scientific, political, or theological—must sooner or later come to grips with the ways in which enmity, absurdity, and tragedy have warped not just the process of working, but the conditions in which all work is undertaken. Even in a well-ordered society, as Amy Veltman concludes, meaningful work simply will not be available to everyone due to the sheer fact of "the social necessity of unfulfilling work." Veltman (and others) are nevertheless convinced that there are things to be done to make bad work

---

[96]Hieronymus Bosch, *The Garden of Earthly Delights*, 1490-1510, oil painting on oak panels, Museo del Prado, Madrid, https://en.wikipedia.org/wiki/The_Garden_of_Earthly_Delights#/media/File:The_Garden_of_earthly_delights.jpg.

better, whether through industrial policy or at the level of business ethics within individual companies.[97]

In the chapter to follow, we shall likewise offer some modest proposals for a constructive theology of work east of Eden, which gestures toward some always-provisional possibilities for redeeming human work, beset though it is by enmity, absurdity, and tragedy. Even so, we contend that a biblical theology of work will always be ambivalent, since, in theological perspective, work is simultaneously a gift of God *and* subject to the curse. To return to Bonhoeffer's vision of work "in the middle": "So the fruit of the field becomes both the bread that we eat with tears and yet at the same time the bread of grace of the one who upholds. . . . Human beings at work live between curse and promise, between *tob* and *ra*, pleasure and pain, but they live before God the Creator."[98] Is there, then, a theology of work for everyone, not just those whose daily work reflects the agency-dignity-power of Genesis 1–2? If there is, it seems to us, it will have to be a theology of work *from and for* "the middle," a theology that does not appeal primarily to protology or eschatology, but is rather generated from the tension between curse and promise, pleasure and pain—a theology in which work, even though it is the bread of tears, may nevertheless become the bread of grace.

---

[97]Veltman, *Meaningful Work*, chap. 5. For an example of a proposal for labor reform at the level of policy, see Standing, *The Precariat*, chap. 7, which argues for a universal basic income, among other measures. For an example of a business ethics approach to labor reform, see Zeynep Ton, *The Case for Good Jobs: How Great Companies Bring Dignity, Pay, and Meaning to Everyone's Work* (Boston: Harvard Business Review Press, 2023), especially chaps. 9-10.

[98]Bonhoeffer, *Creation and Fall*, 134.

6

THE GOODNESS OF FINITE
AND FALLEN WORK

*Insofar as human creatures' ultimate context is God's utterly
gratuitous continual relating to the quotidian, the sheer existence
of the quotidian, and they with it, is in some sense a gift.*

David H. Kelsey, *Eccentric Existence*

FROM THE MIDDLE, FOR THE MIDDLE:
TOWARD A QUOTIDIAN THEOLOGY OF WORK

As we have shown, the biblical narrative characterizes all human experience existing in a state of rivenness. There is some grave rupture between God and humans, and subsequently between humans and everything else: other humans, the natural world, our own selves. And yet throughout the entire ordeal, we remain what we always were: finite, contingent, and radically dependent creatures. But the fall has also resulted in a cloudiness of vision that obscures our apprehension of God's original intent for creation and for human existence, what Helmut Thielicke calls a "loss of perspicuity." Not only can we no longer walk with God *in* the garden, we cannot say with certainty how the memory of the garden recorded for us in Genesis 1–2 might possibly be realized in our fallen state. "To try to make a 'direct' transfer from the primal state into our own world is to be as ridiculous as the man who tries to drive his automobile down the lines of longitude from the North Pole to the South."[1] We take this loss of perspicuity to imply that a theology of work that proceeds primarily by envisioning a repristination of Eden or speculating about the new Jerusalem will falter in speaking to the experience of the majority of workers.

We have already detailed ways in which many evangelical theologies of work operationalize protology, but much faith and work literature also draws heavily on an (overrealized) eschatology. In this respect, Andy Crouch's remarks in *Culture Making*, in which he catalogues the various cultural artifacts he hopes to see in the eschaton, are representative: "Bach's *Mass in B Minor*, Miles Davis's *Kind of Blue*, and Arvo Pärt's *Spiegel im Spiegel*; green-tea crème brûlée, fish tacos, and bulgogi; *Moby-Dick* and the *Odyssey*; the iPod and the Mini Cooper."[2] It is difficult to see what kind of exegetical warrant this kind of speculation might claim. On this point, we find it best to follow Reinhold Niebuhr's advice: it is unwise for Christians to claim much knowledge of the "furniture of heaven or the temperature of hell; or to be too certain about any details of the kingdom of God in which history is consummated."[3] Speculation aside, such an eschatology fails to appreciate how the production of these cultural artifacts is inextricably bound up in enmity, absurdity, and tragedy. An iPhone, for example, is hardly an unambiguous cultural good.

Moreover, this kind of thinking both rests on and reinforces a romanticized and unrealistic view in which work and worship are conflated. This becomes especially problematic when eschatology becomes the criterion for judging the value of our present work: "Are we creating and cultivating things that have a chance of flourishing in the New Jerusalem?"[4] For the

---

[1]Helmut Thielicke, *Theological Ethics*, ed. William H. Lazareth (Grand Rapids, MI: Eerdmans, 1979), 1:403, 405.

[2]Andy Crouch, *Culture Making: Recovering Our Creative Calling* (Downers Grove, IL: InterVarsity Press, 2008), 170. N. T. Wright also imagines listening to Bach in heaven. See N. T. Wright, *Surprised by Hope: Rethinking Heaven, the Resurrection, and the Mission of the Church* (New York: HarperCollins, 2008), 208-9. For a similar line of eschatological thinking, see also Tom Nelson, *Work Matters: Connecting Sunday Worship to Monday Work* (Wheaton, IL: Crossway, 2011), 73.

[3]Reinhold Niebuhr, *The Nature and Destiny of Man*, vol. 2 (New York: Charles Scribner's Sons, 1943), 294.

[4]Crouch, *Culture Making*, 171.

overwhelming majority of workers—from the lower reaches to the precariat to the upper echelons of the power brokers of global commerce—the answer to that question must be no. It is, to be sure, a breathtaking vision, but such a question is meaningful only for those workers who are in a position to "create culture." It is not cognizant of workers for whom an eternal destiny of more work—even if it is redeemed work—would be a disappointing reward indeed, especially compared to that great sabbath rest promised to the people of God (Heb 4:9). In short, this is not a theology that speaks to life in the middle.

What kind of theology might?

In this chapter, we hazard some constructive possibilities for a theology of work in the real world. Having emphasized the recovery of creational finitude as a genuine good of creation (and a genuine good of our working lives), and having proposed a methodology that grounds the theology of work primarily in chapter two of the grand narrative rather than chapter one, we now turn our attention to a positive account of the value of finite work in a fallen world. As we have insisted throughout, the exigencies of finitude constrain all human work, and the phenomenology of sin distorts all human work. Accordingly, any realistic theology of work will, in the first place, need to take finitude seriously, which we will attempt to do by exploring the Creator/creature relationship as it pertains to work, with particular attention to God's freedom with respect to space, time, and knowledge and his sustaining presence as mediated to and through human labor. At the same time, a realistic theology of work will also need to reckon with the manifold impacts of fallenness. With these impacts in view, we pursue a robustly quotidian theology of work that seeks to privilege the instrumental value of work by highlighting biblical voices that approach work as a thoroughly ordinary (rather than a protological or eschatological) reality. To round out the argument, we will set forth a christological account of human personhood, which confers an enduring dignity and value on human persons quite apart from what they happen to do for a living.

BOTH ENOUGH AND MORE: FINITUDE,
WORK, AND THE PRESENCE OF GOD

In the interest of constructively contributing to a theology of work for the real world, we must give due attention to the Creator of the real world, the Creator of workers. While a theology of work must richly account for both the creation within which work is carried out and the workers who carry out that work, as was our burden in chapters two and three, it must do more. Theology of work, if it is to genuinely be *theology of work*, must richly attend to God, the Creator. Moreover, this Creator is not *only* Creator but, acknowledged as such or not, is also the sovereign Sustainer and Lord of the world in which all work is done. Thus, a theology of work for the real world must engage not only the immanental realm of creation but also the transcendent reality of the Creator.

Furthermore, work is part of life. This may seem unnecessary to say, but sometimes it is important to state the obvious because the obvious can unthinkingly come to be regarded as insignificant. Work is part of life, and that is significant for our present considerations because *what is true of God in the rest of life is true of God in relation to work*. There is not God and also a God-of-work. The God who is, is (Ex 3:14). Whether acknowledged as Lord or not, he is in all of life, in all of work.[5] Because of this there is a real sense in which much theology of work is simply theology.[6] If any particular exercise in theology speaks truly about God it will share much common ground with other exercises in theology. Without apology, and in the hope that what is said speaks truly about God, in the pages that immediately follow there is much that will be said that is not unique to a theology of work. At the same time, because God is the God of all of life, we believe that what is said about God here is indeed of great significance for work and human beings as workers.

---

[5]Something like an analogous continuity is also true of human beings. Human beings are what human beings are, whether engaged in work or in any other activity or arena of life.
[6]In principle, this is true of any "theology of _____."

We desire to contribute in some small measure to a genuinely *theo-logical* theology of work.[7] Thus, we here move from focusing primarily on creation—space, time, and human capacities—to focus on the Creator, to focus on God. We will first make some general observations about the freedom of God. Then we will think about God in relation to the human experience of working within the finitude of space and the finitude of time. Finally, we will ponder two divine attributes and their significance for work: God's power and God's knowledge.[8]

The freedom of God. God is free. God is utterly free. Were it not so, he would not say "I AM WHO I AM" (Ex 3:14). Were it not so, the psalmist would not proclaim, "Whatever the LORD pleases he does, in heaven and on earth, in the seas and all deeps" (Ps 135:6; also Ps 115:3). Were it not so, the prophet Isaiah would not testify to the words of God, "I have spoken, and I will bring it to pass; I have planned, and I will do it" (Is 46:11). Were it not so, the apostle Paul would not assure the Ephesian Christ-followers that God "accomplishes all things according to his counsel and will" (Eph 1:11). Even King Nebuchadnezzar knows that God "does what he wills with the host of heaven and the inhabitants of the earth. There is no one who can stay his hand or say to him, 'What are you doing?'" (Dan 4:35 NRSVA). Karl Barth describes God's freedom in both "negative" and "positive" terms. Negatively, God's freedom is manifest in "the absence of limits, restrictions, or conditions." Positively, God's freedom is manifest both in being "grounded in [His] own being, to be determined and moved by

---

[7]The phrase "theological theology" was introduced into contemporary theological discourse by John Webster, originally in his inaugural lecture as Lady Margaret Professor of Divinity, Oxford University, in 1997. See "Theological Theology" in John Webster, *Confessing God: Essays in Christian Dogmatics II* (London: Bloomsbury T&T Clark, 2016), 11-31. Also see R. David Nelson, Darren Sarisky, and Justin Stratis, eds., *Theological Theology: Essays in Honour of John B. Webster* (London: Bloomsbury T&T Clark, 2015).

[8]In discussions of divine attributes, God's relationship to space and time are usually considered in conjunction with discussions of attributes such as omnipresence and eternality. Corresponding to the structure of our two chapters on finitude (chaps 2 and 3), we here discuss omnipresence and eternality in conjunction with our discussions of space and time. Other selected divine attributes will thus be considered below under the heading "God, Power, Knowledge, and Work."

[Himself]" and in being "unlimited, unrestricted and unconditioned from without."[9]

We are not free. Human beings are not, have never been, and will never be free in the ways that God is free. This is one of the fundamental differences between the Creator and creatures, including human beings. God is the Potter, we are the clay.[10] "Woe to you," Isaiah warns, "who strive with your Maker, earthen vessels with the potter!" (Is 45:9 NRSVA; also Is 64:8). Through his prophet Jeremiah the Lord says to Israel, "Can I not do with you, O House of Israel, just as this potter has done? says the LORD. Just like clay in the potter's hand, so are you in my hand, O house of Israel" (Jer 18:6). The apostle Paul rhetorically asks the Christians of Rome, "But who indeed are you, a human being, to argue with God? Will what is molded say to the one who molds it, 'Why have you made me like this?' Has the potter no right over the clay, to make out of the same lump one object for special use and another for ordinary use?" (Rom 9:20-21 NRSVCE). While these passages include words of warning and judgment, the imagery of potter and clay is not employed to render judgment on clay as clay—on human beings as human beings. Nor is the image employed to make a point about human beings only. The point and the power of the imagery is in the comparison, the contrast between potter and clay, the contrast between God and human beings, and the emphasis of the message is on God. As a potter is with clay, so God is with His creation—utterly sovereign. He is sovereign over the circumstances, the lives, and the work of human beings, and ultimately there is nothing human beings can do to thwart God's will. God is utterly free. We are

---

[9]Karl Barth, *Church Dogmatics*, vol. 2, pt. 1, *The Doctrine of God*, ed. G. W. Bromiley and T. F. Torrance, trans. T. H. L. Parker et al. (London: T & T Clark International, 2004), 2.1:303. While God's freedom is manifest in these ways, God is free "in Himself quite apart from His relation to another from whom he is free." He is free in and of himself. "The loftiness, the sovereignty, the majesty, the holiness, the glory—even what is termed the transcendence of God—what is it but this self-determination, this freedom, of the divine living and loving, the divine person?" (302).

[10]Interestingly, this is an image adapted from a very concrete form of human work.

not. We are contingent, limited, finite. We are creatures of God's *good* design and making.[11]

Yet God's freedom is not manifest only in His relationship to human beings. It is cosmic in scope. God's freedom is manifest in His relationship to the entire creation. The psalmists know this well. "The earth is the LORD's and all that is in it, the world, and those who live in it" (Ps 24:1). "For the LORD is a great God, and a great King above all gods. In his hand are the depths of the earth; the heights of the mountains are his also. The sea is his, for he made it, and the dry land, which his hands have formed" (Ps 95:3-5). "Our God is in the heavens; he does whatever he pleases" (Ps 115:3). In this the psalmists are echoing their tradition. Moses had exhorted the Israelites, "So acknowledge today and take to heart that the LORD is God in heaven above and on the earth beneath; there is no other" (Deut 4:39). Thus, it is not surprising that Jesus teaches his followers to pray to their Father in heaven, "Your kingdom come, your will be done, on earth as it is in heaven" (Mt 6:10). God is free and his freedom knows no limits. The freedom of the Creator is manifest in relationship to all and everything that he has created, and his freedom belongs not only to the past or the present, but also to the future. His will will be done (see Job 42:2; Eph 1:11; Rev 19:6).

God's freedom is inherent to who he is—just one dimension of the goodness and glory of who he is. The finitude of creation is inherent to what it is. Finitude is part of what renders us not-God. The contrast between God in his freedom and creation in its finitude is *not fundamentally quantitative but rather qualitative.*[12] God is not the same kind of being as human beings only "more" or perfect. He is Other. Thus, for example, Michael Horton observes that, "To say that God is infinite is not to say that he is infinitely extended throughout time and space. . . .

---

[11]Gen 1:26. Since God created human beings in his image, how could it be otherwise? And were human beings not good by creation design, would God have given humans the work of dominion over creation?

[12]Michael Horton, *The Christian Faith: A Systematic Theology for Pilgrims on the Way* (Grand Rapids, MI: Zondervan, 2011), 256; and Michael Allen, "Divine Attributes," in *Christian Dogmatics: Reformed Theology for the Church Catholic*, ed. Michael Allen and Scott R. Swain (Grand Rapids, MI: Baker Academic, 2016), 69-70.

Rather, it is to say that God *transcends the very categories of* time and space."[13] "Transcends" expresses God's freedom, and it signals the uniqueness of God's freedom. God's freedom is not primarily a question of Him having more freedom than creation and its creatures but rather of being a different kind of Being and thereby having a different kind of relationship, a unique relationship to the creation and its creatures. In the freedom of who he is, the Creator transcends creation.

"'Finite' means 'limited.' Creaturely being is limited being," writes David Kelsey. "This is an ontological claim. The entire creaturely realm taken as a kind of whole . . . and each particular physical creature that is a part of such contexts, including human creatures, are *limited in being*."[14] The finitude of space and the finitude of time, at least with respect to human beings, is inherent to space and time. It is characteristic of the very nature, it is part of the created essence, of space and time. The finitude of human capacities is inherent to who we are as creatures. It is not a result of the fall. It is not a corruption of human being. It is not a defect to be denied or an evil to be overcome. It is inherent to who we are as created by God. As previously observed, finitude is part of the grain of the universe. When we try to work "without limits" we are going against the grain. Human beings are best served, and serve best, when we seek to work with that grain. Yet a vision of work is incomplete if the vision of the grain of the universe does not include God, both immanent and transcendent. God is present and at work within the grain of the universe (his creation) while also transcending it (he is the Creator). God is the Creator and Sustainer of the grain of the universe while being completely free with respect to it.

God, space, and work. God is free with respect to space. He is neither limited by nor captive to it. Moses declares that "heaven and the heaven of heavens belong to the LORD your God" (Deut 10:14). As important as the temple was to the people of Israel, they are reminded more than once that the temple does not, indeed cannot, "contain" God. In his wisdom Solomon

---

[13]Horton, *Christian Faith*, 256.
[14]David H. Kelsey, *Eccentric Existence: A Theological Anthropology* (Louisville, KY: Westminster John Knox, 2009), 1:201, emphasis added.

proclaims, "But will God indeed dwell on the earth? Even heaven and the highest heaven cannot contain you, much less this house that I have built!" (1 Kings 8:27; also 2 Chron 2:6). Not surprisingly then, Israel's worship includes the declaration that "The LORD is high above all nations and his glory above the heavens. Who is like the LORD our God, who is seated on high," and "To you I lift up my eyes, O you who are enthroned in the heavens!" (Ps 123:1; see Ps 113:4-5). The prophet Isaiah is keenly aware of God's exalted dwelling: "Thus says the LORD: Heaven is my throne and the earth is my footstool; what is the house that you would build for me, and what is my resting place?" (Is 66:1 NRSVCE).[15] In light of this Jewish knowledge of God, it is not surprising that the Messiah's coming to earth is heralded by the heavenly host with "Glory to God in the highest heaven, and on earth peace among those whom he favors!" (Lk 2:14). The apostle Paul makes known to the Athenians at the Areopagus that the "unknown god" whom they worship is in fact "the God who made the world and everything in it, he who is Lord of heaven and earth" and this God "does not live in shrines made by human hands, nor is he served by human hands, as though he needed anything" (Acts 17:24-25).[16]

God is not only free *from* space, He is free *within* space. He is free to be in and act in space. There is no place beyond his reach, no place that he cannot "go." The term *immanence* is often used to refer to this

---

[15]The book of Acts reports that the apostle Stephen quoted this passage in his address to the Jewish council in Jerusalem (Acts 7:49).

[16]Just as it was prudent earlier to include an interpretive word on the scriptural contrast between the potter and clay, so too a brief note is offered here regarding some of the comparisons in some of the verses cited above, such as the comparison between *heaven* and *earth*, or between *above* and *below*. If as suggested above the difference between God the Creator and creatures is not fundamentally quantitative but qualitative, then care needs to be taken when drawing on human categories, perspectives, and language to interpret and describe the divine. As Michael Allen suggests, "Any attribution of terms from human to divine or in reverse must traverse an analogical path." See Allen, "Divine Attributes," 70; also Horton, *Christian Faith*, 255. Just as scriptural imagery of God as a "potter" with "clay" is intended to exalt the greatness and sovereignty of God, so too statements affirming that, for example, God is enthroned in heaven are not statements of physical or spatial geography suggesting that God is not present on earth. Rather, they are attempts, within the limits of human language, to exalt the sovereignty and freedom of God in relation to the earth and its inhabitants. They do not indicate God's absence from the creation and creatures but rather God's freedom with respect to them.

dimension of God's freedom. The first biblical testimony that we cited above regarding God's freedom with respect to space was a portion of Deuteronomy 10:14. Here is the entirety of that verse plus the following verse: "Although heaven and the heaven of heavens belong to the LORD your God, the earth and all that is in it, yet the LORD set his heart in love on your ancestors alone and chose you, their descendants after them." Here we see the both-and of God's freedom from and freedom within space. The God of heaven is also the God of earth. The God of heaven is actively, relationally *present on earth*.[17] Psalm 113 praises the Lord who is "high above all nations," who is "seated on high," who "looks far down on the heavens and the earth." But the Lord not only looks down. The same psalm also proclaims that he "raises the poor from the dust, and lifts the needy from the ash heap. . . . He gives the barren woman a home, making her the joyous mother of children" (Ps 113:4-9). The heavenly praise celebrating the earthly arrival of the Messiah did not end with "Glory to God in the highest heaven" but concluded with "and on earth peace among those whom he favors!" (Lk 2:14). Having proclaimed at the Areopagus that God "does not live in shrines made by human hands, nor is he served by human hands, as though he needed anything," the apostle Paul goes on to declare that this God "is not far from each one of us." Adapting the language of a Greek poet, he goes so far as to say that "in him we live and move and have our being" (Acts 17:24-28). God is free with respect to space, and very much present in the world.

It is important to highlight the fact that the Scriptures' testimony to absolute freedom in relation to space is not a statement about some force or principle or dimension of the universe. It is a statement about the living God. The one who is omnipresent and free to act in and beyond space is the Creator and Sustainer of the universe. The Scriptures' statements about

---

[17]As the title of Scott Duvall and Daniel Hays's book *God's Relational Presence* indicates, many of the biblical affirmations and descriptions of God's presence make it clear that his presence is not mere presence but relational presence. See J. Scott Duvall and J. Daniel Hays, *God's Relational Presence: The Cohesive Center of Biblical Theology* (Grand Rapids, MI: Baker Academic, 2019), 10n17.

God's freedom in relation to space are not offered as solutions to philosophical or metaphysical questions, but are given primarily to inspire awe
and worship, to reassure and guide, to comfort or encourage, to humble
and in some instances bring about repentance. When the psalmist prays, "If
I ascend to heaven, you are there; if I make my bed in Sheol, you are there.
If I take the wings of the morning and settle at the farthest limit of the sea,"
he is not engaged in a metaphysical musing or playing some kind of cosmic
game. These expressions of God's transcendence of space are the foundation for his expression of assurance, "even there your hand shall lead me,
and your right hand shall hold me fast" (Ps 139:8-10). One commentator's
observation about Psalm 139 is applicable to many of the Scripture passages
that speak of God's freedom with respect to space: "Any small thoughts that
we may have of God are magnificently transcended . . . yet for all of its
height and depth it remains intensely personal from first to last."[18]

By contrast, as we observed in chapters two and three, we human
beings are placed. We are always somewhere, including being somewhere when we work. This is not bad, not a manifestation of fallenness.
The fact that we are always somewhere in space when we work is (simply)
one manifestation of God's design of embodied creatureliness, and it
has the potential to be the context for many good gifts, not least when
space becomes place, with meaning and experiences and relationships.

Wherever we work, God is present. Wherever. God's freedom with respect to space means that he can be wherever, literally, we work. We never
work completely alone. We never work beyond or outside the presence of
God.[19] Furthermore, in the context of remote work, God is also present to
the other people with whom we are working. In our finitude we are always
here, not there, but God is not limited in this way. He can indeed be at work
both here and there. One of the major agendas of the faith and work

---

[18]Derek Kidner, *Psalms 73-150*, Tyndale Old Testament Commentaries, vol. 16 (Downers Grove,
IL: IVP Academic, 1975; reprint ed., 2008), 500.
[19]Scott Duvall and Daniel Hays write that "as the biblical story unfolds and as God seeks to relate
to his people, almost by definition . . . immanence takes center stage in how God reveals himself (although transcendence still hovers about continuously)" (Duvall and Hays, *God's Relational Presence*, 6).

movement in recent decades has been to challenge, if not reject, the so-called sacred/secular divide in which there is a hierarchy, however explicit or implicit, in which "sacred" work is more highly valued than "secular" work, with the associated tendencies to value the "spiritual" over the "bodily" and "material" and the "eternal" over the "temporal."[20] In response to this, the faith and work movement in recent years has sought to erase, or at least render very thin and porous, this "divide" and robustly affirm the goodness or the potential goodness of all forms of work.[21] However, whether or not one embraces such an approach to sacred/secular questions, what can be affirmed with clarity and confidence with respect to our focus here—human finitude within space—is that wherever one works and in whatever form of work one engages, that place and that work are not beyond the reach of God. In this respect there is no sacred/secular divide. God is omnipresent—He is utterly free with regard to space and that includes the spaces, the places, where we work.[22]

God, time, and work. God is free with respect to time. He is neither limited by nor captive to it.[23] Authors in both the Old and New Testament clearly regard God as eternal—that is, transcending time.

---

[20]From outside the faith and work movement, Andrew Lynn identifies and critiques a variety of faith and work responses to the sacred/secular divide. See Andrew Lynn, *Saving the Protestant Ethic: Creative Class Evangelicalism and the Crisis of Work* (Oxford: Oxford University Press, 2023), 30, 36, 54, 164, 205-13.

[21]E.g., Crouch, *Culture Making*, 252-56; Os Guinness, *The Call: Finding and Fulfilling the Central Purpose of Your Life* (Nashville: Thomas Nelson, 2003), 27-35; and Gordon T. Smith, *Courage and Calling: Embracing Your God-Given Potential*, rev. ed. (Downers Grove, IL: InterVarsity Press, 2011), 34-36 and 43-47. R. Paul Stevens implicitly addresses the sacred/secular distinction by rejecting conventional clergy/laity distinctions—both Roman Catholic and Protestant—and formulating a view of Christians as a people without laity and without clergy. See R. Paul Stevens, *The Other Six Days: Vocation, Work, and Ministry in Biblical Perspective* (Grand Rapids, MI: Eerdmans, 1999).

[22]We continue our focus here on *creational, prelapsarian* finitude. In the longer unfolding of the grand narrative, this affirmation of the presence of God needs to consider the various postures in which God can be present and on the absence of God in judgment. As Michael Horton comments, "Of course, God is omnipresent in his essence, but the primary question in the covenantal drama is whether God is present for us, and if so, where, as well as whether he is present in judgment or in grace" (Horton, *Christian Faith*, 255). Also see, for example, sections on divine judgment in chap. 3, on the Old Testament prophets, in Duvall and Hays, *God's Relational Presence*, 113-65.

[23]For a critique of and alternative to the traditional understanding of God's relationship to time, see R. T. Mullins, *The End of the Timeless God* (Oxford: Oxford University Press, 2016).

Testifying to the making of a covenant at Beer-sheba, Abraham "called on the name of the LORD, the Everlasting God" (Gen 21:33). In the doxology with which the apostle Paul concludes his epistle to the Romans, he attributes the revelation of the gospel of Jesus Christ and its disclosure to the Gentiles to "the command of the eternal God" (Rom 16:26). Paul concludes another doxology, this one in the opening paragraphs of his first letter to Timothy, with praise "To the King of the ages, immortal, invisible, the only God, be honor and glory forever and ever." Before the letter is finished, Paul adds to this affirmation a doxological statement, "It is [God] alone who has immortality . . . to him be honor and eternal dominion" (1 Tim 1:17; 6:16). Not surprisingly, God's utter freedom with respect to time, so different from the human relationship to time, calls forth imaginative language in attempts to affirm and describe God's unique freedom. For example, several Old Testament authors, some in prose, some in poetry, employ merismus in affirming God's freedom with respect to time.[24] As recorded in Nehemiah 9:5, the people of Israel are called on to "bless the LORD your God from everlasting to everlasting." The psalmists frequently employ this phrase or similar ones: "Blessed be the LORD, the God of Israel, from everlasting to everlasting"; "Your throne, O God, endures for ever and ever"; "Before the mountains were brought forth, or ever you had formed the earth and the world, from everlasting to everlasting you are God" (Ps 41:13; 45:6; 90:2).

This last verse from Psalms also introduces another way that God's freedom with regard to time is presented in Scripture. God is described as living "before the mountains were brought forth, or ever you had formed the earth and the world." Time came into existence in conjunction with the events of the original creation, and both the Old and the New Testaments include descriptions of God's life and work as

---

[24]Merismus is a literary device that "mentions the extremes of some category in order to portray it as a totality—that is, the opposites and everything in between them." See William W. Klein, Craig L. Blomberg, and Robert L. Hubbard Jr., *Introduction to Biblical Interpretation*, 3rd ed. (Grand Rapids, MI: Zondervan, 2017), 394. In the case of the examples cited here, the poles— "everlasting"—are extreme in and of themselves ("ever") before they are employed as poles in merismus.

existing prior to creation, thus prior to the existence of time. Time began. God already was.[25] The apostle Paul testifies that the wisdom of God was "decreed before the ages" and that God chose followers of Christ "before the foundation of the world" (1 Cor 2:7; Eph 1:4). Furthermore, whatever the ultimate future of time is, the future of God is never-ending. A psalmist testifies, "Long ago you laid the foundation of the earth, and the heavens are the work of your hands. They will perish, but you endure. . . . You are the same, and your years have no end" (Ps 102:25-27). Ringing a note of hope amid the reality of judgment, near the conclusion of the book of Lamentations the author says, "But you, O LORD, reign forever; your throne endures to all generations" (Lam 5:19). We noted earlier that even Nebuchadnezzar had some understanding of God's relation to space, and the same is true with respect to God and time. Following his grass-eating humiliation, when "reason returned" to him, he praised God saying, "I blessed the Most High, and praised and honored the one who lives forever. For his sovereignty is an everlasting sovereignty, and his kingdom endures from generation to generation" (Dan 4:34). The author of Hebrews, speaking of the Son of God, echoes the wisdom of Psalms 45; 102, proclaiming, "'In the beginning, Lord, you founded the earth, and the heavens are the work of your hands; they will perish, but you remain; . . . you are the same, and your years will never end'" (Heb 1:10-12). Also speaking of the Son, in the opening of the book of Revelation the apostle John says, "'I am the Alpha and the Omega,' says the Lord God, who is and who was and who is to come, the Almighty" (Rev 1:8; also see Rev 4:8).

As was the case with the Bible's testimony to divine transcendence within and beyond space, so too is it the case with the testimony with regard to God and time. The Bible does not proclaim God's freedom in relation to time as a way of asserting a fine point of theology or making

---

[25]We acknowledge that the wonder of God's relationship to time here outstrips, if you will, the capacities of human language. For example, words like "prior to" or "before" or "was" are associated with and reflect temporality . . . which temporality is what God, in his freedom, transcends.

an abstract metaphysical claim. The Bible proclaims God's eternality because it is true, and the eternality in which the Bible is interested is the eternality of the one and only living God. These are not proclamations about a principle or force or dimension of the universe. They speak of the eternal Lord, personally engaged in the lives of human beings. The call in the book of Nehemiah to praise "the LORD your God from everlasting to everlasting" is embedded within a story of confession and renewal of relationship with God, within which God is repeatedly referred to in relational terms as "their God" and "your God" (Neh 9:1-5). The concluding praise to God "from everlasting to everlasting" in Psalm 41 follows praise to God for delivering, protecting, and healing the poor, and thanks to God for rescuing the psalmist and settling him "in your presence forever" (Ps 41:1-12). As celebrated in Isaiah 40, the Lord who is "the everlasting God" "gives power to the faint, and strengthens the powerless." Those who "wait for the Lord shall renew their strength, they shall mount up with wings like eagles, they shall run and not be weary, they shall walk and not faint" (Is 40:28-29, 31). The apostle Paul reassures the Christians at Rome that the "eternal God" is able and ready to "strengthen" them (Rom 16:25-26), and he teaches the Christians at Ephesus that the God who chose them "before the foundation of the world" (Eph 1:4) lavishly, graciously provides redemption, bestows on them a glorious inheritance, and "marked [them] with the seal of the promised Holy Spirit" (Eph 1:13; also Eph 1:4, 7-8, 11). The one whom Paul describes as "immortal, invisible, the only God" "strengthened" him, "appointed" him to His service, was merciful to him, loved him, saved him, and was patient with him (1 Tim 1:12-17). This is not a principle or force that transcends time. This is the living, active God who lives and acts, for good, both within and beyond time.

For the Christian, thinking about and responding to the reality of work within the bounds of human finitude in relation to time needs to be completed and shaped by the fact that God is free with regard to time. He has been, is, and will be living and active in what to us is past, present, and future. To adapt James K. A. Smith's phrase, God is never "nowhen."[26] Stanley Grenz accurately and helpfully enriches our understanding of God's sovereignty when he observes that "God's eternality encompasses three related attributes, omnipresence, omniscience, and omnipotence."[27] If in our work we find ourselves wondering, "How did I get here?" we can be assured that our past is known to God and that he was there. If our work at present is very trying, we can be assured that God is present and knows and is at work . . . today. Now. And if we think ahead and wonder about the outcomes of our work, we can be assured that God knows and God will be there, at work in the world.

God, power, knowledge, and work. God's freedom is manifest with respect to every reality in relation to which we are limited. In the previous two sections we began to glimpse the wonder of the attributes of God, focusing on God's relationship to space and time. We will now consider two other divine attributes and their significance for our understanding and experience of work: God's power and God's knowledge.[28]

The prophet Isaiah sees very clearly, in juxtaposition, both the limits of human power and the limitless power of God. "Even youths will faint and be weary, and the young will fall exhausted." But the everlasting God, the Creator of the ends of the earth, "does not faint or grow weary." Moreover, fully aware of our finitude, our Creator "gives power to the faint, and strengthens the powerless" (Is 40:28-30). God is free with respect to power. He is all-powerful, and eternally so. There is no force, no being, no creature, nothing in creation that can thwart God. Throughout our considerations of finitude we have made repeated reference to *creation* and *the Creator*. While God's power is manifest in myriad ways in all of his works—as Sustainer, Redeemer, Coming King, to name just three—his work of creation *ex nihilo* is primal and awe-inspiring. In perhaps the

---

[26]James K. A. Smith, *How to Inhabit Time: Understanding the Past, Facing the Future, Living Faithfully Now* (Grand Rapids, MI: Brazos, 2022), 4.

[27]Stanley J. Grenz, *Theology for the Community of God* (Grand Rapids, MI: Eerdmans, 2000), 92.

[28]Grenz identifies the association among the four attributes we are considering here: omnipresence, eternality, omnipotence, and omniscience (Grenz, *Theology for the Community*, 92).

greatest understatement in all of human writing, we read several times in Genesis 1 that "God said . . . and there was" (Gen 1:3, 6, 9, 11, 14, 20, 24, 26). However one interprets the genre of Genesis 1, these are understatements of power beyond full comprehension. It is not surprising, then, that this primal exercise of God's power is recalled in Scripture when other exercises of God's power are in view. "Will you question me about my children, or command me concerning the work of my hands?" the Lord rhetorically asks through the prophet Isaiah, "I made the earth, and created humankind upon it; it was my hands that stretched out the heavens, and I commanded all their host" (Is 45:11-12). God's work of creation is the foundation, Jeremiah's first words, in a prayer in which he recounts a litany of God's redemptive works: "Ah Lord God! It is you who made the heavens and the earth by your great power and by your outstretched arm! Nothing is too hard for you" (Jer 32:17). Nothing is too hard for God . . . including the Son of God taking human nature on himself and coming to earth as the God-Man. When the angel brought Mary the news that she would bear the Son of God, the one through whom creation itself was realized, he concludes his announcement with "For nothing will be impossible for God" (Lk 1:37). God is all-powerful.

God is free with respect to knowledge. He is all-knowing. "Our knowledge," writes Michael Horton, "is partial, ectypal, composite, and learned, but God's is complete, archetypal, simple, and innate."[29] Our knowledge related to any form of work is finite. The point here, however, is *not* that our knowing is bad—it is partial, limited, must be learned over time. In other words, our knowledge is creaturely, appropriate to creatures. The more important point here is that God's knowledge is complete, perfect, without limits. His knowledge can be described as both macro and micro, both cosmic and intimately personal. God knows and understands the grandest and most expansive realities. Even one of Job's companions, Elihu, observed this about God: "Do you know the balancings of the clouds, the wondrous works of the one whose knowledge is perfect?"

---

[29]Horton, *Christian Faith*, 259.

(Job 37:16). The psalmist praises God because "he determines the number of the stars; he gives to all of them their names. Great is our Lord, and abundant in power; his understanding is beyond measure" (Ps 147:4-5). God's free creative power does not outstrip or go beyond his knowledge.[30] Not surprisingly, the Creator has intimate knowledge of all his creation work, both cosmic (such as the clouds and stars) and personal (such as human hearts and minds). Praying words of comfort and assurance, the psalmist says, "O LORD, you have searched me and known me. . . . You discern my thoughts from far away. . . . Even before a word is on my tongue, O LORD, you know it completely" (Ps 139:1-2, 4). The apostle Peter well knew that God "knows the human heart" (Acts 15:8). Indeed, "before him no creature is hidden, but all are naked and laid bare to the eyes of the one to whom we must render an account" (Heb 4:13). Finally, God's knowing is shaped by his goodness. God is wise. Knowledge and wisdom are not strictly synonyms, but wisdom entails knowledge. It entails the right use of knowledge. As J. I. Packer observes, God's wisdom is "the power to see, and the inclination to choose, the best and highest goal, together with the surest means of attaining it."[31] God always acts on and employs his knowledge for good.

These two, knowledge and power, are sometimes linked together when biblical authors describe the work of God. We cited above Isaiah's clear vision of God's power as set forth in Isaiah 40. In the midst of this description of the power of God he cannot help but also note that "his understanding is unsearchable" (Is 40:28). The apostle Paul testifies to a similar combination when instructing the Christians at Corinth. Early in his first letter to the Corinthians he says, "God's foolishness is wiser than human wisdom, and God's weakness is stronger than human

---

[30]This is but one manifestation of what is sometimes referred to as divine simplicity. Whenever one ponders a divine attribute, it is important to bear in mind that, as Millard Erickson observes, "God is unitary, not a composite" of parts, and that, despite how it may appear in light of our experiences as human beings, "there is no fundamental tension among the attributes, and they are ultimately aspects of the one divine nature." See Millard Erickson, *Christian Theology*, 3rd ed. (Grand Rapids, MI: Baker Academic, 2013), 269.

[31]J. I. Packer, *Knowing God* (Downers Grove, IL: InterVarsity Press, 1973), 80.

strength" (1 Cor 1:25). Paul here both associates the exercise of knowledge with the exercise of power and, though he does not here describe God's knowledge and power as limitless, he does contrast God's knowledge and power with human knowledge and power.

We have previously observed that when in Scripture God's divine perfections are compared and contrasted with the capacities of human beings the intention is not always to make the point that human beings are bad. In fact, often the primary point is not about human beings at all but rather about God and his ways. So too, here in 1 Corinthians. Immediately making the comparison between God and the Corinthians, Paul does not tell them that they are not qualified to participate in God's redemptive work in the world. Rather, he tells them that it is precisely the foolish and the weak, that which is "low and despised in the world," that God chooses to carry forward his redemptive work in the world (1 Cor 1:26-31). God does not abandon us or remain aloof from us because of the differences between his divine attributes and our finite capacities as humans, whether those finite capacities are physical or cognitive or spiritual. He is present, always, and for those who rely on him, he is ready in his freedom to renew their strength so that they might "run and not be weary . . . walk and not faint" (Is 40:31).

GOOD ENOUGH (BUT NOT EDEN): WORK IN A FALLEN WORLD

A theology of work from and for the middle, then, takes seriously human finitude, but it will also be rooted, as we have said, in "the quotidian," which, as David Kelsey argues, is the dominant frame of the biblical wisdom literature. In other words, the Judeo-Christian wisdom tradition typically does not appeal to protology (although it may assume it), nor does it envision a concrete eschatological teleology that humans are striving to realize. Instead, says Kelsey, it concerns itself with what we have described as *phenomenology*: "'the creation' denotes the lived world as the quotidian, the everyday finite realities of all sorts—animal, vegetable, and mineral—in the routine networks that are constituted by their ordinary interactions."[32] The Bible's wisdom literature of course recognizes the fallenness of the world, even if it does not explicitly thematize a "fall" event. Even so, the quotidian is never devalued or rejected, thorns and thistles notwithstanding; the creation theology of these texts interprets the world as basically good, basically ordered, and basically suitable for flourishing—in short, good *enough*, but not Eden. Simply put, the wisdom tradition, especially the book of Ecclesiastes, represents a theology in and for the middle: "[The quotidian's] dignity lies not in the fact that it inherently refers beyond itself to transcendent reality, nor in its having an ontological depth more meaningful than itself, but simply in being just what God creates in all its everydayness."[33]

Critically, the biblical writers often (though not exclusively) situate their accounts of work within the everydayness of the quotidian. While Genesis 1–2 undoubtedly represents one stream—perhaps even the primary stream—of the Bible's theology of work, there are other voices too. Indeed, to adopt a taxonomy first introduced by Jacques Ellul, some biblical writers, principally Qoheleth, place work in the "realm of necessity," not the "realm of freedom." Put crassly, work is something that all of us *must* do, and perhaps would choose not to do if we had the freedom, but it is not intrinsically redemptive. Ellul takes a rather extreme position:

> Work is a natural exercise of human activity which sets man in a relation to creation that is either positive, as in Eden, or negative, as after the break with God. In the latter case work is laborious and necessary to survival. Either way, however, it is not presented as service of God. It has to be done, and the Bible is realistic enough not to overlay this necessity with superfluous spiritual ornamentation. Moreover, the Bible displays

---

[32]Kelsey, *Eccentric Existence*, 1:190. In the same passage, Kelsey notes that "mainstream Wisdom's creation theology generally lacks any account of cosmic origins. . . . It simply does not touch on the question of how creation came to be. Nor does it suggest that the present context of our lives is a decline and fall from an actual paradisiacal state that God first created" (190).

[33]Kelsey, *Eccentric Existence*, 1:191.

no essential interest in the situation of work. Work is the painful lot of all men but it is not particularly important.[34]

Ellul goes on to argue that, even "if not in the purest sense, at least in the form in which we know it, work is a result of the fall." In our view, Ellul overstates the case; we must stop short of affirming that "work is a simple necessity" with "no specific value."[35] Still, it is an argument worth hearing, if only for the purpose of offering a corrective to overly optimistic theologies of work. After all, as Ellul shows quite convincingly, this quotidian vision of work—toilsome yet necessary—is just as biblical as the magnificent cultural mandate of Genesis 1–2.

Instrumental, not (just) intrinsic: work as means to an end. A realistic theology of work will need to attend more closely to the quotidian by recovering an *instrumental* view of work. While it is certainly true that the Bible does present work as having intrinsic dignity and value, it is equally true that it can also speak of work in purely instrumental terms. For our purposes, we shall take only two examples: the earthy theology of work found in Ecclesiastes and the apostle Paul's directives to the Thessalonian church, where he commends work as a means to an end rather than an end in itself.

Qoheleth has more to say about work than any other biblical author; fittingly, Ecclesiastes does feature in many theological accounts of work, though sometimes only peripherally.[36] However, we propose that several of the themes that emerge in Ecclesiastes ought to be central to any realistic theology of work. Like every other reality under the sun, the purpose of work is both obscured and frustrated by *hebel*, but it would be a mistake

---

[34]Jacques Ellul, *The Ethics of Freedom*, trans. Geoffrey W. Bromiley (Grand Rapids, MI: Eerdmans, 1976), 495.

[35]Ellul, *The Ethics of Freedom*, 496.

[36]See, for example, R. Paul Stevens, *Work Matters: Lessons from Scripture* (Grand Rapids, MI: Eerdmans, 2012), chap. 13. Representative titles also include John Mark Comer, *Garden City: Work, Rest, and the Art of Being Human* (Nashville: Thomas Nelson, 2017), 168-70; James M. Hamilton, Jr., *Work and Our Labor in the Lord* (Wheaton, IL: Crossway, 2017), 48-52; Timothy Keller with Katherine Leary Alsdorf, *Every Good Endeavor: Connecting Your Work to God's Work* (New York: Penguin, 2016), chap. 6.

to conclude that Qoheleth basically has a negative view of human labor. One thing we can say for certain is that the book's theology is thoroughly quotidian, above all because it recognizes that we are in the middle.[37] No human technique will ever reproduce the conditions of Eden: "Whatever my eyes desired I did not keep from them; I kept my heart from no pleasure, for my heart found pleasure in all my toil, and this was my reward for all my toil. Then I considered all that my hands had done and the toil I had spent in doing it, and again, all was vanity and a chasing after wind, and there was nothing to be gained under the sun" (Eccles 2:10-11). Significantly, these melancholy ruminations on the futility of work come as Qoheleth reflects on his grand-but-failed attempt to re-create Eden in 2:1-8, which is dense with allusions to and the vocabulary of the garden narratives of Genesis 1–2.[38] Since there is no going back to Eden, then, Qoheleth turns to an instrumental view of work, which recurs throughout the entire book: "There is nothing better for mortals than to eat and drink, and find enjoyment in their toil. This also, I saw, is from the hand of God; for apart from him who can eat or who can have enjoyment?" (Eccles 2:24-25; cf. Eccles 3:12, 22; 8:15). This theology of work is supremely realistic: work is something that must be done, but it is also something from which we can derive great purpose and enjoyment. Whether we enjoy it or not, though, the way of wisdom is to see work for what it is: a genuine good of creation that is constrained by finitude and beset by fallenness. "These observations," explains Ellul, "enable us to see work within its limitations, which do not lead us to deny its existence or despise it. . . . [but] work for the sake of work makes no sense."[39]

---

[37]Tyler Atkinson has engaged this motif at length in his insightful study of Qoheleth's understanding of labor, arguing for an interpretation of Ecclesiastes that "hold[s] protology and eschatology together through christology." See Tyler Atkinson, *Singing at the Winepress: Ecclesiastes and the Ethics of Work* (London: Bloomsbury T&T Clark, 2015), 190. Although Atkinson develops these concepts differently than we do here, his approach represents one promising way to operationalize Qoheleth's quotidian theology of work. See *Singing at the Winepress*, chap. 4.

[38]See Craig G. Bartholomew, *Ecclesiastes*, Baker Commentary on the Old Testament (Grand Rapids, MI: Baker Academic, 2009), 133.

[39]Jacques Ellul, *Reason for Being: A Meditation on Ecclesiastes*, trans. Joyce Main Hanks (1987; repr., Eugene, OR: Wipf & Stock, 2021), 94-95.

We find a similarly gritty theology of work also in the New Testament, this time from the pen of Paul, apostle to the Gentiles by day, tentmaker by night. Paul's most concentrated theology of work emerges in the Thessalonian correspondence, where across both letters he counsels the saints in Thessalonica with a quotidian understanding of labor. "But we urge you, brothers," he writes, "to mind your own affairs, and to work with your hands, as we directed you, so that you may behave properly before outsiders and be dependent on no one" (1 Thess 4:10-12). Similarly, in 2 Thessalonians 3:6–12, Paul offers an extended discourse on the purpose and value of work, which includes an admonition to "the idle," those who had disregarded his counsel in 1 Thessalonians 4:9-12 and, perhaps in expectation of the Lord's imminent return, have quit their jobs.[40] "Now such persons we command and encourage in the Lord Jesus Christ to do their work quietly and to earn their own living" (2 Thess 3:12). Significantly, Paul makes no appeal whatsoever to protology or eschatology to ground his theology of work. In fact, this quotidian approach to toil is arguably presented to *remedy* an overeager eschatology. On any reading, however, there is absolutely no suggestion that the Thessalonians' labor will somehow endure into the age to come. Rather, it is simply something that must be done to serve various instrumental purposes—providing for one's kin, for instance, or contributing to the financial life of the body of Christ—in the middle. To drive home the point, Paul holds up himself as an example of one who works instrumentally: "For you yourselves know how you ought to imitate us; we were not idle when we were with you, and we did not eat anyone's bread without paying for it; but with toil and labor we worked night and day, so that we might not burden any of you" (2 Thess 3:7-8 NRSVA). Paul made tents (which, note, he describes as *toil*),

[40]Paul does not explicitly link some Thessalonians' aberrant eschatology with their refusal to work, but it has been common for commentators to make this connection in the history of interpretation. Although this reading has been contested, it remains a plausible interpretation of the passage. For a summary of the state of the debate, see Gordon D. Fee, *The First and Second Letters to the Thessalonians*, New International Commentary on the New Testament (Grand Rapids, MI: Eerdmans, 2009), 157n5, and Jeffrey A. D. Weima, *1–2 Thessalonians*, Baker Exegetical Commentary on the New Testament (Grand Rapids, MI: Baker Academic, 2014), 296-97.

but not because he understood tentmaking to be a participation in God's own work; he made tents because that's what he had to do to support his apostolic ministry (Acts 18:1-4; cf. 1 Cor 9:8-15; 2 Cor 11:7-11).

In sum, an account of work that is not only theologically sound but also thoroughly biblical will need to recover an instrumental view of work as a tool in our pastoral toolkits, which can supplement (but not replace) an intrinsic view of work. Such a recovery is vital, we argue, if the faith and work movement is going to speak to a broader range of workers, all of whom toil in the middle, having heard only a rumor of Eden and not yet at the open gates of the new Jerusalem. What is needed is a *carpe diem* theology[41]—a theology for the time being, a *today* theology, in addition to a *yesterday* theology (protology) and a *tomorrow* theology (eschatology). What might it look like to activate such a theology in concrete terms? For a start, this would involve a pastoral theology in which, simply put, the saints are encouraged to "aspire to live quietly, to mind [their] own affairs, and to work with [their] hands" (1 Thess 4:11). Such a theology will need to situate work in the "penultimate sphere" rather than the "ultimate sphere," to use Bonhoeffer's terms.[42] Put another way, a realistic theology of work will put work in proper perspective: a penultimate reality that can be good and purposeful but also futile and fruitless, but in neither case salvific in any ultimate sense in and of itself. Otherwise, we run the risk of freighting our jobs with existential weight they simply cannot bear: "A serious perversion of the truth takes place when a whole society claims to provide satisfaction for the soul through work! Such talk can produce nothing but a huge vacuum, which all other passions will rush to fill up."[43]

Ecce Homo, *not (just)* **homo faber:** *Deconstructing toxic work mythologies.* In our view, such revisions will be necessary to open up redemptive possibilities for workers who feel the limitations of finitude

---

[41]Bartholomew uses this phrase to designate Qoheleth's general theological outlook, which is not a despairing hedonism but an attentiveness to God's good gifts given in the present, elusive and transitory though they are. See *Ecclesiastes*, 150.

[42]See Dietrich Bonhoeffer, *Ethics*, trans. Neville Horton Smith (1949; repr., New York: Simon & Schuster, 1995), 125-32.

[43]Ellul, *Reason for Being*, 96.

most acutely and whose daily labor is mired in enmity, absurdity, or tragedy. We contend that such a theology will be more pastorally viable for people whose work does not "participate in God's work" in an obviously redemptive way or for whom the concept of co-laboring with God simply does not resonate. In fact, in our experience, emphasizing the instrumental value of work—the ways in which it provides for material needs even if it is not especially fulfilling—takes the pressure off workers who find their jobs futile or frustrating, or whose daily tasks are bound up with unjust systems and structures. Most critically, though, a realistic theology of work will situate work within a *broader anthropology* that does not identify the *imago Dei* with autonomy, creative capacity, or the ability to co-create with God. To anticipate, we shall now argue for an *Ecce Homo* anthropology, a vision of human life and flourishing that is grounded above all in the person of Jesus Christ, who *is himself* the truly human one, to supplement (and perhaps supplant) a *homo faber* anthropology, in which human dignity and purpose is found mainly in working and building. Such an anthropology promises meaning and purpose in multiple dimensions of human personhood, displacing work as the prime means of defining human identity. With respect to a theology of work, therefore, an *Ecce Homo* anthropology must deconstruct two toxic work mythologies, which are sometimes (perhaps unintentionally) reinforced by some theologies of work: You Are What You Do and Do What You Love.

"Behold the man!" (Jn 19:5 KJV). Thus speaks Pilate of Jesus Christ, pointing to the truly human one, the only one who fulfills the human vocation. Indeed, Pilate says more than he knows, as the consistent witness of the New Testament is that Jesus Christ is *the* image of the invisible God in human flesh (Col 1:15; cf. 2 Cor 4:4; Phil 2:6; Heb 1:3) and, as such, is himself the key that unlocks human image-bearing, enabling it to realize its ultimate *telos*, as Kathryn Tanner has shown. "There is only one perfect or express image of God—the second person of the trinity—and that perfect image becomes the creature's own by way of a close relationship with it, the closer the better, a closeness consummated in Christ.

Jesus Christ is more than a paradigm for what is involved here; he has become for us the very means."[44] Any Christian anthropology, then, will inevitably draw on Christology in its account of what it means to be human. It is fully appropriate therefore that faith and work literature has appealed to the person of Jesus to substantiate its claims about the theological value of work. These approaches make much of the fact that Jesus of Nazareth is the son of a *tektōn*—a carpenter or a builder, someone who works with their hands (Mt 13:55; cf. Mk 6:3). R. Paul Stevens, for example, styles Jesus as an "artisan" who "might have made houses, boats, cradles or ox-yokes."[45] It is common for writers in this stream to emphasize that it is only natural that the incarnation would put the Logos to work in the field or the shop, since the God of Israel is himself a worker, in glaring contradistinction to the idle idols of the ancient Near East. "A workman's jacket was a fitting garment for the God whom the biblical revelation had all along represented as himself a worker."[46]

It is of course indisputable that Jesus of Nazareth presumably worked as a *tektōn* with Joseph. What is up for debate, however, is what kind of theological implications we can draw from this fact. Appealing to the occupation of Jesus to bolster a theology of work is more complicated than it might appear. For a start, as Jacques Ellul has pointed out, the gospels never actually *show* Jesus working, nor do the evangelists seem to have any interest in thematizing Jesus' daily work as theologically significant: "Jesus never calls upon anyone to work. On the contrary, he constantly takes the men he calls away from their work, e.g., Peter, James, Levi . . . It is possible that Jesus himself worked, but this is by no means certain, and even if he did, it proves nothing. Like others he obeyed the necessities of human life."[47] Jesus' own labor, on this account, has less to do with the intrinsically redemptive value of work and more

---

[44]Kathryn Tanner, *Christ the Key*, Current Issues in Theology (Cambridge: Cambridge University Press, 2010), 14.

[45]R. Paul Stevens, *The Other Six Days: Vocation, Work, and Ministry in Biblical Perspective* (Grand Rapids, MI: Eerdmans, 1999), 115.

[46]Alan Richardson, *The Biblical Doctrine of Work* (London: SCM Press, 1952), 48.

[47]Ellul, *Ethics of Freedom*, 496.

to do with the eternal Son's willingness to identify, in humility, with the lot of all humans, who eat their bread only by the sweat of their brows. In other words, the fact that Jesus of Nazareth worked may simply mean that he subjected himself to the same conditions, finitude and fallenness, which each of us faces east of Eden—and nothing more.

In that case, the question now becomes: *how* does Jesus Christ image the invisible God? To pose the question in an anthropological frame, what does Jesus reveal about what it means to be truly and fully human? We contend that much faith and work theology relies on a Christology that assumes and reinforces a *homo faber* understanding of the image of God, which could in turn imply that those without meaningful work may not be imaging God fully. Conversely, though, if we suppose an *Ecce Homo* anthropology, then it appears that work is by no means central to human personhood, since it is not central to the gospel accounts of Jesus' life. Put another way, the vision of authentic human personhood made manifest in Jesus Christ does not have work—understood as vocation or occupation— as its essence. Accordingly, a sound theology of work will de-center work from the core of human identity and worth, principally by interrogating alternative accounts of work that identify work with the *humanum* itself.

The first of these toxic mythologies to be scrutinized is "You Are What You Do" a view in which work is the primary means by which humans present themselves to the world and attempt to solidify their identities.[48] As we have seen, this mythology animates enmitous work, as people expend enormous energy to "give a legitimate account of themselves," to return to Robert Wuthnow's phrase, by piling up work accomplishments on their résumés.[49] Decades ago, Dianne Fassel warned that the church was fueling the workaholism epidemic through a theology that empha- sizes industriousness as a cardinal theological virtue. She laments that the church, which should be an "oasis of sanity" in a frenetic culture of

---

[48]For an overview of this phenomenon in the modern era, see Al Gini, *My Job, My Self: Work and the Creation of the Modern Individual* (London: Routledge, 2012), chap. 1.

[49]Robert Wuthnow, *Poor Richard's Principle: Recovering the American Dream Through the Moral Dimensions of Work, Business and Money* (Princeton, NJ: Princeton University Press, 1996), 225.

overwork, has actually contributed to the problem: "Think of the renaissance if people could look to the church as a place of rest, nurture, and justice rather than a treadmill of frantic activity."[50] Is it possible that the faith and work movement has been unwittingly reinforcing work addiction by asking work to do *too much* and giving it *too much attention*, loading it with existential weight it was never meant to bear? It's at least a question worth asking. Perhaps the task of a realistic theology of work in such a context is to challenge the church to be an "oasis of sanity."

Indeed, a Christian anthropology must object to the logic of "You Are What You Do" not just on pastoral grounds, but on theological grounds as well. The Christian faith insists that work is not the only way, nor even the best way, for humans "to give a legitimate account of themselves." In fact, to state the issue in these terms is already to have taken a wrong turn, since, according to the Bible, it is *God* who gives account of human beings. It seems to us that, in a culture of neurotic work obsession, a great deal of pressure could be relieved if people were reminded that they do not have to generate their own identities. From the very beginning, as the Bible tells it, human identity is conferred, not constructed. We should note that, to begin with, human beings, having just been created in God's image, receive the divine benediction not after having undertaken the cultural mandate by exercising their capacities to co-create with God, but *before they do anything at all* (Gen 1:28). Rather than a set of capacities, the image of God is an alien dignity, an *alienum*, which is simply conferred on humans from beyond themselves according to God's good pleasure. To the extent that image bearers reflect the glory of Jesus Christ, they do so with what Helmut Thielicke calls "borrowed light": "Never for a single moment does [humanity] have a light which is its own, appropriated by it as an 'attribute' or 'property.'"[51] This is true not only at the level of

---

[50]Diane Fassel, *Working Ourselves to Death: The High Cost of Workaholism and the Rewards of Recovery* (New York: HarperCollins, 1990), 118.

[51]Thielicke, *Theological Ethics*, 1:177. John Kilner has likewise argued that the image of God is an indelible status that gives humans dignity by virtue of their connection to God. See John Kilner, *Dignity and Destiny: Humanity in the Image of God* (Grand Rapids, MI: Eerdmans, 2015), 113-23.

protology, but at the level of eschatology as well, since it is the resurrected and glorified Christ who gives the saints their true names (Rev 2:17) so they need not try in vain to make a name for themselves (Gen 11:4).

A sound anthropology, then, must insist that work is merely something humans do, not something humans are. This will inevitably involve introducing a broader anthropological framework to supplement the *homo faber* account of the *imago Dei* with other aspects of image-bearing. Such a revision rests on a recovery of alternative accounts of the *imago Dei* that do not prioritize agency, power, productivity, and creativity as the key criteria of human purpose and value. There are several directions such a revision could take, but we contend that an ecclesial interpretation of the *imago Dei* holds great promise for correcting some of the excesses of a *homo faber* anthropology, since the potential to relate intimately to God in and through the Christian community is available to all people in equal measure, regardless of what they do for work. For example, Orthodox theologian Alexander Schmemann has argued that before we are builders or culture-makers, we are worshipers, *homo adorans*.[52] If the fundamental character of humanity is doxological—if humans are worshipers before they are creators—then the image of God can be realized just as fully in those whose work is dynamic, purposeful, and interesting as in those whose work is enmitous, absurd, or tragic.

Ultimately, the You Are What You Do mythology is a cruel ideology, not least because it is an affront to the dignity of persons made in the image of God who either cannot work or who find themselves in employment that is degrading or otherwise unsatisfying. As Gilbert Meilaender has pointed out, "there is something tyrannical about [interpreting work as co-creation with God], as if we must find fulfillment in work or suffer a meaningless existence. Tyrannical too—and too narrow—is a view that seems to leave little place for those too young, too old, or too disabled to work, not to mention those unable to find

---

[52] Alexander Schmemann, *For the Life of the World: Sacraments and Orthodoxy*, St Vladimir's Seminary Press Classics Series (Yonkers, NY: St Vladimir's Seminary Press, 2018), 22.

employment."[53] Such a mythology is also too small to do justice to the manifold beauty and brilliance of human beings, who are much more than just workers, and must be transcended and relativized by a more compelling vision in which we are not, in the end, professors or plumbers or painters, but "ecclesial selves" being drawn into the very life of the triune God by virtue of our union with Jesus Christ.[54]

We come now to the second work mythology to which a realistic theology of work must address itself: Do What You Love. Over the last half-century, Americans have looked to work to fulfill more and more of our most fundamental human longings. Derek Thompson summarizes this trajectory succinctly: "Here is the history of work in six words: from *jobs*, to *careers*, to *callings*."[55] This narrative of work—which, we should note, moves from an instrumental to an intrinsic understanding of labor—would have been inconceivable to most workers even a generation ago, but it has since become the standard way in which younger Americans especially think about their professional trajectories, a "new mantra for the college-educated."[56] We might identify Apple founder Steve Jobs's commencement address at Stanford University in 2005 as a turning point in the evolution of attitudes toward work:

> You've got to find what you love. And that is as true for your work as it is for your lovers. Your work is going to fill a large part of your life, and the only way to be truly satisfied is to do what you believe is great work. And the only way to do great work is to love what you do. If you haven't found

---

[53] *Working: Its Meaning and Its Limits*, ed. Gilbert C. Meilaender (Notre Dame, IN: University of Notre Dame Press, 2000), 4. Compare also the remarks of Hannah Arendt: "The blessing of life as a whole, inherent in labor, can never be found in work and should not be mistaken for the inevitably brief spell of relief and joy that follows accomplishment and attends achievement." See Hannah Arendt, *The Human Condition*, 2nd ed. (Chicago: University of Chicago Press, 1958), 107.

[54] See Stanley J. Grenz, *The Social God and the Relational Self: A Trinitarian Theology*, The Matrix of Christian Theology (Louisville, KY: Westminster John Knox, 2001), 312-28. For an interesting study at the intersection of ecclesiology and the theology of work, see Dylan Parker, "Faith and Labor: An Ecclesiology of Blue-Collar Participation," *Ecumenical Trends* 53, no. 3 (2024).

[55] Derek Thompson, *On Work: Money, Meaning, Identity*, Atlantic Editions (New York: Zando, 2023), ix, emphasis original.

[56] The phrase is Jeff Haanen's. See "God of the Second Shift," *Christianity Today*, December 2018.

it yet, keep looking. Don't settle. As with all matters of the heart, you'll know when you find it.[57]

As we have already seen, critics of this ideology have observed that, while it sounds nice, it can easily be put to exploitative use. Journalist Simone Stolzoff has likened the "Do What You Love" mantra to "frosting on a burned cake," since it can be used to obscure adverse working conditions or to discourage workers from bargaining collectively. "The implication that love is a suitable stand-in for job security, workplace protections or fair pay is a commonly held belief, especially in so-called dream jobs like writing, cooking and working in the arts, where the privilege to do the work is seen as a form of compensation itself."[58]

Not only is this work mythology prone to exploitative interpretations, however, it also rests on dubious theological foundations. Even so, faith and work literature risks proffering a baptized version of the same thesis, bound up in a problematic understanding of vocation. Specifically, faith and work discourse commonly assumes that each person has a *particular* or *specific* calling that God has created them to fulfill, typically under-stood as a (usually paid) occupation. This notion stretches at least as far back as the Puritans. To take only one example, the Puritan writer William Perkins distinguished between a "general" vocation and a "particular" or "personal" vocation: "The general calling is the calling of Christianity which is common to all that live in the Church of God. The particular is that special calling that belongs to some particular men: as the calling of a magistrate, the calling of a minister, the calling of a master, of a father, of a child, of a servant, of a subject, or any other calling that is common to all."[59] On the face of it, such a theology of calling seems innocuous enough, and indeed consistent with the teachings of the Protestant

---

[57]Steve Jobs, Stanford University Commencement Address (Palo Alto, CA, June 12, 2005), https://news.stanford.edu/2005/06/12/youve-got-find-love-jobs-says/, accessed April 30, 2024.

[58]Simone Stolzoff, "Please Don't Call My Job a Calling," *The New York Times*, June 5, 2023.

[59]William Perkins, "A Treatise of the Vocations or Callings of Men," in *The Work of William Perkins*, ed. Ian Breward, Courtenay Library of Reformation Classics 3 (Abingdon, Berkshire, UK: Sutton Courtenay Press, 1970), 451. This distinction has been widely adopted and adapted in faith and work literature. For example, see R. Paul Stevens's tripartite schema

reformers, who aimed to recover a robust doctrine of the priesthood of all believers. However, some formulations of calling language can manifest in a problematic vision of work that is unattainable for most workers.

In the first place, it is worth asking whether some notions of calling are genuinely biblical or whether they represent a Christian adaptation of the "Do What You Love" mythology. Take, for instance, Dorothy Sayer's interpretation of vocation in her essay "Vocation in Work," which has exercised a great deal of influence in faith and work circles. "Man," she says, "is *homo faber*—man the craftsman. . . . Man is a maker, who makes things because he wants to, because he cannot fulfill his true nature if he is prevented from making things for the love of the job. He is made in the image of the Maker, and he must himself create or become something less than man."[60] One may ask where such a vision leaves workers who do not make things because they want to (but because they have to) and do not make them for the love of the job (but for the paycheck). While surely not Sayers's intention, the implication is that those who are not engaged in lifegiving, creative work are not fulfilling their true nature—not just wasting their lives, but actually becoming something less than human. For the same reason, Frederick Buechner's romantic definition of vocation— "the place where your deep gladness and the world's deep hunger meet"[61]— will fail to resonate (or worse) with most workers.

More recently, Amy Sherman has refreshed Buechner's conception of vocation in her concept of the "vocational sweet spot," which workers are to discern by doing an inventory of the various dimensions of their

---

of "personal calling—Christian vocation—human vocation" in *The Other Six Days*, chap. 4 and Os Guinness's "primary calling"/"secondary calling" taxonomy in *The Call*, 31-32.

[60]Dorothy Sayers, "Vocation in Work," in *A Christian Basis for the Post-War World*, ed. A. E. Baker (New York: Morehouse-Gotham, 1942), 90.

[61]Frederick Buechner, *Wishful Thinking: A Theological ABC* (New York: Harper & Row, 1973), 95. Buechner's definition has proven influential in faith and work literature. R. Paul Stevens modifies Buechner's conception slightly with the language of "heart call," which is defined by an experience of "inner oughtness" that draws Christians to particular tasks (*Other Six Days*, 81-82). Likewise, Ben Witherington III explicitly adopts Buechner's aphorism in his definition of work, although he does qualify it. See Witherington, *Work: A Kingdom Perspective on Labor* (Grand Rapids, MI: Eerdmans, 2011), ix, 12-14.

"vocational power." "The sweet spot is the place where our gifts and passions intersect with God's priorities and the world's needs. To the
greatest extent possible, Christians should seek to work there."[62] While
Sherman does qualify that not all workers have the luxury of working
in their "sweet spot," the implication is that Christians should not work
jobs commonly (and wrongly) characterized as menial or trivial unless
there are extenuating circumstances.[63] These interpretations of vocation
are open to scrutiny on both exegetical and practical grounds. In a
recent study on biblical calling language, William Klein and Daniel
Steiner have identified several problems with the uses to which calling
language has been put in faith and work conversations, noting that
Buechner's (and others') conception of vocation has unwittingly

> (1) reinforced a significant divide that already exists within our culture,
> whereby a person's significance and worth are determined by the sort of
> work that they do; (2) declared certain sorts of work to be worthy of God's
> leading and others not; (3) emphasized that it is primarily in our gainfully
> employed work that we can live out God's calling; and (4) taught that
> faithfulness is conditioned by personal gladness.[64]

The agency-dignity-power narrative works well for those whose work
is creative and satisfying; it is less clear whether these ideas help people
whose work is degrading or unfulfilling. To put it bluntly, many
workers—perhaps the majority of workers—would score extremely low
on a "vocational power assessment." Though unintended, a romantic
vision of calling patronizes workers who have no means of working at
the intersection of their deep gladness and the world's deep hunger.

---

[62] Amy Sherman, *Kingdom Calling: Vocational Stewardship for the Common Good* (Downers Grove,
IL: InterVarsity Press, 2011). The various dimensions of "vocational power" include knowledge/
expertise, platform, networks, influence, positions, skills, reputation/fame (121-26).

[63] For example, Sherman concedes that, hypothetically, a Christian could work at a dog food
factory if the benefit package were needed to care for a "severely disabled daughter" (*Kingdom
Calling*, 111). One wonders why such extreme circumstances would be needed to justify working
in a dog food factory.

[64] William W. Klein and Daniel J. Steiner, *What Is My Calling? A Biblical and Theological Exploration of Christian Identity* (Grand Rapids, MI: Baker Academic, 2022), 23.

"Do What You Love" is likewise a cruel ideology, since for many workers, this is simply not an option. Even if it were, it would still not do justice to human dignity and human destiny as the Bible sees it. Christianized versions of the Do What You Love mythology must be dislodged by a realistic theology of work, which rests on an anthropology that accords dignity and purpose to human beings, whether or not they ever find their calling. In the end, this romanticized understanding of calling, conclude Klein and Steiner, suffers on practical grounds, as it "sounds rather elitist." But the most serious problems are exegetical, since it depends on muddled thinking about how the biblical writers use calling language. "Most important, it is not what the Bible means by God's call on a person's life." As they go on to show, when the Bible uses calling language, it is overwhelmingly to describe a person's calling into union and communion with Jesus Christ, not an individual task or occupation.[65] It is here where an *Ecce Homo* anthropology can make a valuable contribution. If it is true that the ultimate calling of the saints is to be conformed to the image of Jesus Christ (2 Cor 3:18; Rom 8:29; Col 3:10; Eph 4:24; 1 Jn 3:1-3), not to find one's ideal paid occupation, then we can dispense with the harmful suggestion (intended or not) that a person who does not find "the thing they were made to do" is wasting their life. To put it simply: every last individual *has been* created to fulfill just one life-purpose: to be in union and communion with Jesus Christ. Every individual can do this no matter what their paid employment (or lack thereof) or quotidian tasks. In the end, if there is one thing we ought to be passionate about—one thing for which we are willing to suffer—it is this; it is not a job or a career or even a vocation. Which means, in turn, that a realistic and sound theology of work must recover an emphasis on the instrumental value of work. Sometimes a job is just a job—and jobs are still worth doing.

---

[65]Klein and Steiner, *What Is My Calling?*, 23, 111-12. Cf. Ellul, *Ethics of Freedom*, 495.

7

WORTH DOING

The End of the Matter

"The end of the matter; all has been heard. Fear God, and keep his commandments, for that is the whole duty of everyone" (Eccles 12:13). Part of what it means to fear God, explains Qoheleth, is to work while we still have the strength to do so, before "the strong men are bent, and the women who grind cease working because they are few" (Eccles 12:3), before "the silver cord is snapped, and the golden bowl is broken, and the pitcher is broken at the fountain, and the wheel broken at the cistern" (Eccles 12:6). But, as we have seen, all work is done within the limitations of finitude, with all its attendant frustrations, and it is refracted through the jagged prism of fallenness. How is one to "accept [one's] lot and find enjoyment in [one's] toil" (Eccles 5:19) in circumstances like these, where we must inevitably leave undone things we had hoped to do and where enmity, absurdity, and tragedy stalk every good endeavor? To endure—and, indeed, to enjoy—the quotidian takes a certain kind of double vision, the sanctified imagination to behold the world not only as it is, but as it once was. The Christian, says David Bentley Hart,

> should see two realities at once, one world (as it were) within another: one the world as we all know it, in all its beauty and terror, grandeur and dreariness, delight and anguish; and the other the world in its first and ultimate truth, not simply "nature" but "creation," an endless sea of glory, radiant with the beauty of God in every part, innocent of all violence. To see in this way is to rejoice and mourn at once, to regard the world as a mirror of infinite beauty, but as glimpsed through the veil of

death; it is to see creation in chains, but beautiful as in the beginning of days.[1]

Like everything under the sun, all of which groans in eager expectation of redemption and renewal (Rom 8:22), work too is subject to this double reality: both beautiful and broken, both fruitful and futile, both good and grotesque. And yet when we face work as we find it in the real world—enmitous, absurd, tragic—and when we come to terms with the kinds of creatures we are—bound, dependent, finite—we may just see what Qoheleth saw: constrained though it is by finitude and haunted as it is by the curse, work is nonetheless a good gift from the good God and therefore worth doing. It is true, as Jesus says, that the "night is coming when no one can work" (Jn 9:4), but each of us can—and should—still make hay while the sun shines.

---

[1]David Bentley Hart, *The Doors of the Sea: Where Was God in the Tsunami?* (Grand Rapids, MI: Eerdmans, 2005), 60-61.

ACKNOWLEDGMENTS

IN A BOOK THAT SEEKS to advance the theology of work, we gladly express our appreciation for the good work and contributions of other people who helped this book come to fruition.

Don Payne and Daniel Steiner collaborated in the earliest conversations about the concept and plan for the book and assisted with initial drafts of two chapters. They helped get the ball rolling. While the shortcomings of the book are ours, many of Don's and Daniel's insights remain in these pages.

For quite a few years, I (David) have been privileged to participate in conversations, grant-funded projects and events stewarded by the Oikonomia Network and more recently the Karam Forum. The interaction I have experienced in these venues has been and continues to be a source of insight and wisdom in the integration of faith and work, as well as the occasion for delightful collegiality. My thanks to Greg Forster for his leadership and encouragement in many of these endeavors. Jeff Haanen and Joanna Meyer generously gave time and thought for insightful conversation. Don Payne and I created and have several times taught a course at Denver Seminary on the theology of work. In ways not reflected in the footnotes in the pages that follow, I learned much from Don and our interaction with the students who worked with us. I also thank the Denver Seminary Board of Trustees, administration, and my Theology Department faculty colleagues for making possible a one semester sabbatical during which I was able to work on my portions of the book.

Many of the ideas that take shape in this book were born of my (Ryan's) time on the staff of the Denver Institute for Faith and Work. I'm grateful to the many brilliant fellows of the 5280 Fellowship whose faithful work in the marketplace continues to be a source of great inspiration. I want also to extend my gratitude to my wonderful colleagues who endured many staff meetings in which I complained that "we don't talk enough about sin": Joanna Meyer, Abby Worland, Dustin Moody, Stephen Blankenship, Pamela Ramon, Catherine Sandgren, Cliff Johnson, and Ross Chapman. Special thanks are due to Jeff Hoffmeyer, Jeff Haanen, and Brian Gray, fine theological minds with whom I work-shopped concepts for the book and received illuminating feedback. Brian in particular, along with Christopher McDermott, has been subject to more than one of my incoherent brainstorming sessions when we should have been discussing the Denver Nuggets and Russian novels. I'm sorry, guys—and thank you.

We thank the good people of IVP Academic who saw fit to add this project to IVP's long-standing contributions to the literature on faith and work—David McNutt, Jon Boyd, and especially Rachel Hastings—as well as the many IVP staff behind the scenes without whose work this book would not have come to be. We both benefited, as we so often do, from the fine work of the staff of the Carey S. Thomas Library of Denver Seminary. Special thanks go to Tom Jacobs and Charlotte Nutter for assistance in tracking down and accessing materials, and for doing so with professional efficiency and personal grace. We also thank and commend Jennay Smith-Wilson for her skilled and insightful research assistance with several topics.

Our respective dedications express our appreciation for and thanks to others without whom this book likely would not have seen the light of day.

APPENDIX
The Rise of Faith and Work

IN RECENT YEARS THERE HAS BEEN a marked increase of interest in exploring and fostering the relationship between religious faith and work, and not least the relationship between Christian faith and work. One of the most well-known and oft-cited studies in this relationship is *God at Work*, by David Miller. Miller describes and analyzes what he refers to as the "faith at work" movement, a "decentralized" social movement "with loosely networked clusters of lay-initiated and lay-led activities that focus on integrating spirituality and work."[1] Focusing on businesses and businesspeople, he identifies three eras in the history of the faith and work movement: the social gospel era, the ministry of the laity era, and the faith at work era. More recently, sociologist Andrew Lynn has published *Saving the Protestant Ethic*, in which he focuses more narrowly on evangelical faith and work endeavors in particular, approaching them "as primarily a case of cultural change and adaptation."[2] Our primary interest in this book is theological. However, theology neither rises from nor exists in a vacuum, so a brief survey of the history of the faith and work *movement*, with help from Miller and Lynn, provides background for our theological explorations.

Miller identifies the first era of the modern faith and work movement as beginning in the 1890s and continuing until the mid-1940s. The emergence and development of the distinct address of work in the Catholic Church unfolded within the context of Catholic social thought and can be seen, in part, in a papal encyclical issued in 1891, *Rerum Novarum*

---

[1]David W. Miller, *God at Work: The History and Promise of the Faith at Work Movement* (New York: Oxford University Press, 2007), 10.
[2]Andrew Lynn, *Saving the Protestant Ethic: Creative Class Evangelicalism and the Crisis of Work* (Oxford: Oxford University Press, 2023).

("The Worker's Charter"). As Darrell Cosden notes in *A Theology of Work*, "With *Rerum Novarum* . . . Leo XIII opened the door and redirected Catholic concern in such a way that broader social-ethical questions which transcend more preservationist concerns could emerge."[3] This encyclical marked a new level of appreciation for the sheer importance of work in the lives of individual persons and in the order and form of societies. Four decades later (1931), Pope Pius XI issued *Quadragesimo Anno* ("The Social Order"), which was considerably "more radical and 'liberal,'" with a larger role seen for the state, than the essentially conservative *Rerum Novarum.*[4] With regard to work in particular, however, *Quadragesimo Anno* basically reaffirmed and sought to carry forward the fuller implementation of the view of work set forth in *Rerum Novarum*.

During this first era, faith and work endeavors within Protestant circles were significantly shaped by the social gospel, in forms ranging from conservative to radical, which focused on addressing the unique challenges raised by industrialization. This was accompanied by the creation of some "special purpose" organizations to address work-related issues and by what Miller refers to as "the popularization of Jesus," rendering Jesus approachable largely through emphasizing the earthiness of his life and ministry.[5] In addition to these efforts, Lynn recounts what he refers to as faith and work endeavors that reflect "the era of conservative Protestant revivalism and fundamentalism," from 1890 to 1929. In contrast to those efforts shaped by the social gospel, a fundamentalist work ethic "channeled spiritual attention and energies toward activities other than economics." The work that mattered to God was "Christian work," which was functionally synonymous with "evangelism and saving souls."[6]

During what Miller identifies as the second era (ca. 1946–1985) the church remained important to faith and work thought and endeavors,

---

[3]Darrell Cosden, *A Theology of Work: Work and the New Creation*, foreword by Jürgen Moltmann (Milton Keynes: Paternoster, 2004), 19-20.
[4]Cosden, *Theology of Work*, 20.
[5]Miller, *God at Work*, 34-37.
[6]Lynn, *Saving the Protestant Ethic*, 43.

but there was a noticeable raising of the profile of laity. Reflecting perspectives that would come to be associated with the Council of Vatican II (1962–1965), in 1961 Pope John XXIII issued *Mater et Magistra* ("Mother and Teacher"), on Christianity and social progress. When it touched on work, it promulgated a greater affirmation of the roles for and work done by lay persons. Furthermore, "the understanding of work presented in *Mater et Magistra* closely corresponds with the idea of the priority of the human (labor) over the material (capital) which later become the foundation for the theology of work found in *Laborem Exercens*."[7] In 1981, Pope John Paul II commemorated the ninetieth anniversary of *Rerum Novarum* by issuing *Laborem Exercens* ("Through Work" or "On Human Work"), but moved distinctively theological questions about work to the forefront, viewing them as "key to the social question."[8] According to John Paul II, "Work is a good thing for man—a good thing for his humanity—because through work man *not only transforms nature,* adapting it to his own needs, but he also *achieves fulfilment* as a human being and indeed, in a sense, becomes 'more a human being.'"[9] Upon this understanding of the necessity of work for the dignity of human being, and in a challenge to both liberal capitalism and Marxist communism, John Paul II advanced "a principle that has always been taught by the Church: *the principle of the priority of labour over capital.*"[10]

During this second era, particularly in Protestant traditions, under greater lay leadership there was an accelerated creation of voluntaristic

---

[7]Cosden, *Theology of Work*, 23.

[8]John Paul II, *Laborem Exercens* (1981), para. 3, www.vatican.va/content/john-paul-ii/en /encyclicals/documents/hf_jp-ii_enc_14091981_laborem-exercens.html (accessed June 8, 2020).

[9]John Paul II, *Laborem Exercens*, para. 9, emphasis original.

[10]John Paul II, *Laborem Exercens*, para. 12, emphasis original. This is followed by an extensive section (paras. 16–23) that identifies and argues for the rights of workers, ranging from the availability of jobs and job-related education to "just remuneration" and provision of basic medical care, from gender-related fairness in employment and respect for agricultural work to the legitimacy of unions and respect for "disabled" workers. For more on the theology of work in Catholic social thought see John M. Todd, ed., *Work: Christian Thought and Practice* (London: Darton Longman and Todd, 1960), and Edmond Malinvaud and Margaret S. Archer, eds., *Work and Human Fulfillment* (Ypsilanti, MI: Sapienta Press Ave Maria University, 2003).

special-purpose groups.[11] This second era also roughly coincides with what historians often describe as the post–World War II rise of neo-evangelicalism, which by the 1960s came to be identified simply as "evangelicalism."[12] Interest among evangelicals in the relationship between Christian faith and work is evident during this period in the variety of organizations, educational programs, and publications that appeared.[13]

The work of campus ministry organizations like InterVarsity Christian Fellowship (1941) and Navigators (1951) encouraged college students to live faithfully throughout all dimensions of life, including their future employment.[14] There were also organized efforts to encourage businessmen to witness for Christ in their workplace.[15] Symbolic of this kind of faith and work ministry is the Full Gospel Businessmen's Fellowship, which was founded in 1951.[16] These early evangelical ministries, and in the case of the Full Gospel fellowship charismatic or Pentecostal ministries, tended to focus almost exclusively on businessmen, rather than a broader range of work, and almost exclusively on the call to evangelism, rather than a more fundamental and organic integration of faith and work.[17]

Regent College (Vancouver) was founded in 1968 as a graduate school of theology particularly for laity. Though not always recognized by observers today, Regent was not founded as a seminary with a focus on professional clergy but as a graduate theological school to equip

---

[11]Miller, *God at Work*, 39-40.

[12]For an informative discussion of the historiography and terminology surrounding these discussions, see Douglas A. Sweeney, "The Essential Evangelicalism Dialectic: The Historiography of the Early Neo-Evangelical Movement and the Observer-Participant Dilemma," in *Evangelicals: Who They Have Been, Are Now, and Could Be*, ed. Mark A. Noll, David W. Bebbington, and George M. Marsden (Grand Rapids, MI: Eerdmans, 2019), 56-73.

[13]For a general analysis of Protestant literature in the theology of work in the second half of the twentieth century, see Cosden, *Theology of Work*, 37-66.

[14]The Navigators organization was founded in 1933, but it did not formally organize its campus ministry until 1951.

[15]At this point in time, businessmen, not businesswomen, were the focus of these efforts.

[16]Miller, *God at Work*, 51.

[17]As was often the case with theologian Carl F. H. Henry, he was an early voice on heretofore neglected issues. Henry devoted a portion of his 1963 Payton Lectures at Fuller Theological Seminary to a Christian view of work. See Carl F. H. Henry, *Aspects of Christian Social Ethics* (Grand Rapids, MI: Eerdmans, 1964; reprint ed., Grand Rapids, MI: Baker, 1980).

students for Christian life and work in whatever paths of employment they might pursue.[18] This focus on the laity was driven in no small measure by the Brethren convictions of many of the founding faculty members, and it meant that Regent pursued theological education with at least one eye intentionally focused on "the marketplace."[19] This orientation of Regent toward the laity, including the marketplace, was manifest as well in the founding of New College Berkeley in 1977.[20]

There were a few popular-level publications, such as *Your Job* by Jerry White and Mary White, and *Secular Work Is Full-Time Service*, published by the Christian Literature Crusade.[21] Perhaps not surprisingly given the still-emerging character of post–World War II evangelical theological scholarship, there was not much scholarly work on questions of faith and work or the theology of work carried out by evangelicals prior to the 1980s. However, looking across the landscape of all forms of faith and work efforts, Miller observes that since the mid-1980s there has been exponential growth in this area,[22] and evangelicals have had a major role in this growth. Similarly, Lynn states that since the 1980s there has been "an unprecedented explosion" of evangelical organizations focusing on the integration of faith and work.[23]

Thus, Miller identifies the third wave, extending from circa 1985 until at least the early 2000s (Miller's book was published in 2007), as the faith at

---

[18]Regent College did not offer the master of divinity degree until 1979, and while the quality of its education was always highly regarded, the school did not seek and obtain accreditation with the Association of Theological Schools of the United States and Canada until 1985.

[19]One of the distinctive marks of the Brethren tradition is its lack of a distinction between clergy and laity. Historically, selected male members of Brethren assemblies fulfill all leadership and teaching responsibilities. Among those people who influenced the founding and shape of Regent were a number of members of the Brethren, including James M. Houston, Donald G. Tinder, W. Ward Gasque, Carl E. Armerding, Walter L. Liefeld, and Paul E. Little.

[20]The first president of New College Berkeley was one of the founding members of the Regent College faculty, the New Testament scholar Ward Gasque.

[21]Jerry White and Mary White, *Your Job: Survival or Satisfaction?* (Grand Rapids, MI: Zondervan, 1977) and Larry Peabody, *Secular Work Is Full-Time Service* (Fort Washington, PA: Christian Literature Crusade, 1974).

[22]Miller, *God at Work*, 106.

[23]Lynn, *Saving the Protestant Ethic*, 90. For a very helpful tabular overview of organizations, 1930–2020, see 91–97.

work era, marked by the quest for "integration." Over the course of the 1980s, Miller observes, there was in business communities an intensifying sense that "faith and work are not meant to be separated or isolated from each other. Businesspeople want the ability to bring their whole selves to work— mind, body, and soul—and are no longer satisfied with sacrificing their core identities or being mere cogs in the machine, nor do they want a discon-nected spirituality."[24] Lynn reports that beginning in the 1980s conferences became a prominent vehicle for advancing this faith and work movement.

Additionally, there were evangelical voices in the 1980s and 1990s who proved to be forerunners to today's proponents of attending to matters of faith and work. In 1985, Paul Stevens of Regent College published *Liberating the Laity*, and, in 1999, *The Other Six Days*.[25] Stevens has de-voted himself to promoting an ecclesiology that does not distinguish between clergy and laity, and, correspondingly, he has written and taught, at Regent and beyond, about "marketplace Christianity" and the divine dignity of "everyday" work. In 1991, Robert Banks, a sometimes-colleague of Stevens, edited *Faith Goes to Work*.[26] In 1987 Doug Sherman and William Hendricks published *Your Work Matters to God*, which set forth a clear case for the value and dignity of all forms of good work, not simply "religious" or "spiritual" work, and Leland Ryken published *Work and Leisure in Christian Perspective*, which was subsequently signifi-cantly revised and significantly expanded as *Redeeming the Time*.[27] It was during this same period that a book that proved to be seminal to English-language discussions of the theology of work appeared in English. In 1991, Oxford University Press published Miroslav Volf's *Work in the Spirit*,

---

[24]Miller, *God at Work*, 74.

[25]R. Paul Stevens, *Liberating the Laity: Equipping All the Saints for Ministry* (Downers Grove, IL: InterVarsity Press, 1985) and *The Other Six Days: Vocation, Work, and Ministry in Biblical Per-spective* (Grand Rapids, MI: Eerdmans, 1999).

[26]Robert Banks, ed., *Faith Goes to Work: Reflections from the Marketplace* (Eugene, OR: Wipf & Stock, 1999).

[27]Doug Sherman and William D. Hendricks, *Your Work Matters to God* (Colorado Springs, CO: NavPress, 1987), and Leland Ryken, *Work and Leisure in Christian Perspective* (Portland, OR: Multnomah, 1987) and *Redeeming the Time: A Christian Approach to Work and Leisure* (Grand Rapids, MI: Baker Books, 1995).

which was based on his doctoral work at the University of Tübingen in the 1980s.[28] Lynn summarizes and documents this phenomenon as an "explosion of evangelical faith and work books" at the end of the twentieth century and leading into the early 2000s.[29]

These publications paralleled a larger and increasing interest among evangelicals in building bridges between faith and work, interest that was also manifest in initiatives in schools and in the creation of numbers of work-oriented organizations and ministries. For example, in the 1990s two major evangelical seminaries established institutes specifically to advance the integration of Christian faith and work. In 1994 Gordon-Conwell established the Mockler Center for Faith and Ethics in the Workplace, and two years later Fuller Theological Seminary founded the DePree Center to serve marketplace leaders.

All these kinds of developments in the arena of faith and work have only multiplied and accelerated since the turn of the new millennium. Many popular-level books were published seeking to support the efforts of Christian laypeople to integrate their faith and work as well as the many parachurch organizations dedicated to serving them. Some of the more widely known books in this genre from this time are Gene Edward Veith, *God at Work*; Darrell Cosden, *The Heavenly Good of Earthly Work*; Tom Nelson, *Work Matters*; Ben Witherington, *Work*; Timothy Keller and Katherine Leary Alsdorf, *Every Good Endeavor*; and Steven Garber, *Visions of Vocation*.[30] Ethical guidance and Christian witness were among

---

[28]Miroslav Volf, *Work in the Spirit: Toward a Theology of Work* (Oxford: Oxford University Press, 1991; reprint ed., Eugene, OR: Wipf and Stock, 2001).

[29]Lynn, *Saving the Protestant Ethic*, 97-100.

[30]Gene Edward Veith Jr., *God at Work: Your Christian Vocation in All of Life* (Wheaton, IL: Crossway, 2002); Darrell Cosden, *The Heavenly Good of Earthly Work* (Peabody, MA: Hendrickson, 2006); Tom Nelson, *Work Matters: Connecting Sunday Worship to Monday Work* (Wheaton, IL: Crossway, 2011); Ben Witherington III, *Work: A Kingdom Perspective on Labor* (Grand Rapids, MI: Eerdmans, 2011); Timothy Keller and Katherine Leary Alsdorf, *Every Good Endeavor: Connecting Your Work to God's Work* (New York: Penguin, 2012); and Steven Garber, *Visions of Vocation: Common Grace for the Common Good* (Downers Grove, IL: InterVarsity Press, 2014). Other books along this line include David Steward and Robert L. Shook, *Doing Business by the Book: 52 Lessons on Success Straight from the Bible* (New York: Hyperion, 2004); Norman Geisler and Randy Douglass, *Bringing Your Faith to Work: Answers for Break Room Skeptics* (Grand Rapids, MI: Baker Books, 2005); John C. Haughey, *Converting Nine to Five: Bringing Spirituality to Your*

the recurring themes. Many of these books focused on the work-world of business. All of them sought to commend and cultivate a positive view of work, locating it, in various ways, within God's work in the world.

In addition to these books, there emerged books that addressed various dimensions of faith and work at a more complex and sophisticated level. Many of the same themes, such as ethics and a focus on business, are reflected in these books. Additionally, matters of economics and a desire to orient the work of Christians toward serving "the common good" become frequent themes.[31] Though not always reflected in the titles, in addition to seeking to ground work in biblical teaching there is increased attention, among both evangelicals and other Christians, to more nuanced and deeper *theological* reflection on work. Some noteworthy books along these lines include Wayne Grudem, *Business for the Glory of God*; Armand Larive, *After Sunday*; Darrel Cosden, *A Theology of Work*; David Jensen, *Responsive Labor*; Amy Sherman, *Kingdom Calling*; Kenman Wong and Scott Rae, *Business for the Common Good*; and James Hamilton Jr., *Work and Our Labor in the Lord*.[32] Between 2012 and 2015 the Christian's Library Press published a series of five books that explored faith, work, and economics from the perspectives of five Christian traditions.[33]

Daily Work (Eugene, OR: Wipf & Stock, 2005); John D. Beckett, *Mastering Monday: A Guide to Integrating Faith and Work* (Downers Grove, IL: InterVarsity Press, 2006); Ken Eldred, *God Is at Work: Transforming People and Nations Through Business* (Montrose, CO: Manna, 2009) and *The Integrated Life: Experience the Powerful Advantage of Integrating Your Faith and Work* (Montrose, CO: Manna, 2010); Christian Overman, *God's Pleasure at Work: Bridging the Sacred Secular Divide* (Bellevue, WA: Ablaze, 2009); and John Knapp, *How the Church Fails Businesspeople (and What Can Be Done About It)* (Grand Rapids, MI: Eerdmans, 2012).

[31] Among Lynn's negative critiques of evangelical faith and work endeavors is their blunting or avoidance of social and economic ethical issues. See, for example, his critique of "de-ethicized Kuyperianism" (Lynn, *Saving the Protestant Ethic*, 218-22).

[32] Wayne Grudem, *Business for the Glory of God: The Bible's Teaching on the Moral Goodness of Business* (Wheaton, IL: Crossway, 2003); Armand Larive, *After Sunday: A Theology of Work* (New York: Bloomsbury, 2004); Cosden, *Theology of Work*; David H. Jensen, *Responsive Labor: A Theology of Work* (Louisville, KY: Westminster John Knox, 2006); Amy Sherman, *Kingdom Calling: Vocational Stewardship for the Common Good* (Downers Grove, IL: InterVarsity Press, 2011); Kenman L. Wong and Scott B. Rae, *Business for the Common Good: A Christian Vision for the Marketplace* (Downers Grove, IL: InterVarsity Press, 2011); and James M. Hamilton Jr., *Work and Our Labor in the Lord* (Wheaton, IL: Crossway, 2017).

[33] Chad Brand, *Flourishing Faith: A Baptist Primer on Work, Economics, and Civic Stewardship* (Grand Rapids, MI: Christian's Library, 2012); David Wright, *How God Makes the World a Better*

As these and other books were being published in the opening decades of the century, many organizations, institutes, and media ventures such as websites and podcasts devoted to faith and work were established. Organizations such as Made to Flourish and the Oikonomia Network seek to equip present and future pastors and church leaders so that they can lead churches in ways that advance whole-life discipleship, particularly discipleship that extends to the workplace. A number of universities and seminaries, including, but not limited to, Seattle Pacific University, LeTourneau University, Wheaton College, Asbury Theological Seminary, Bethel Seminary (Minnesota), Sioux Falls Seminary, Talbot Theological Seminary, and Western Seminary (Oregon), have established institutes or programs specifically addressing matters of faith and work, and increasing numbers of schools are addressing faith and work in the context of other initiatives.

Local, city-specific yet substantial faith and work organizations have arisen in numbers of cities, such as San Diego (Flourish San Diego), Denver (the Denver Institute for Faith and Work) and Nashville (the Nashville Institute for Faith and Work). Some of these originally local organizations are expanding their impact by establishing chapters in other cities, such as the networks of the Redeemer Center for Faith and Work and the Faith and Work Movement. There are an increasing number of gap-year and fellows programs primarily for students who graduate from secular schools, such as the Gotham Fellowship of the Redeemer Center for Faith and Work (New York City), the SURGE Network (Phoenix), 5280 Fellows of the Denver Institute for Faith and Work, New City Fellows (Raleigh, North Carolina), Circle City Fellows (Indianapolis), and the Fellows Initiative. And there are numbers of organizations that have arisen largely to develop and provide resources for all these kinds of

---

Place: A Wesleyan Primer on Faith, Work, and Economic Transformation (Grand Rapids, MI: Christian's Library, 2012); John Bolt, *Economic Shalom: A Reformed Primer on Faith, Work, and Human Flourishing* (Grand Rapids, MI: Christian's Library, 2013); Charlie Self, *Flourishing Churches and Communities: A Pentecostal Primer on Faith, Work, and Economics for Spirit-Empowered Discipleship* (Grand Rapids, MI: Christian's Library, 2013); and Gene Edward Veith Jr., *Working for Our Neighbor: A Lutheran Primer on Vocation, Economics, and Ordinary Life* (Grand Rapids, MI: Christian's Library, 2016).

faith and work endeavors, some of which also conduct or collaborate on periodic equipping events. One of the largest and most widely connected is the Theology of Work Project, founded in 2007 under the leadership of William Messenger. Among the many resources developed by the TWP is a commentary on the entire Bible that provides information and insight related to work. Increasingly, issues related to faith and work are being addressed through blog sites and podcasts, such as The Green Room blog, the Patheos faith and work channel, the RightNow Media faith and work channel, and the Gospel Coalition faith and work channel. Addressing the particular and distinctive interests and needs of women, 4Word facilitates and provides resources for a network of local groups across the country in which women discuss and address work-related issues in the home, in church, and in the marketplace.

The faith and work movement as analyzed by David Miller is not a theological movement per se. It is a "dynamic, decentralized, loosely networked, informal, and unstructured" social movement made up primarily of individual actors and voluntaristic special-purpose organizations, and devoted to engagement with people and organizations more than pondering ideas.[34] This does not mean, however, that theology is not important. As Miller himself observes, "Understanding FAW groups and participants is aided by an awareness of their theological emphasis," and theological considerations, amid others, are woven throughout his discussion of the implications and proposals flowing from his research, and suggestions for further research.[35] As noted above, Andrew Lynn's *Saving the Protestant Ethic* is a sociological study of cultural change and adaptation, but he recognizes that there are distinctively theological dimensions of evangelical faith and work efforts.[36] Indeed, *theology* is at work in faith and work movements. And it is to the theology of work that we seek to contribute in this book.

---

[34]Miller, *God at Work*, 105.
[35]Miller, *God at Work*, 116 and 143-52.
[36]See Lynn, *Saving the Protestant Ethic*, chap. 4, "The Four Evangelical Theologies of Work," 122-54.

GENERAL INDEX

SCRIPTURE INDEX